J. M. W. TURNER

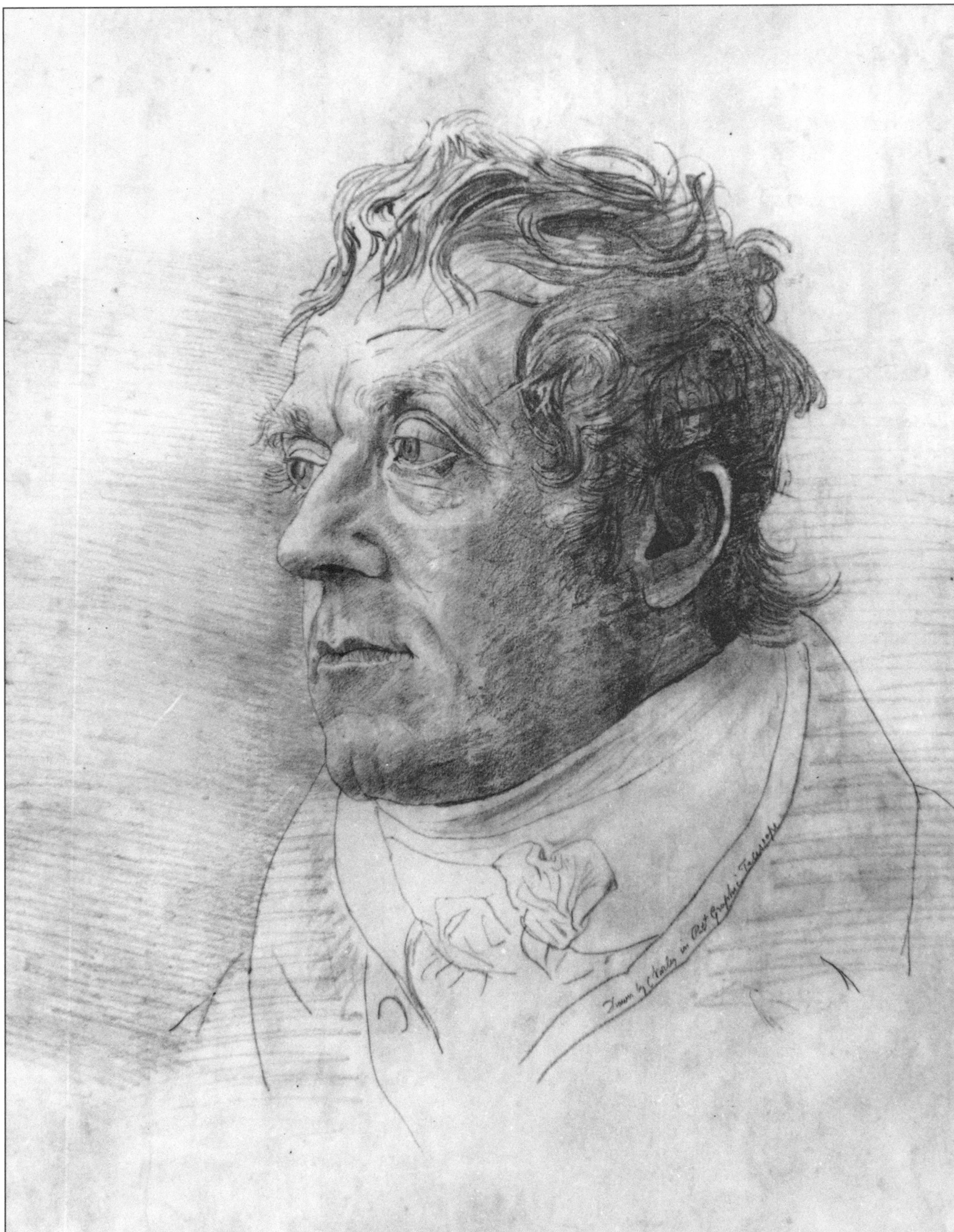

HORST KOCH

JOSEPH MALLORD WILLIAM

# TURNER

Artline Editions

*Artline Editions*

Translated by Stephen Gorman


Printed in Germany — Imprimé en Allemagne
ISBN 1 8714 8708 0

# CONTENTS

»I feel that Turner is a man of outstanding genius who takes a place among the English landscape painters as Byron does among the modern English poets. In fact, until now, no landscape painter with such a varied talent has ever existed. His historical landscapes show a most exquisite feeling for beauty of line and light effect. At the same time he has the means of allowing this effect to express the most different atmospheres of nature - grandness, deep, sombre melancholy, sunny cheerfulness and peace or the turmoil of the elements. His treatment of architecture is also outstanding and even the many aspects of the ocean yield to his magic brush. His views of certain cities and regions fill the observer with poetic feelings which no other has been able to do to the same extent. This can mainly be attributed to the choice of an exceptional artistic viewpoint and the beauty of the lighting. Finally he treats the most ordinary objects, such as a group of trees, a meadow, a shadowed stream with such an artistry that they gain the most artistic stimuli. Because of this I must recognize Turner as the greatest landscape painter without hesitation . . .«

Gustav Waagen, 1854

## INTRODUCTION

In the considerable life's work of William Turner, the colour symphonies of his late paintings must have had an irritating effect on contemporaries of the great artist. The struggle between air and water, the transcendence of the elements fire, water, air and light, reproduced in a style of painting where emotion almost allows the contours of what is being represented to disappear in favour of dynamism. It was an art of expression which forgot everything time-honoured and which must have confused the people at the beginning of the Victorian era.

The artist met with a general rejection of his most mature works although he himself had absolutely no doubt as to their exceptional importance for the development of western art. Even helping friends such as the author John Ruskin, who vehemently defended Turner's later work in his book *Modern Painters*, failed to recognize the artist's ability and were more concerned with making excusing explanations than attempting to understand the spiritual depth of these paintings and successfully interpreting them.

His artistic path, his attempts at form, colour and movement in his late works, his struggle to implement Goethe's theory of colour in his paintings developed logically and corresponded to his artistic genius. However, as the subject often was so much integrated with the weaving of the elements that it was difficult to recognize it, he was generally misunderstood. When the object could not be recognized, the painting remained inaccessible to the observer. No one understood the visionary aspect of this art, one wondered about the eccentric old man, who in the course of his long artistic life had once painted such classically beautiful paintings, but now seemed no longer to have the strength to produce a clear artistic design.

Turner was a Romantic and beside Constable the most important English Romantic. It is difficult, however, to place him in this art- historical category. He comes — and his early paintings show this clearly — from the classical French art movement, which was his starting point and also the breeding ground for his first creative years. Claude Lorrain was an obvious model on which he based his early works. Turner's landscape work *Liber studiorum* was conceived from Claude Lorrain's *Liber Veritas*, and later Turner insisted that his paintings be hung alongside those from Claude Lorrain in museums.

In comparison, the late Turner is basically at the start of impressionism, and he began and anticipated something which only eyes in this century got used to seeing. To draw the sensory impression at the instant of painting, the immediate feelings the artist has at the moment of creative action, was one of the prevailing thoughts of the impressionists who endeavoured to find a theoretical formulation for this basic idea.

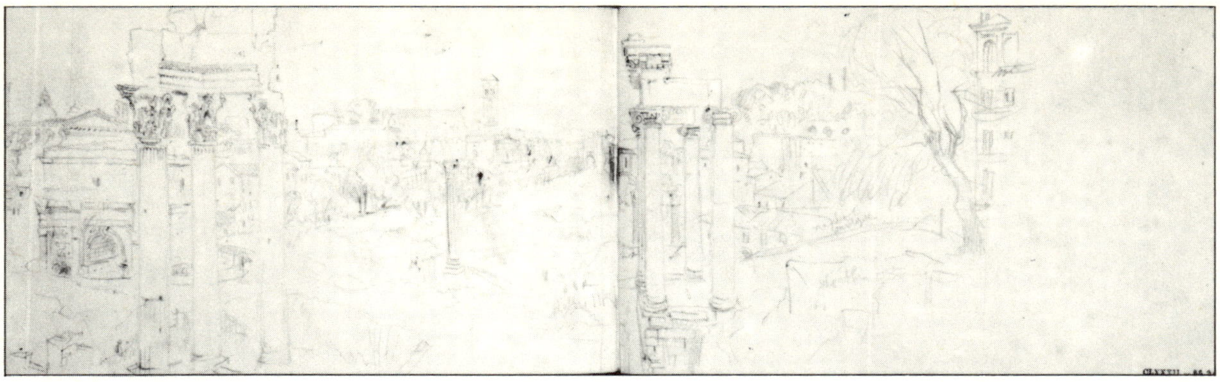

Turner had the thought much earlier and painted accordingly. Although Turner knew other laws, such as those of classical painting, he confidently ignored them when it seemed sensible to him for the achievement of his artistic aims. Many of his works followed the traditional rules in picture construction, harmony and perspective; however, especially in his later works he went in new directions, completely detached himself from form and consequently used light and colour for the creation of the atmosphere he wished to obtain.

In spite of this, Turner's basic attitude was that of a Romantic artist, even when he covered a considerably broader spectrum in his painting. From his art a path leads directly to Delacroix and from there to the impressionists. Without Turner's paintings, impressionism would have had a less sure, groping, poorer start.

Turner lived a busy, not especially outstanding life and created a great amount of paintings in which he developed from a master of charming, scenic miniature paintings to a visionary prophet with supernatural graphic qualities. What Turner attempted to express in his late work could also be articulated in the form of music or in poetry. The spiritual content of his art would not especially have been tied to painting. The judgement of art historians was negative well into the 20th century: one regarded Turner as a very virtuous deliverer of pretty topographical views who had lost his ability in later years through trying too hard, who had been thwarted by the impossibility of representing atmospherical elements in the landscape.

»It is less the abstractness of paintings such as ›The Sea-Monster‹ than the fact that we are hardly capable of interpreting the symbolical colour effects which Turner intended should produce physiologically pure colours, in fact we cannot appreciate these colour contrasts as harmonic. With an almost monomaniac, some think direct pathological one-sidedness, the late Turner had certain speculations which he dedicated himself to following Goethe's theory of colours, and while they remained with our Philipp Otto Runge a more literary programme, they were carried to an extreme by Turner and because of this led ad absurdum — something one feels when one has to look at too many of these shimmering canvases next to each other.«

Turner began completely in the traditional style with a great preference for landscape painting and with the ambition to achieve something exceptional in painting. Popular opinion at that time was that a mastering of historical themes was necessary for a true artistic format. And, in the connection between historical painting and landscape, an intensification of the artistic workmanship was possible. Historical painting showed historic events which were often meant to be understood as symbols for an idea (e.g. the numerous romantic presentations of themes which more or less secretly carried the notion of freedom, the struggle against oppression and patronage). At the same time the landscape components which were brought into the painting supported the pictorial statement with their atmospheric description. The landscape virtually became a stage on which dramatis personae were represented whose action was a symbol for intense feelings, dreams and expectations. Turner's contemporaries regarded this as the way in which the cycle was completed to a valid work of art.

While Turner's precursor, Reynolds, attempted to develop the portrait to heroic figure painting, where the large-scale figure also left room for spiritual statements, Turner gladly took up the challenge of the age, without this part of his work being able to take a special place in his complete works. Landscape and historical scenario were also areas in which Turner's contemporaries admired him and considered him one of the very best.

That his later paintings are complete attestations of a new spiritual art, that they form the sum of an intensively lived artistic life are realizations of a more recent date.

## THE EARLY WORKS

Joseph Mallard William Turner, as he is properly called, born in London in 1775, began his artistic career at a very young age. His father, a barber in Maiden Lane, Covent Garden, recognized the unusual talent of his son very early and did everything possible to encourage him.

In 1789, when Turner was only fourteen years old, he was accepted in the Royal Academy which, having only been founded twenty years previously, was still a young, but respected institution. It had two aims: firstly, to offer British artists appropriate exhibition possibilities and, secondly, to serve as a training facility for hopeful young talents. Here Turner received a thorough training in drawing from models as well as in perspective and in the other crafts necessary for a basic knowledge of art.

He also received a small supplement to his livelihood by working for the architect and topographer Thomas Malton where he also gained a certain amount of knowledge in architectural representation. Turner retained a stylistic characteristic of Malton's in choosing unusual standpoints to achieve dramatic perspectives in his own work and later perfected it. Malton, who placed great importance on artistic detail in his work and was never satisfied with simple architectural pictures, was an exemplary ideal.

In 1790, Turner first took part in an exhibition at the Royal Academy where he exhibited regularly from then on. Although the young man had to absolve a general programme of learning at the academy, he consequently trained at the same time to become a topographer in the field of architecture as well as in landscape painting. The sudden turn to landscapes is astonishing and shows that this theme was a true concern of the young artist. Turner grew up in the narrow back streets of London — and Maiden Lane is even today not the most respectable area. His first contact with the countryside came late for the youth but then suddenly and with a grasping vehemence.

Until Turner's era, only historical painting had been regarded as real art; Reynolds, however, made the portrait an equally worthy theme. However, landscape painting was considerably lower in status. At first, in order to be accepted by the public, it had to prove itself worthy of being displayed by including historical scenarios as adornment. In a transitional period it required the historical theme in order that the accessory »landscape« could be accepted. However, in the course of a few years, public taste changed and the picturesque landscape began to attract interest. At this point in development Turner made his entrance with his decorative landscapes. From then on it was more or less en vogue to see landscapes with different eyes and even to see every natural beauty artistically idealized. It went so far that an auxiliary device was developed which became popular for use with landscapes — a so-called Claude-glass. It was an optical glass which

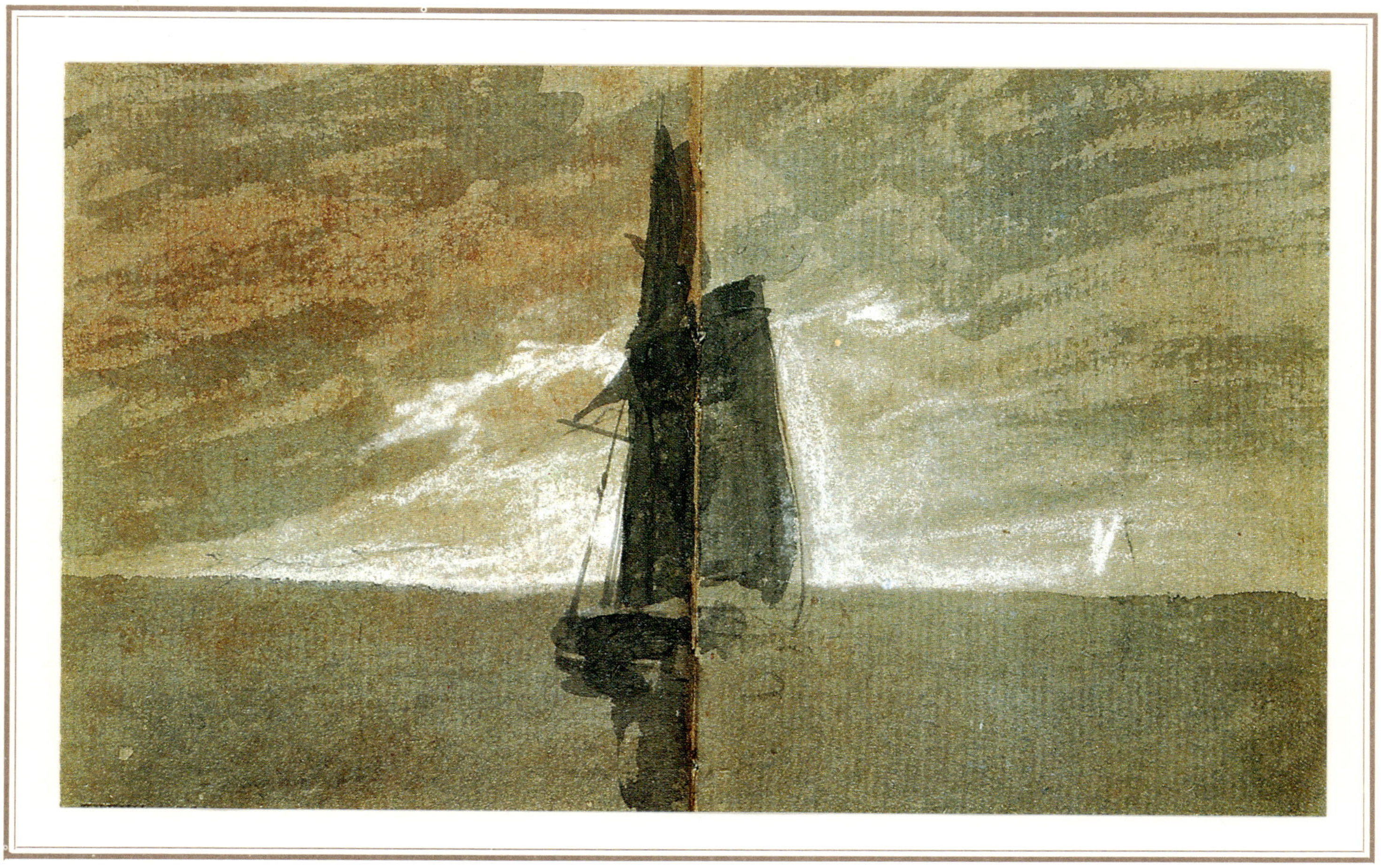

Plate I

Sailing vessel at sea. 1796–97

Watercolour, gouache and pencil,
11.3 x 18.6 cm
Sketchbook XXXVII, page 66–67

reduced the landscape to the proportions of a painting and gave the shading of the scene the colour effect of old varnish and subdued light which matched that of the studio.

English painting was now incredibly popular as Dutch painting had been before with Rembrandt and the other artists of the *Golden Age*. Gainsborough still lived from portrait painting; although he very much wanted to paint landscapes, his commitments in English society left him absolutely no time and frustrated almost every departure from tradition: the portrait earned him his living.

Turner was able to secure a private area for the artistic activities which he tended towards within a short time: the landscape painting including architecture and animated life in the landscape. In 1792, Turner followed the tracks of Richard Wilson, one of the first English landscape painters, to his home country Wales. So the artist began a career which he was to practise for many years to come.

Turner's love of the country and the logical path he followed to landscape painting was astonishing. As mentioned before, the youth grew up in a narrow busy back street in the centre of London where life pulsated strongly, admittedly not in a refined manner. It would have been suitable for the style of the era if Turner had chosen to sketch the colourful masses of people from this environment with his pencil. Instead, while still a young boy, his attention was drawn to architecture and landscape which he sketched from engravings. It is reported that the father exhibited his son's drawings in his barber's shop and was overjoyed at every sale. It was one of the barber's customers who directed young William's way to the art school of the Royal Academy. The boy can thank his enormous talent that he was admitted while still so very young. The regulations of the institute denied students of his age the right to join the classes where female nudes were painted and sketched. It is not reported if these rules were enforced in Turner's case. Turner's father supported the artistic career of his son to the best of his ability and after the mother's death dedicated himself even more to his son. When his son's career began to be financially successful, he closed his barber's shop and helped his son, with whom he lived for the rest of his life, with various preparatory work.

William Turner never married. He declared that his paintings were his children, and in his later years he kept several biographers and newspaper reporters occupied with his various eccentricities, which were, of course, watched with great interest because of his popularity. It appears that he had close contact with two women without approaching a legalization of the relationship in either case. He kept his private life secret, and this, of course, caused all sorts of journalistic speculation.

Turner's obvious conviction as to the value of his paintings had already caused annoyance in his younger years, and soon he had the reputation of being arrogant and slightly rapacious. When he realized that the participation in the annual Academy exhibition with one painting did not offer him the extent of publicity he required, he decided to open his own gallery in his house in the very respectable Harley Street. From the very beginning this astute decision guaranteed him an income which freed him of all financial worries. Soon he was able to afford a house on the outskirts of London where he lived together with his father. At this time he already had the reputation of being an uncouth, overambitious and unfriendly character. In reality he was probably much too fixated on his work to give the distractions of mundane society life even the slightest attention. He refused to attach himself to society, like Constable, who had gained no obvious benefits from this association.

In the annual exhibition of the Royal Academy the artist was allowed — as in many other similar events into this century — to make corrections to the hung paintings up to the official opening. When one realizes how much the effect of a painting differs when the surroundings are changed, this seems a reasonable custom. Turner often took this chance to make last changes to his paintings. He altered his pictures in front of a half-official public who, because of their position or connections, were already admitted to the room. He worked with full concentration, nose pressed close to the canvas without once stepping back. Not in the least bothered by the bustle of people around him, he painted with phenomenal competence. Then he would suddenly close his paint box and leave quickly, as if fleeing, without casting a single glance at the finished work. He knew exactly when the painting was completed. The *Guild of St. George* in London possesses a sketch which shows Turner working in the gallery. Closely watched by colleagues, the small figure stands in front of his painting dressed in frock coat and top hat. He has his palette, paintbrush and spatula in his hands and paints unwaveringly.

## TRAVELS IN ENGLAND

Political events at the time made visits to the continent impossible for a long time for the young Turner and all other private travellers. Until 1802 and from 1806 to 1813 the middle-European ports were unattainable to English travellers.

For William Turner, who had already made topographical views in his area of work in his younger years, the impossibility of reaching picturesque places in foreign lands was most unbearable. Fortunately he had an exceptional affection for his home country and a great concern for the places of interest in Britain. He used the years between 1792 and 1802, a full decade, for intensive study trips in Britain. After his first journey through Wales followed a trip to the Midlands. In 1795, he was in South Wales and on the Isle of Wight. Two years later, he visited Yorkshire, Northumberland and the Lake District, 1798 Bristol and North Wales. In 1799 followed Lancashire and again North Wales.

It was not just the English landscape which fascinated Turner, but also the changeable weather, the quickly changing climate and the constantly altering atmosphere. He realized the great advantage and inestimable stimulus of these moods and absorbed them quickly, only sketching in the landscape. When he was a professor at the Royal Academy, he placed this advantage before his pupils' eyes. »In our changing climate, where one day is enough to experience the four seasons, where a complete hazy abandon covers the subjects' countenance, where nature appears to play a game and gives the artist's study unexpected incidents . . . how lucky the situation of the landscape painter is, how every change of nature excites him from minute to minute — a nature which does not allow tiredness, not even in the effects which it displays before his eyes, unremittingly imperiously demanding admiration and exploration so that the artist can retain every change of place and time in his soul.«

Between all his travels, which had to be arduously covered by coach, there were long periods in which Turner worked in his studio, elaborated on his innumerable travel sketches, created patterns for engravings or simply painted. In 1790, he began to paint in oil, also on a larger scale. In this year he did not set out on any journey, probably because of the new tasks in hand and the corresponding involvement with painting.

In the same year, two important paintings by Claude Lorrain which found great interest among the public came to London. Turner was also very impressed, as his origins had been considerably influenced by the great French master. However, it was not just Claude Lorrain who had acted as a stimulant, a study of the Dutch masters had also been very important for Turner's artistic development. A painting from 1796, an early masterpiece, shows an intimate knowledge of Rembrandt's work. Turner's painting *Fishermen at Sea* has the same light effect on the central events of the picture as Rembrandt's *Rest during the Flight*. In both paintings there is also a sky with intense indirect moonlight so that both the light areas in the picture correspond most charmingly in what is otherwise a dark painting.

In the sketches which he made on his travels, Turner obviously did not just allow himself to be led along by the artistic effects of attractive views, but realized very much that certain scenes would sell well later when he executed them as water colours or oil paintings. It seems that he considered the commercial use of his work at a very early stage in his travel sketches. Of course from the publishers who commissioned series of engravings there would also have been certain thoughts as to which scenes could not be excluded or which would sell especially well in the art trade.

Turner felt especially drawn to the medium of the aquarelle. He did not just use watercolours for sketching but endeavoured his whole life, increasingly so in old age, to make a work of art of the carefully arranged aquarelle which could be placed next to the oil painting and have a completely equal status. When Turner worked on a landscape out of doors, he mostly drew in his sketch books. Several times he made attempts at creating oil paintings outside, but it seems that it did not satisfy him. He definitely preferred working in the studio.

His sketches were often just fleeting shorthand notes in ink, crayon or pencil, recorded in rather small drawing books. Sometimes he used two sides for an oblong sketch. When he wished to capture a landscape or architectural elevation exactly in all its perspective details, he would often use a wash so that he could also note the atmospheric conditions. These quickly drawn impressions were often later elaborated on in his lodgings or at home in his studio to become meticulous watercolours. They retained a sketchy character as their basis was, in a manner of speaking, a drawing. Certainly he also captured motifs in the landscape in coloured sketches with watercolours, but mainly when it just dealt with a representation in which he was concerned with retaining the essence of the landscape and the corresponding mood. He did not dispense with the meticulousness of his drawing pen for architectural subjects and only used coloured shading to raise the graphic quality with light and shadow. It is, however, astonishing to think how much care Turner, who was able to see and capture on paper so incredibly exactly, used in the elaboration of his sketches. In order to reproduce the optimal precision of an elevation or contour of a building, he used a variety of memorabilia, which helped him guarantee the topographic exactness apart from the compositional elaboration through dramaturgical, picturesque scenarios, which as accessories had the task of rounding off the representation. A few periods in his life have been recorded where he organized more comfortable working conditions for himself out of doors so that he could work on his sketches. For instance, once an artist colleague placed his considerable portable

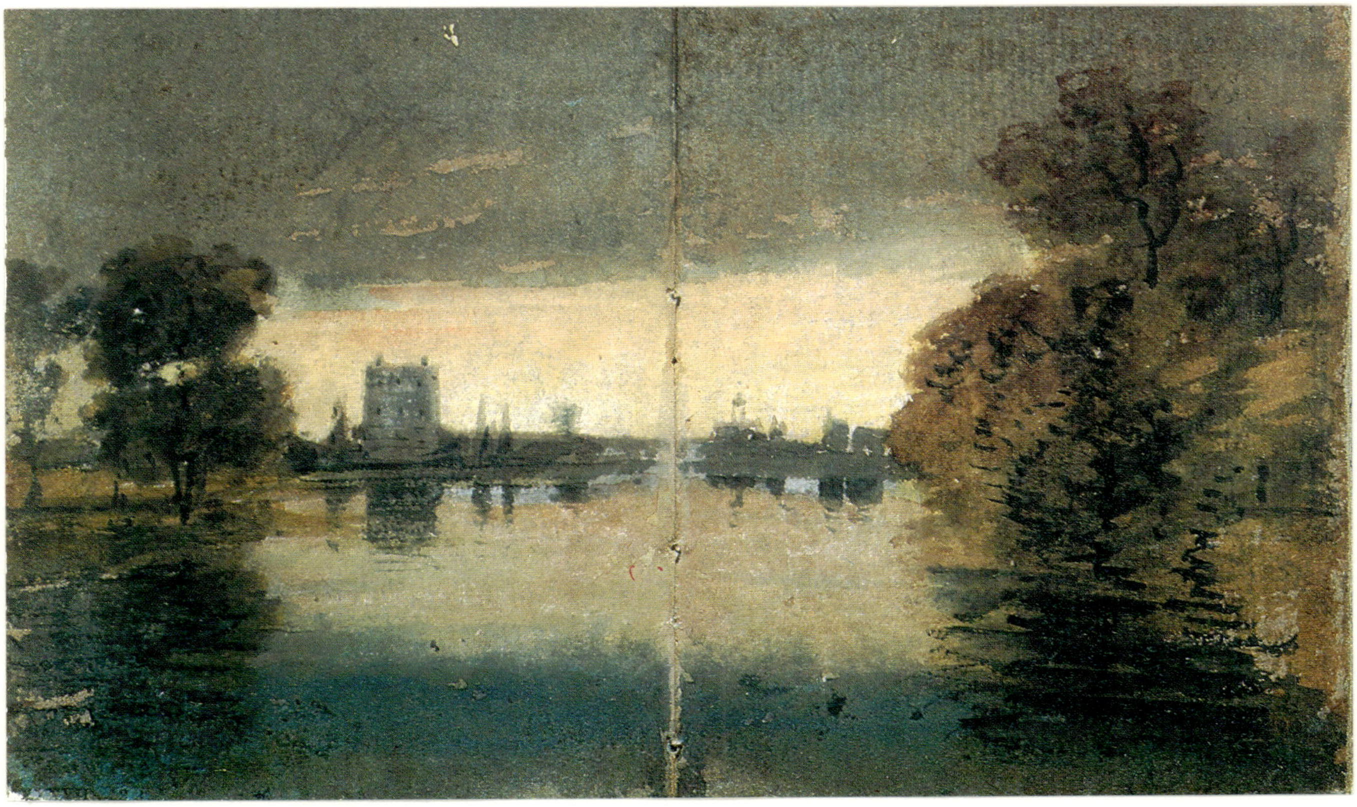

Plate II

River Scene, Evening effect. 1796–97

Watercolour, gouache and pencil,
11.3 x 18.6 cm
Sketchbook XXXVII, page 22–23

painting utensils at Turner's disposal and also helped to carry them. For a time, Turner even worked from a boat which he had brought to moorings on the Thames and the Wey. Independent from the quick sketches, made while travelling, Turner was also concerned with making the aquarelle a valid pictorial form through very careful design. He made many varied attempts at fully utilizing the possibilities of this beloved technique. Admittedly he clearly recognized the limits of the material as well as its benefits and also the relative impossibility of doing justice to many objects. J. Farlington described some of the technical measures which Turner used in his watercolours in excerpts from his journal, which Andrew Wilton cited in his famous book on Turner. For example, Farlington described the method by which Turner created highlights in his aquarelles. »One creates highlights by going over the areas which are to become light with a paintbrush which has been dipped in water (after a general dark ground has been applied where necessary), then raising the paint which has been moistened with blotting paper; then the areas are highlighted with breadcrumbs . . . an extremely matt appearance can be achieved when one goes over the area with an almost dry camel-hair brush which only tickles the moisture in the area which has been touched; and the light areas are made partly visible with blotting paper.«

In his long creative career, William Turner understood how to elevate the studio aquarelle to an equal position with oil painting, to create, in the eyes of the public, watercolours which were of equal value. Although contemporaries of Turner who also tended towards landscape painting stood before similar problems and dedicated a great amount of attention to aquarelle painting, only Turner achieved an outstanding artistic and technical perfection.

In 1799, the young artist was accepted as an Associate of the Royal Academy and he was probably one of the youngest members in this illustrious circle ever. He was admired and employed as a creator of pleasant landscapes as well as highly dramatic historical scenes rich in landscape accessories and also as a topographically skilled designer of artistic patterns for engravings. In his younger years he was already very successful, something for which he could thank the eminent diligence with which he brought his rich talent to advantage. Of course the appointment as an Academy member gave his artistic ambition a decisive impetus. One can read from his work that from this point onwards he attempted larger and thematically more demanding paintings with a different self-confidence. The outer recognition gave him the assurance that he was now a master with the right to set himself all kinds of artistic tasks.

In the years of his travels in England, Turner created an enormous treasure of sketches. As well as these there are also many aquarelles and oil paintings of numerous places, river landscapes and castles. There are very few picturesque corners of the country which do not appear in his work. Especially informative are motifs which Turner painted at the beginning of his career and again in later years: now more experienced, more practiced, richer in narrative details, but also more complex and considerably more fastidious in colour. The numerous series of engravings made to his design harbour a wealth of country views. Turner was a fantastic preparer for this technique. As he had expert knowledge of the manual techique used in the production, he could give the engraver detailed instructions with his designs which would show his work to the best advantage, almost without exception. Turner's printed graphic work covers over 800 items, which admittedly were not produced directly by him alone as was customary at that time. In those days the artist usually made the design and trained engravers carried out the manual work. Turner corrected very carefully with exact knowledge of the possibilities available in this technique. Printing was also entrusted to specialists. The term original graphic, as we understand it today, is quite recent, it was only towards the end of the 19th century that a value was placed on the craftsmanship of the artist. Turner's large portfolio works were widely distributed, the romantic view corresponded exactly with popular taste at the time, the prints were supposed to show topographical views, but as far as possible be picturesque and not without a dramatic accent, all demands which Turner's artistic temperament was able to satisfy fully. Probably the most ambitious project which Turner created in the area of graphic printing was his *Liber studiorum*, a collection of over 80 mezzotint engravings. In this collection Turner wished to show on the one hand his full ability, the variety of his manual skills and at the same time to document with a multitude of different pictorial motifs how rich our world is. The title of this work was chosen in imitation of Claude Lorrain's *Liber Veritatis*. »While this work on which Turner based his own was never meant for public showing, as Claude only wanted to capture his pictures in sketches, Turner's ambitious project had a pronounced didactic character and was meant to present, as a collection of his representative works, compositions and themes from various categories of landscape painting to the art-theoretical expectations of the picturesque or the majestic in his time. A direct study of nature and an empathy with classical masterpieces are the principals from which Turner worked on in *Liber studiorum*. These prints are therefore to be seen as evidence of his confident consideration of tradition, his attempts to surpass it, to be greater than the history to which he still felt completely attached. Nothing could have been further from his mind than a complete break between him and the art of the past.« (Henning Bock)

In the beginning Turner carried out the mezzotint work himself on the first prints and was excited by the beauty of this technique which is rich in nuances. He had a tendency to work thinking in sequences; undoubtedly a characteristic which helped him in these series of engravings. However, Turner also worked in sequences in his aquarelles and in many of his oil paintings so that several works viewed together can be seen as one unit.

Series such as *Picturesque Views of the Southern Coast of England* and the *Picturesque Views in England and Wales* are magnificent and varied achievements in which Turner's great ability can clearly be seen. He already considered the possibilities of transforming his aquarelles for the graphical engraving technique as he was always concerned with the quality of the engravings which were made from his works. As he grew older he enlivened his landscapes and architectural works with genre scenes in the foreground for which he made an endless amount of sketches.

## TRAVELS ON THE CONTINENT

The Treaty of Amiens, which was negotiated between England and France, was really more of a temporary truce than a proper conclusion of peace. It enabled the British people to undertake short trips to Europe from spring 1802 onwards. Turner took the opportunity immediately and was most anxious to see the Swiss mountains with his own eyes as they had occupied him for some time in his work. From July to October he travelled through France to Switzerland and, as was to be expected, was overwhelmed by the gigantic mountains. He drew a great number of sketches, however, oddly enough, only relatively few found use in later paintings.

The artist chose his return journey so that he could remain in Paris for a few weeks where he spent a great deal of time with an intensive study of paintings in the Louvre. The Louvre had been converted a short time before from the royal gallery into the status of a public museum, and the young state energetically attempted to unite all of the great names of the art world in this one place. Especially Napoleon's marauding expeditions brought a tremendous amount of works of art for the museum.

However, it was also Napoleon who prevented Turner from carrying out further study trips on the continent after his first great journey in foreign lands with his Continental System: Between 1805 and 1815 it was practically impossible for private English travellers to reach a European port on the continent. In 1817, Turner was eventually able to travel through Belgium and Holland and on the Rhine in August and September. He stayed for longer periods in Cologne and Mainz and visited all the picturesque areas between these two cities.

Apart from Switzerland, Italy was also a favourite country for British travellers. Turner had already created a number of works which had Italian landscapes as their theme, however, they had all been patterned on paintings by other artists. In 1817, for example, he painted a highly dramatic, immensely colourful aquarelle of the eruption of Vesuvius, solely from a drawing made by a friend. In August 1819, the time had finally come: Turner was able to set out on a long journey to Italy from which he only returned to England in the spring of the following year. He journeyed through Turin and Como to Venice, then on to Rome and Naples. The return journey took him through Florence. Several important friends had encouraged him to make this trip, among others Thomas Lawrence amd James Hakewill who Turner was able to convince to help him on the work *Picturesque Tour of Italy.* The latter also equipped the artist with a detailed map, which even included information as to which points enabled one to obtain the most beautiful views of cities and landscapes. The care with which Turner prepared his journey in order that he could carry out his plans with his individual

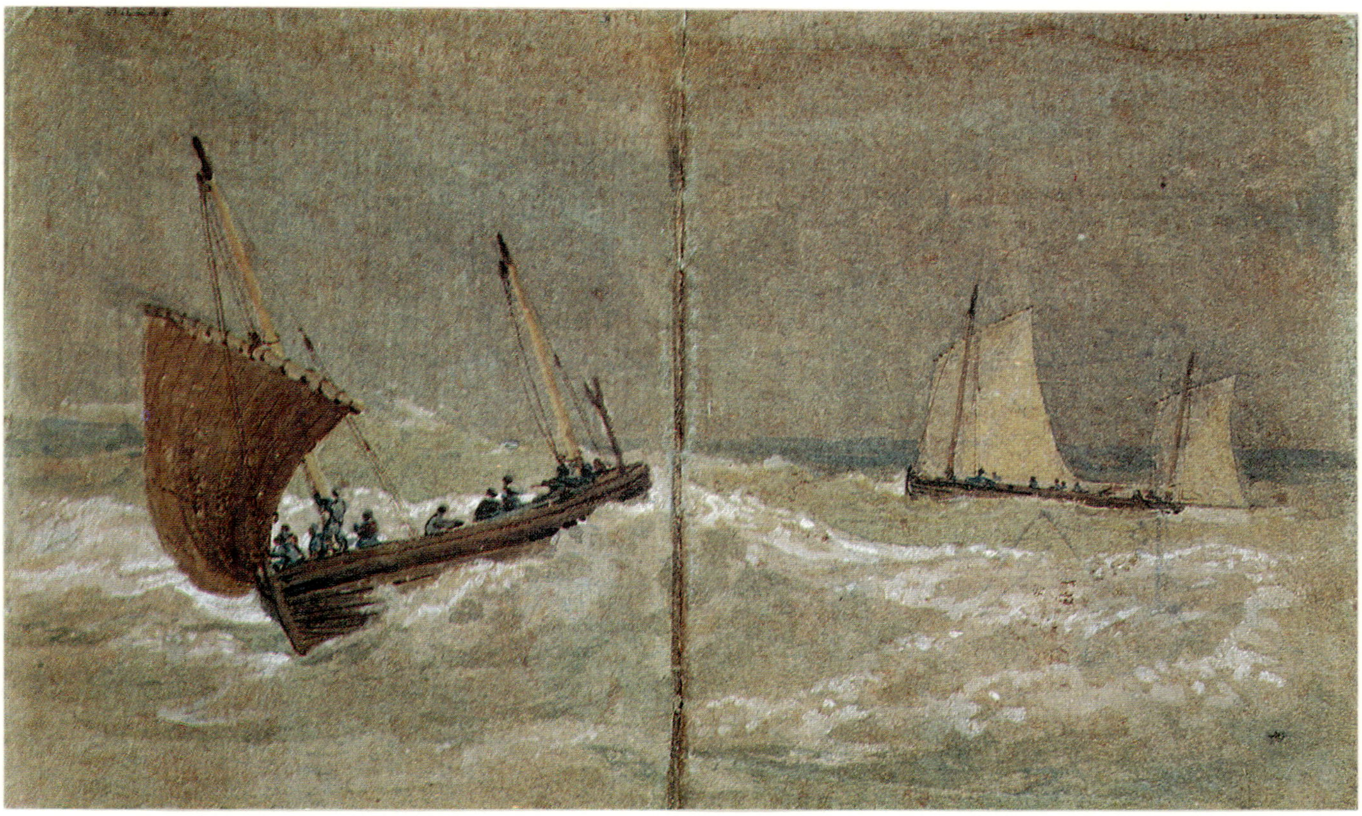

Plate III

Sailing boats at sea. 1796–97

Watercolour, gouache and pencil,
11.3 x 18.6 cm
Sketchbook XXXVII, page 106–107

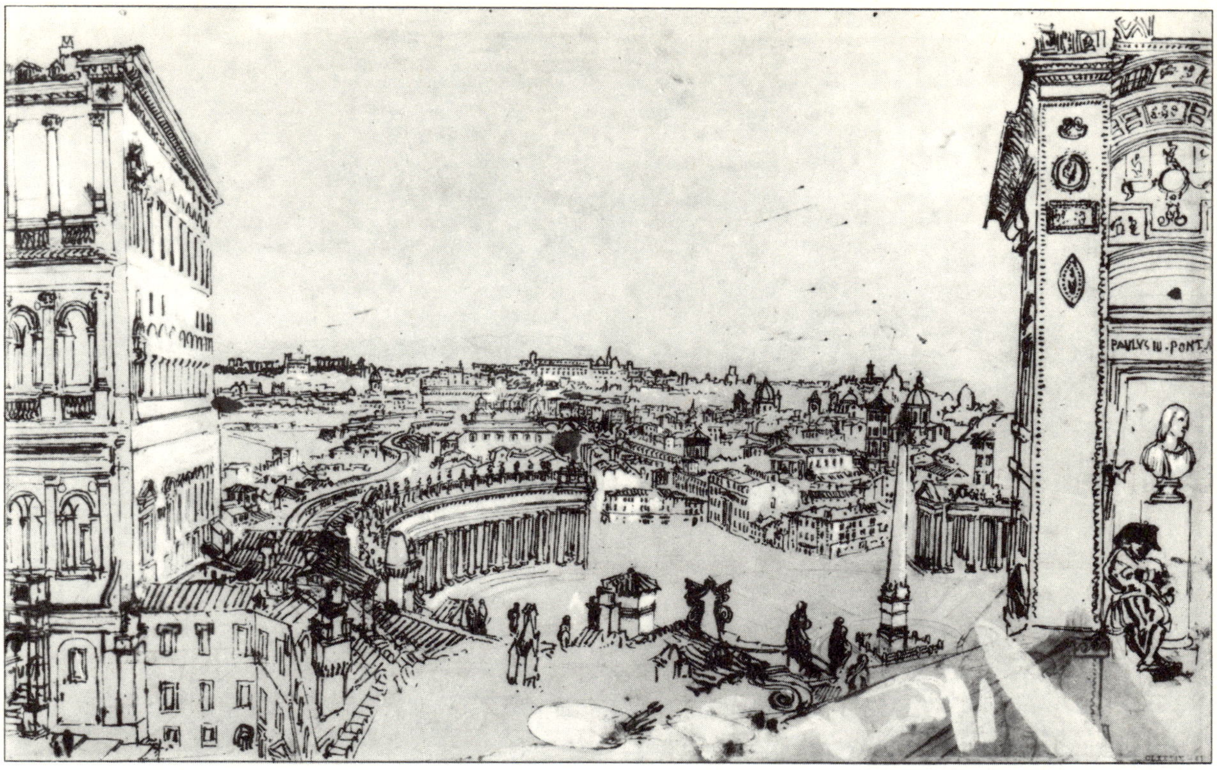

meticulousness is shown in a book of travels which has been preserved with instructions and information in which Turner, while still at home, had transferred references from other sketch books in tiny notes. Obviously he doubted whether his receptiveness would be enough for the wealth of pictorial impressions which awaited him. Actually he filled more than twenty sketch books himself on this journey.

In 1828 he undertook a second journey to Italy. Before this the artist, who was very fond of travelling, had in 1825 journeyed again to Holland, Belgium and also on the Rhine. In the following year he travelled along the rivers Maas, Mosel and Loire. He also visited Paris several times, for example, in 1829 when he also saw Normandy and Brittany. Obviously he did not shy from the rigours which a traveller had to expect in those days. So it was that he went once again to Paris in summer 1833, in 1834 he was again on the Maas, the Mosel and the Rhine and in 1835 he again visited Venice. This time he seems to have chosen a very unusual route, from the port of Szczecin through Berlin, Dresden, Prague and Vienna. He made his last journey to Venice in 1840, this time travelling there on the Rhine and on his homeward journey through Munich. He also spent the summer months of 1841, 1842 and 1844 on the continent, once again on the Rhine and in Switzerland. He was always drawn to water, rivers, lakes and the coast. He was fascinated by the reflection of light on water and reproduced it in transparent colours. Even in his paintings from Switzerland it is obvious that he did not paint the romance of the mountainous region, but gave priority to the atmosphere on and above the great lakes. The picture material which he collected on his travels in Switzerland was most important for the reputation of a leading landscape artist, as Switzerland was regarded as having an especially vivid landscape. Turner had attempted for years to imagine the greatness of the Swiss mountains from paintings by other artists. Now he was eventually able to fill this sensitive gap in his topographical knowledge.

When one considers that between his travels on the continent he also travelled extensively in Britain, one can see how consequently the artist's life was organized around his work. However, of all his travels the place which made the most lasting impression on the artist was the favourite destination of British travellers at that time: the lagoon city of Venice. It had been almost imperative for educated travellers to Italy to visit this city since the 17th century. The splendid city life, the festivities with magnificent displays of pomp, the carnival and the great religious celebrations appeared especially picturesque to the protestant or anglican people from the north. They attracted visitors as much as the unusual position of the city on water, the splendid buildings and the Oriental ambience. The artistic treasures of Venetian painting were enormous and art was rated very highly in the city state.

However, in Turner's time this flair already belonged to the past, since, as history tells us, immeasurable damage had been inflicted on the splendid city by interests from other countries, through wars and plundering. But the British, who were used to living and thinking traditionally, remained true to the city in spite of its apparent impoverishment and the prevalence of dirt and ruin. Venice belonged unchangingly to the most important destinations of a British traveller in Italy — and it was no different for Turner. Of course, as mentioned, he visited Rome and the southern sites of antiquity, but Venice always remained something special to him, even into the later years of his travels. In his paintings of this city the past comes to life again. The observer is drawn into the excitement of lagoon festivities, the pomp and bustle, the life and grace as if all this is happening before his eyes. In Turner's first sketches amd paintings from Venice, architecture and colourfulness still dominate the scenes. In the later paintings, one feels how much he experienced the carefree Venice of the past, forgetting the present and only representing the shimmer of the elements, water, light and heat in their relaxed state.

It was not just chance which made Turner turn to the pure study of colour in these paintings which were mainly painted at home from memory. »In those days, he painted watercolours which were stimulated by the colour atmosphere of the lagoon, without a real representational resolution, mostly in the colours blue, pink and yellow, painted on top of each other in horizontal stripes.« (Ursula Prinz) In many paintings the colour is so far removed from reality that one is unable to connect it with actual situations of light or nature. But it is especially these prints which are very dense in atmosphere. Venice is not literally represented but it is nonetheless immensely present.

Canaletto, the famous Venetian artist, had a great deal of admirers and customers for his paintings in England. This caused him to visit this country to paint for a time there so that he could better his finances. However, the English painters did not like the competition from an artist who surpassed them in many ways, and therefore he was soon compelled to leave the country. Turner admired the great master and documented this by a monument which he erected to him in one of his paintings: *Bridge of Sighs, Ducal Palace and Customhouse, Venice: Canaletto Painting*. It is highly probable that this painting was made at the suggestion of Lord Byron, whose *Childe Harold's Pilgrimage* was illustrated by Turner. Byron was one of the many English admirers of the lagoon city, he lived in Venice from 1816 until 1819. The opening line in *Childe Harold's Pilgrimage* is famous, »I stood in Venice on the bridge of Sighs, a palace and a prison on each hand.«

Without the experience of Venice, Turner's work would most certainly not have achieved the originality which so deeply impresses us today.

## THE LATE WORK

Turner's extraordinary perception for the expressiveness of colour for its own sake and not in combination with other decorative media such as form, perspective or composition often led him in his later years to a style of painting in which the play of colours almost completely dissolved the representational motif. Venice was crucial for the experience of a transparent play of colours. Most of the paintings were not made in front of the motif but from memory in the guarded atmosphere of the studio. Essential here was not the local description of a place but rather the emotional consternation of a creative artist who felt that the statement in colour and light was more important than the original observed expression.

In Turner's late work, colour had absolute priority. First he created its well-balanced structure, then, more by chance, a suggestion of objective realism set in. A colleague of his criticised this course of action quite early: he paints »as if one is looking into a coal-fire or at an old wall, the variety and uncertain structures of which stimulate ones fantasy to see things which are not there.« The expressive colour took up his whole interest. He knew the colour theories of Newton and Goethe well and attempted to translate them into painting. »The colourist Turner discovered in this constructed world from light and colour the possibilities of transforming the sensations and poetical experiences of nature and world into a hymn in praise of colour. No one else in this century had developed the impressive use of colour so far and so close to abstraction as this artist.« (Werner Haftmann)

As has been mentioned before, William Turner freed himself more and more from the object in his paintings as he became older. A transcendental experience of atmosphere, light, water and wind and the transformation of those into colour gained an overwhelming importance in his paintings and aquarelles. The pictorial motif as an object of expression did not become less important, it continued to be of central significance, but Turner was no longer concerned with its recognizability.

The tragedy in his life was the fact that he — as most artists — needed public response for his paintings. With old age he became an unfriendly and sourly character, who made life difficult for his friends. In his personal life, he isolated himself, became crotchety and possibly even turned to alcohol. In his work he became more self-willed and stubbornly concentrated only on things which he considered to be important for his art, without bothering about anyone else. However, neither his friends nor the interested public were able to follow him on this path of artistic spiritualization and outer aloofness. The paintings which came from his studio often met with rejection or, at the least, were misunderstood. The public loved the Turner who painted decorative historical paintings,

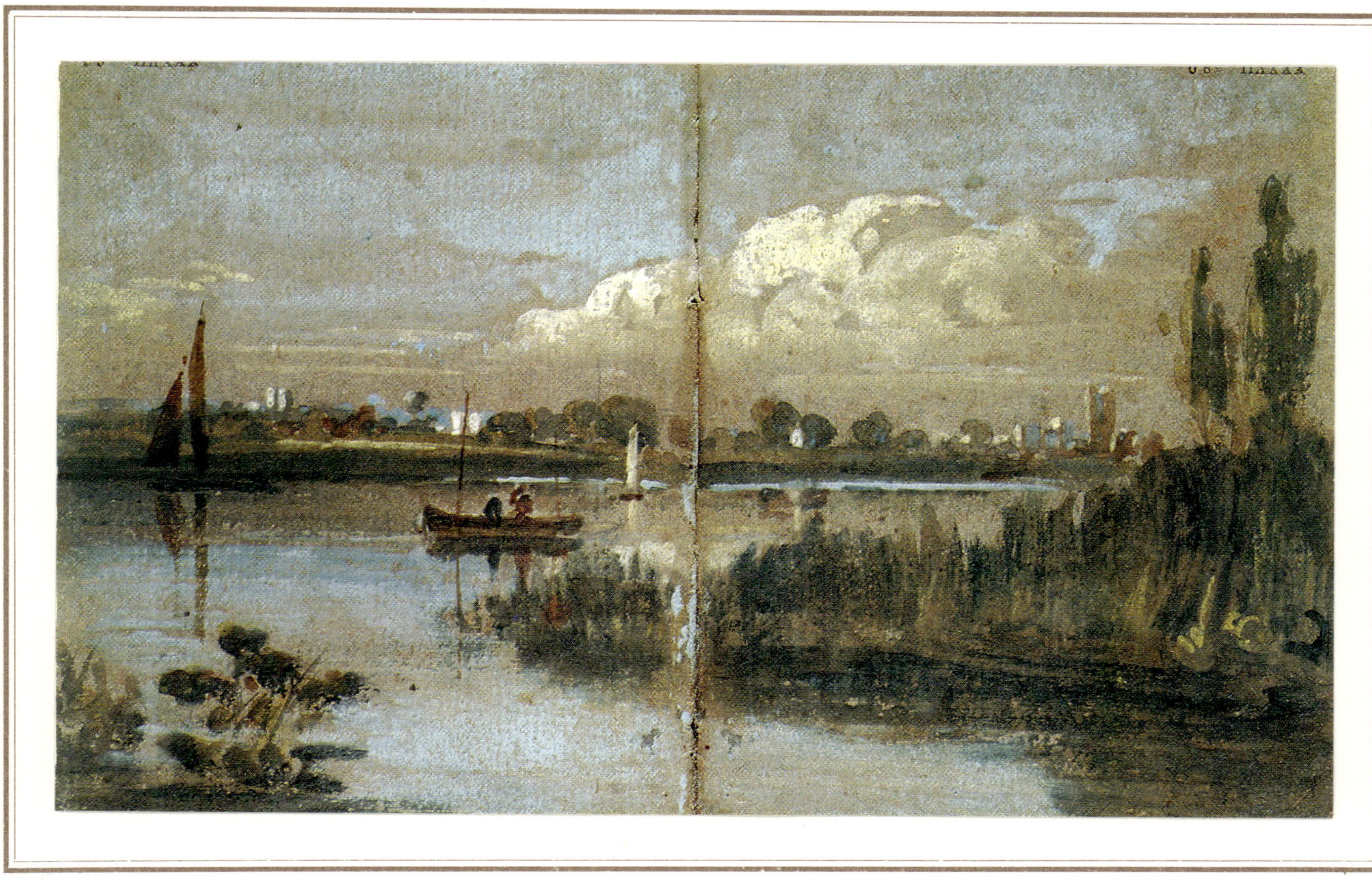

Plate IV

River scene with boats. 1796–97

Watercolour, gouache and pencil,
11.3 x 18.6 cm
Sketchbook XXXVII, page 80–81

they loved the tense drama and the landscapes with their incomparable well-balanced tranquility. In his late work, when access to the subject matter of the paintings was made more difficult, those who had been interested turned away. Criticism was, at first, sceptical, but soon became very negative. Turner was for the whole of his life dependent on the approval of his friends and the acclaim and enthusiasm of his clients. His ambitiousness had become used to this. Even though he was very self-confident, he was often insecure when it came to judging his own work. It was never enough for him to view the paintings which he wanted to be just as they were and no other way — with an inner satisfaction, the lack of a positive reaction from outsiders would give him time and time again a feeling of insecurity. The gruffness of his manner, his overplayed vacillation, of course, also impeded all possibility of understanding. He was often accused of being smug. In reality he was very insecure and always in doubt as to the rightness of his way. In old age he suffered terribly under the lack of approval. He became more lonely with every intellectual step forward.

It is a strange phenomenon that several great artists in history, whose early work was well accepted by their contemporaries for most of their lives, in old age developed their art styles in such a way that future generations, with the interval between, saw it as a completely logical step, while their contemporaries were unable to comprehend the way of such a »new« art, they could only see a deformation of the traditional, a malformation. The artists' reaction to the inevitable misunderstanding was mostly seclusion and a reluctance to explain or to enlighten their purest results of artistic development to outsiders. This was the case with Rembrandt and Tizian and even the aged Dürer only grudgingly allowed mankind to share in the knowledge which he gained in his later years.

That Turner created a very clear picture of his artistic path can be seen in the fact that he retained all the paintings which seemed important to him for the documentation of his career — he even bought paintings back when, in retrospect, these appeared important. In his will he left this general account of his creative development to the public. This complete documentation shows the logical way to his art of light and colour. »Light-symbolism — modern art has not reached this goal because an opposite style — centred on line and colour — crossed the impressionistic movement. Light was not just a physical power for Turner. He used it as an expression of metaphysical atmosphere in the same way as Böcklin and Klinger achieved this with line and colour. The sun rejoices in his *Morning after the Flood*. The new-born earth shines with a paradisiacal brightness . . . Turner is a phenomenon who one faces shuddering as if before a force of nature . . . the man who did not leave his dark hermitage for weeks and months on end carried a world of light in his head; . . . Turner is probably the only one of those who risked the flight of Icarus to the sun and arrived there.« (Richard Muther)

Friends also tried to follow Turner on his way to abstraction, but to no avail. John Ruskin, who was the first to recognize the extraordinary importance which Venice had for Turner, followed the artist's late work with appreciation and great enthusiasm. But even he had problems understanding the master artist. On the other hand, Turner also found somewhat sullenly that his friend's explanations of his paintings amazed him. Ruskin had given the works content which the artist had never thought of. Ruskin reported, ». . . the lack of appreciation affected him deeply, especially the fact that his statement was not understood. Once he took the greatest trouble for a quarter of an hour in allowing me to guess what he had done in a painting before it was exhibited; he gave me one hint after the other, but I could not guess and he did not want to tell me.« A psychological barrier kept the artist from putting the secret of his creation into words. The elementary forces fire, water, light and air occupied his spirit and it was also the spiritual truths of those which he became clear-sighted towards in his later years, without being able to express himself any other way but in his paintings. Ruskin recognized the way which Turner took in the endeavour »that the yearning to raise our existence out of the dominance of rationalism, logic, exactness of the material deliberations and interests to a sphere of freedom, beauty and joy, that the way dedicated to art, purged, leads us back to our life's source.« Turner's last words are said to have been, »The Sun is God.«

# ILLUSTRATIONS

THE EARLY YEARS

LIBER STUDIORUM

Fishermen at sea (detail). 1796
Oil on canvas, 91.5 x 122.4 cm
The Tate Gallery, London

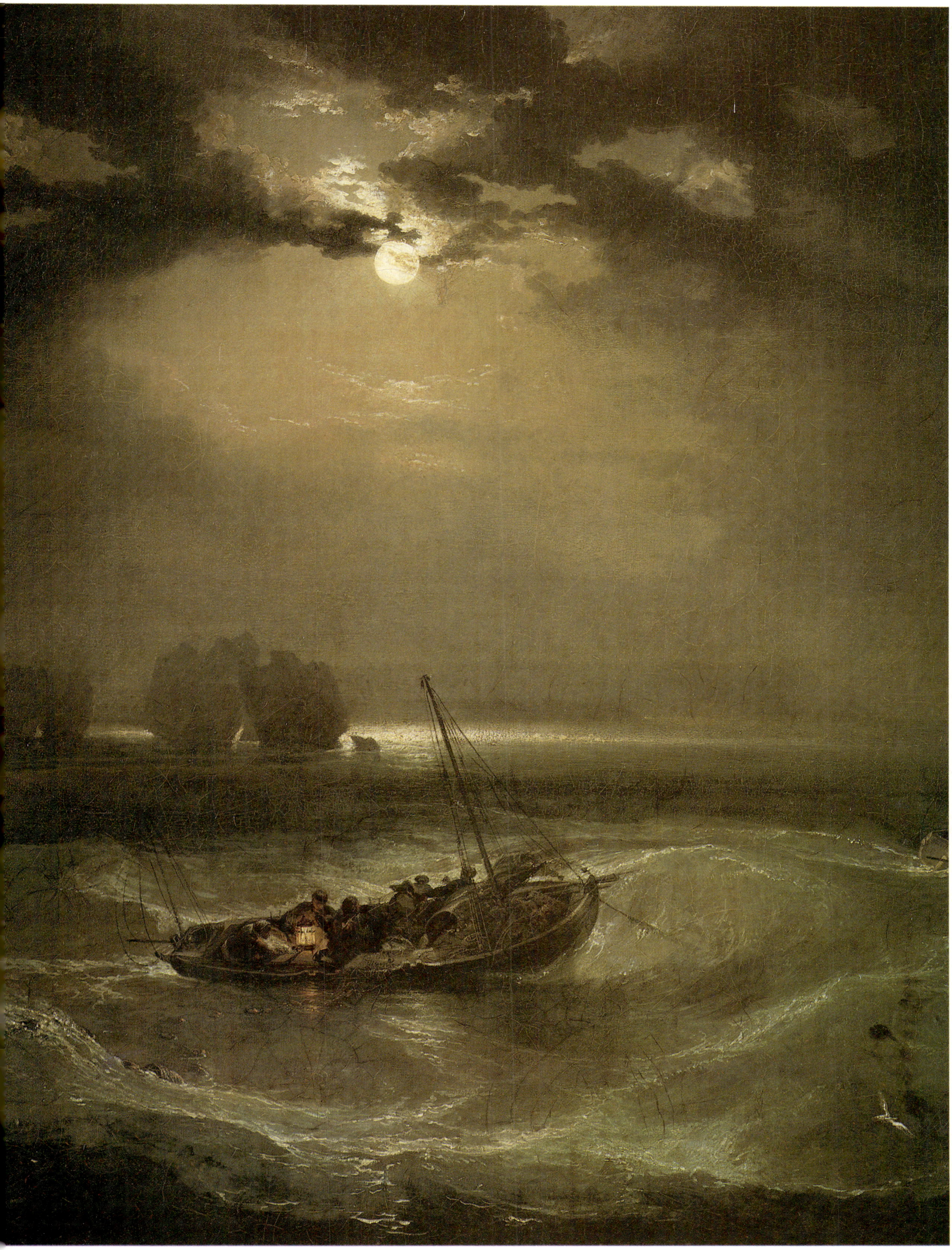

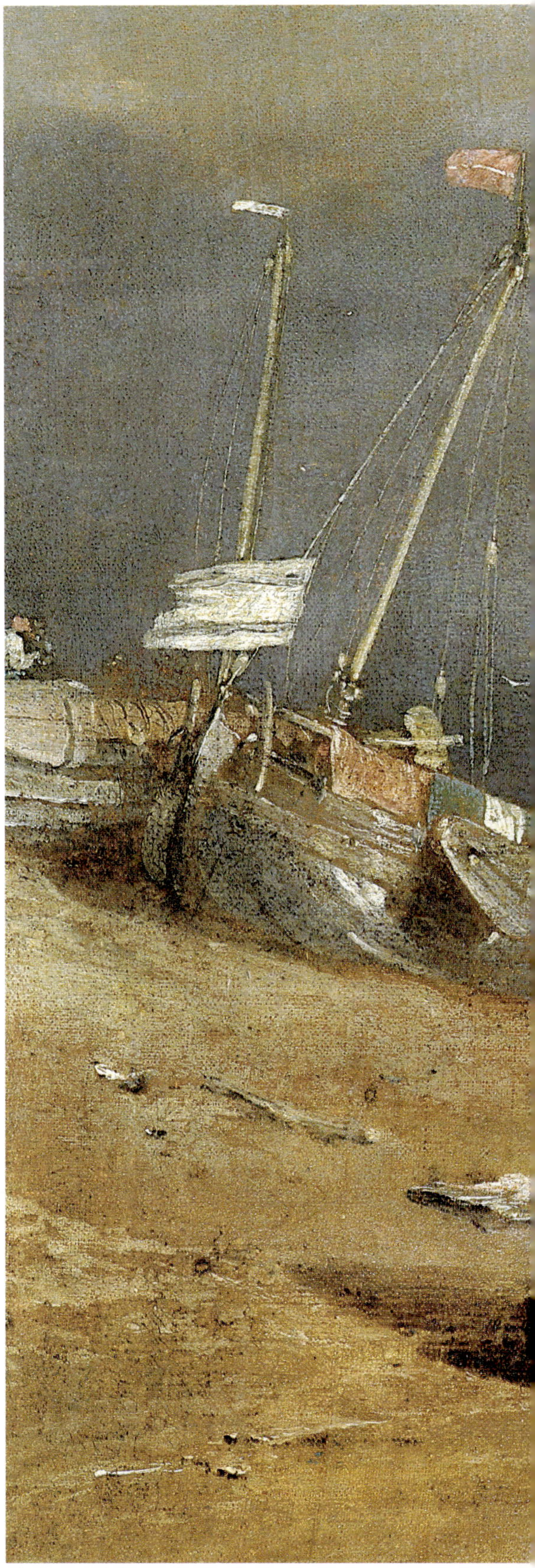

Fishmarket on the beach. 1802-1804
Oil on canvas, 43.2 x 58.4 cm
Private collection

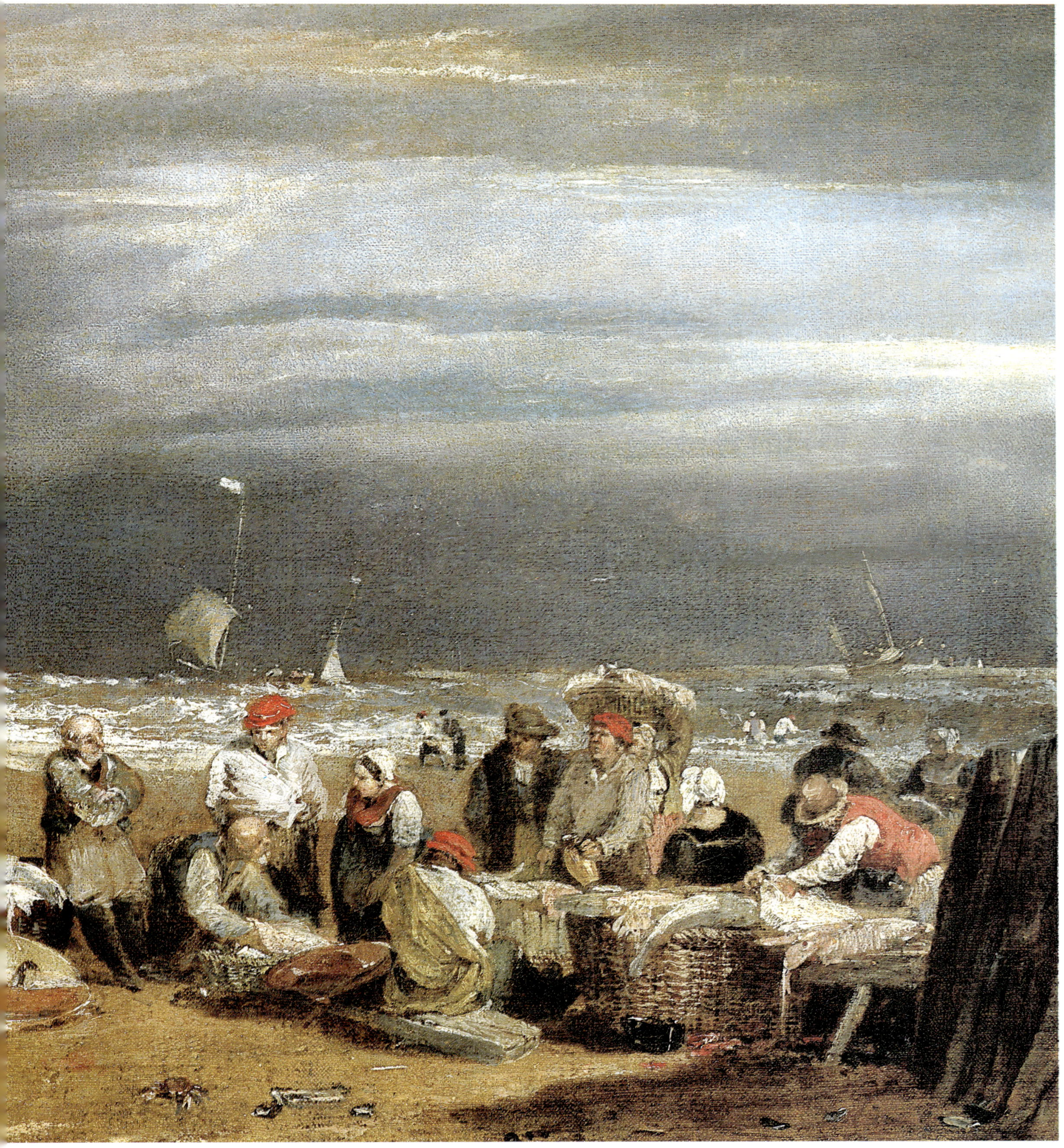

Calais Pier, with French poissards preparing for sea: an English packet arriving (detail) 1803

Oil on canvas, 172 x 240 cm

The Tate Gallery, London

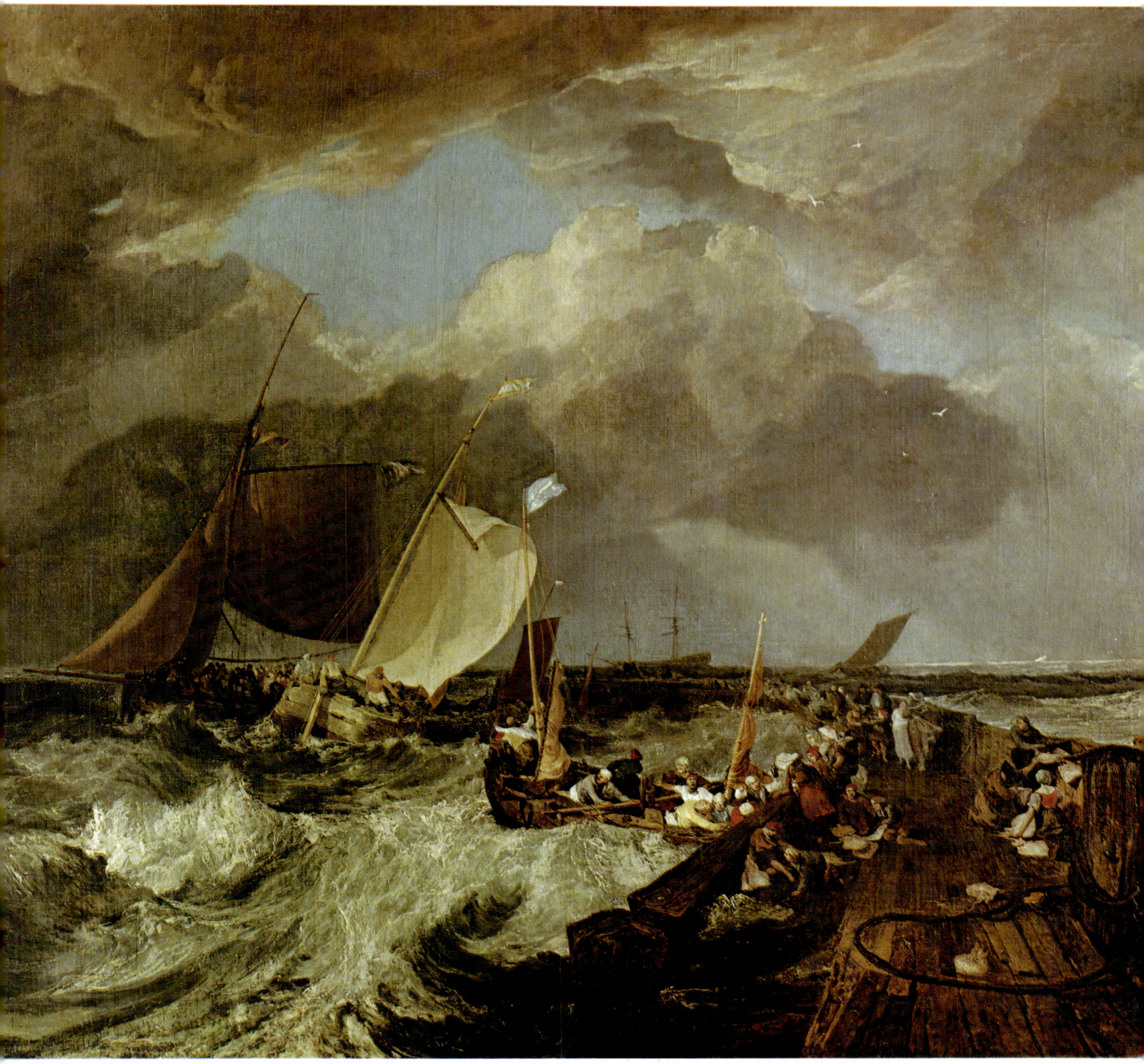

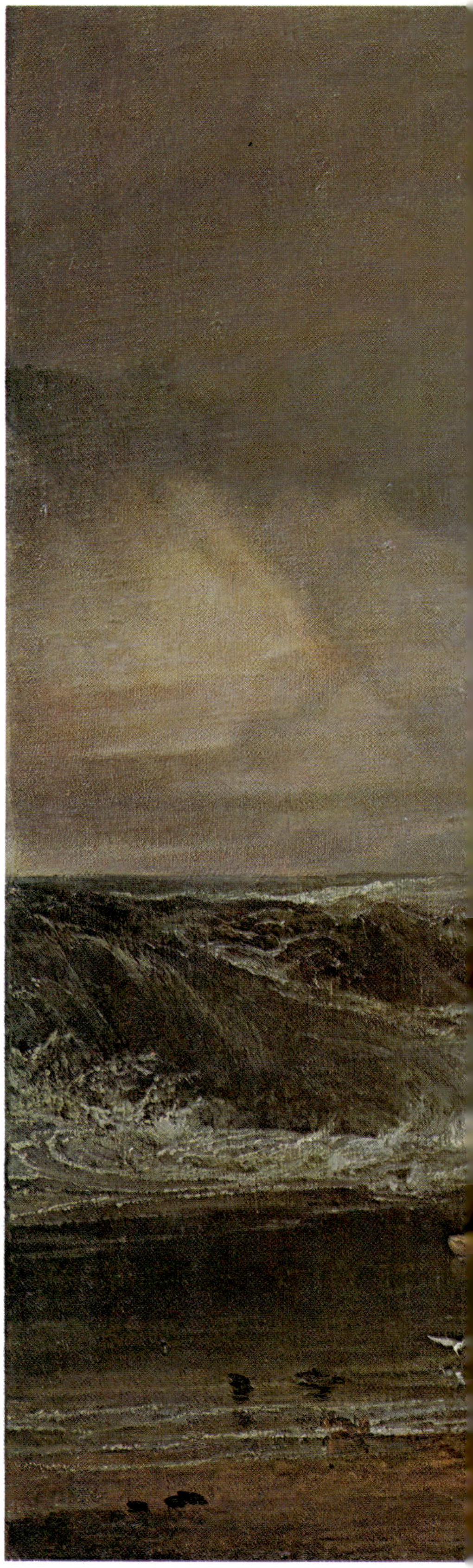

A coast scene with fishermen hauling a boat ashore. (The Iveagh Sea Piece). 1803—1804
Oil on canvas, 91.4 x 122 cm
The Iveagh Bequest, Kenwood, London

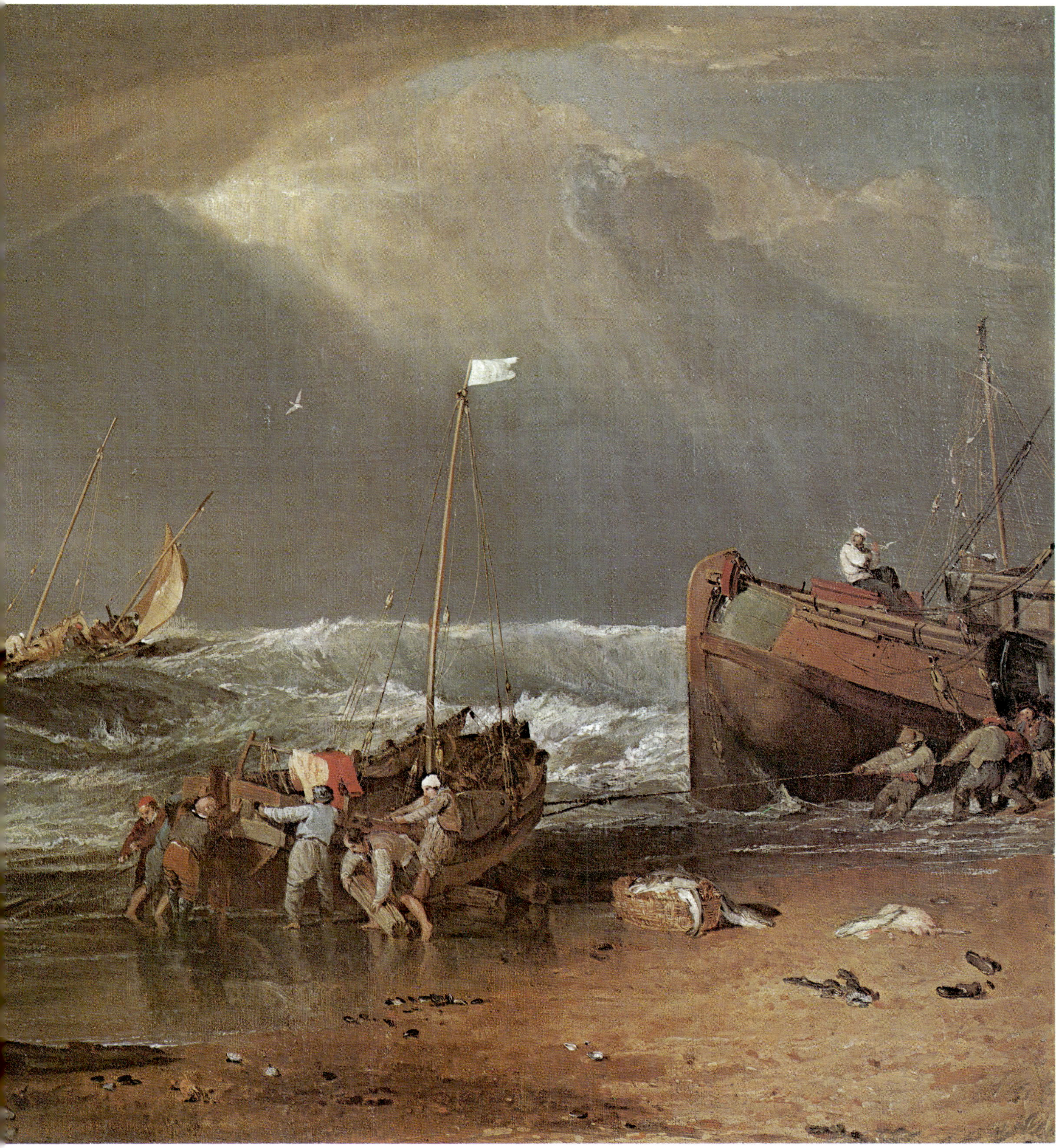

The Shipwreck (detail). 1805
(Turners Gallery)
Oil on canvas, 170.5 x 241.5 cm
The Tate Gallery, London

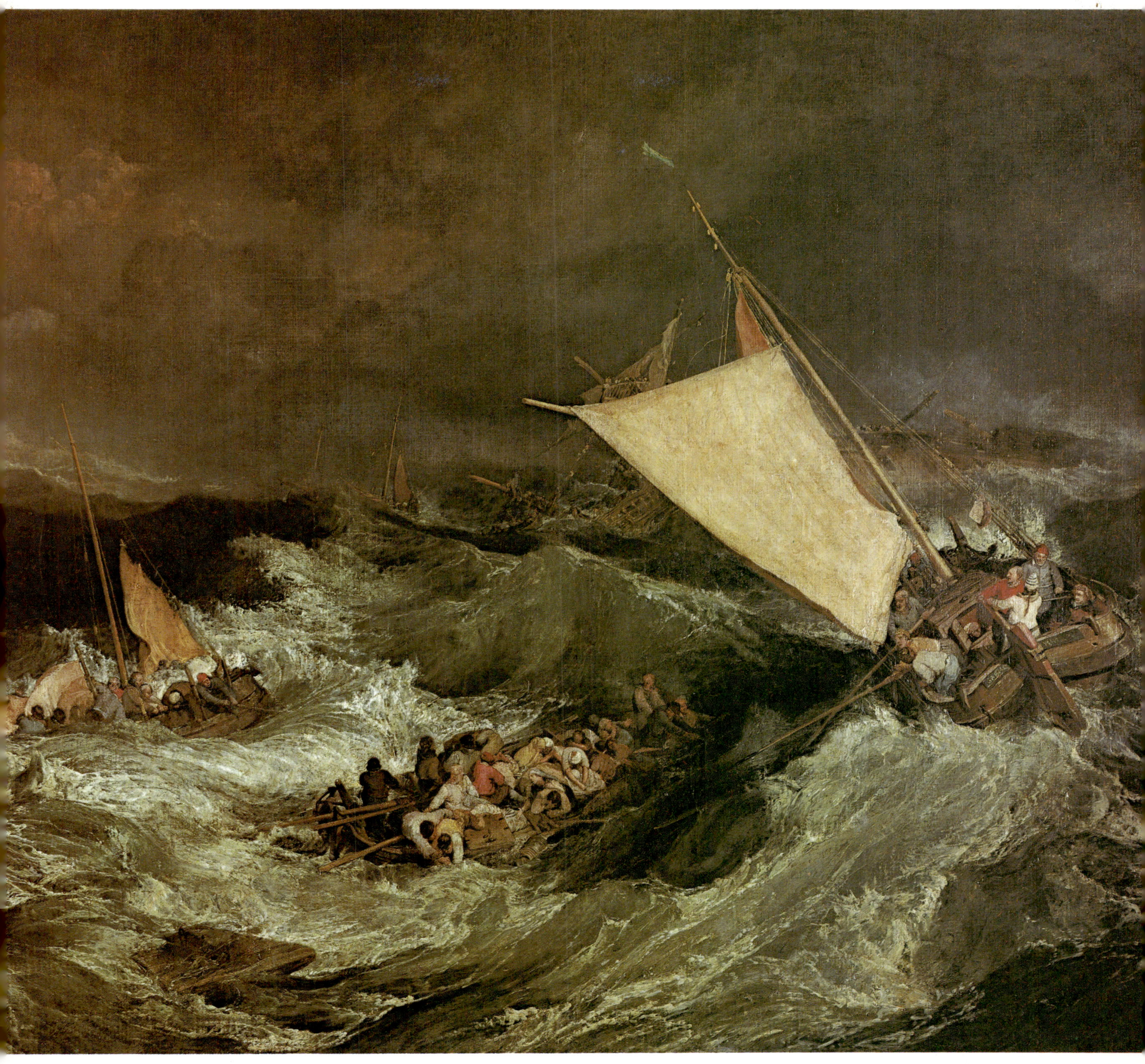

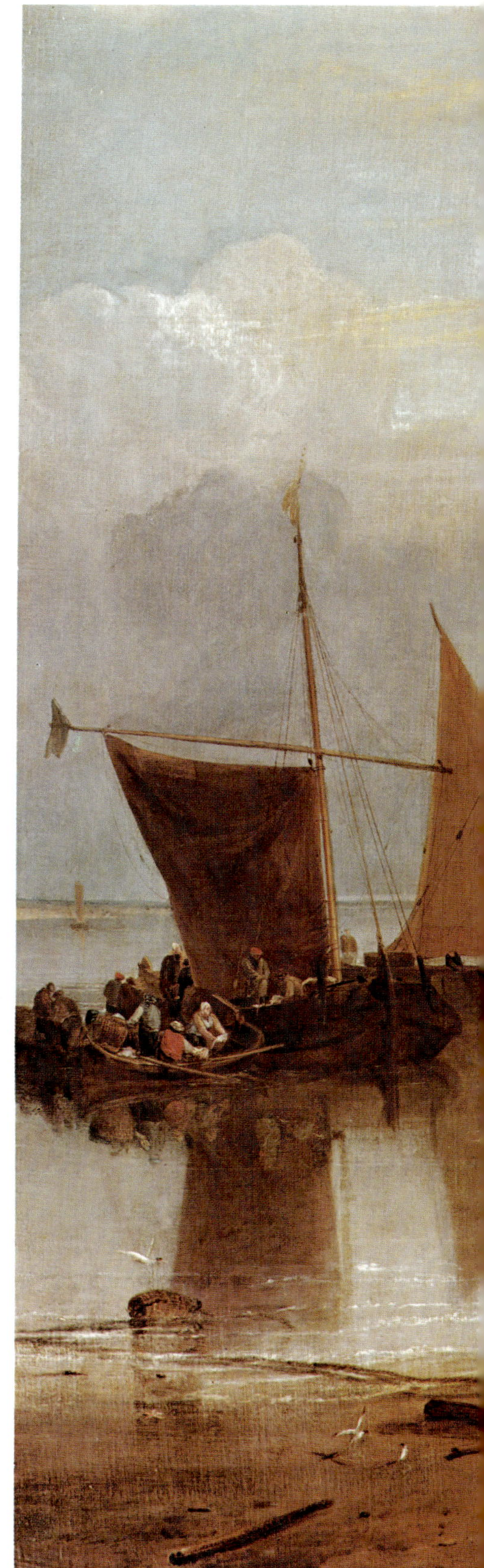

Sun rising through vapour;
Fishermen cleaning and selling fish. 1807
Oil on canvas, 134.5 x 179 cm
Turner Bequest, National Gallery, London

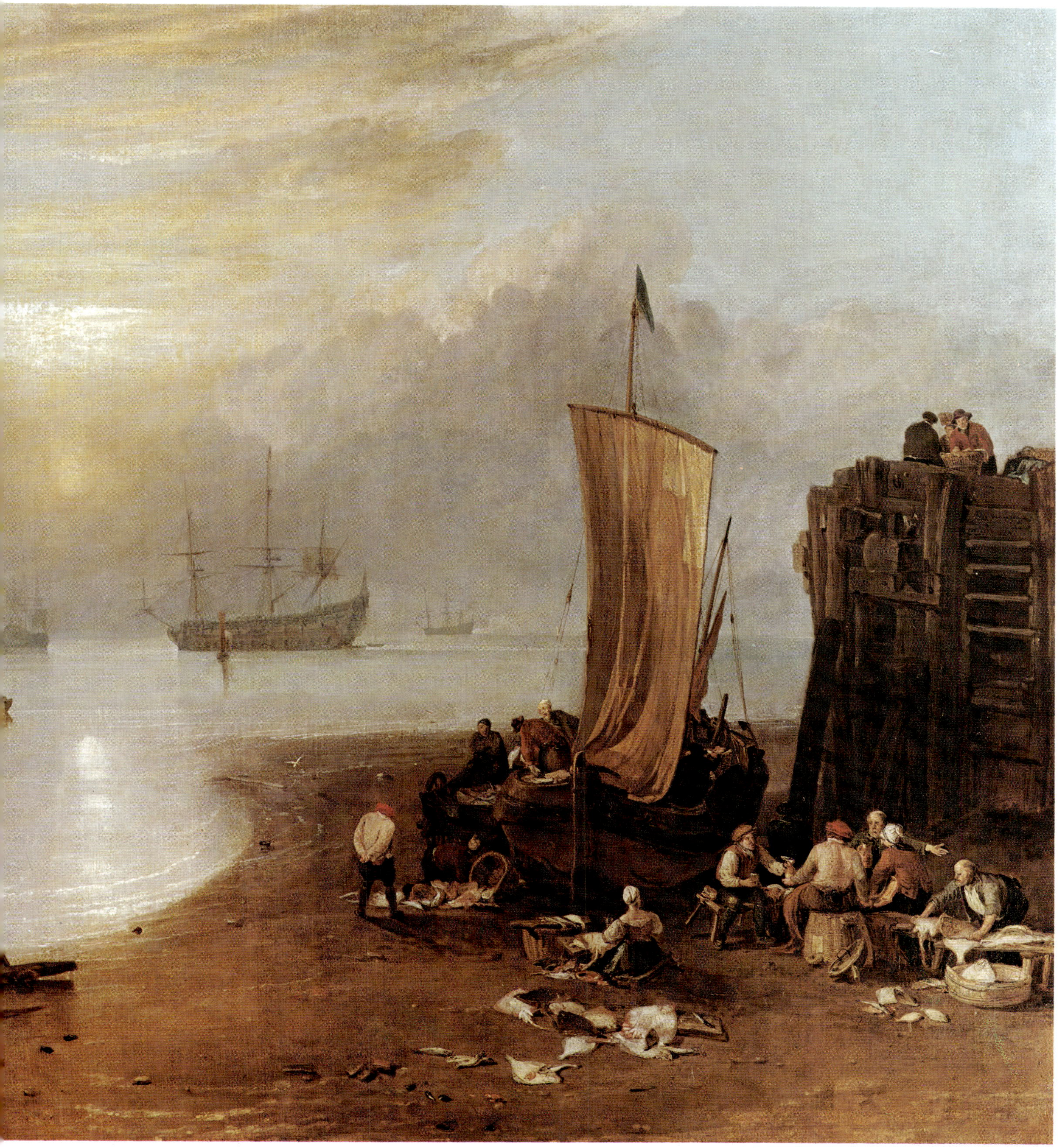

A country blacksmith disputing upon the price of iron, and the price charged to the butcher for shoeing his pony. 1807
Oil on fir-plank, 55 x 78 cm
The Tate Gallery, London

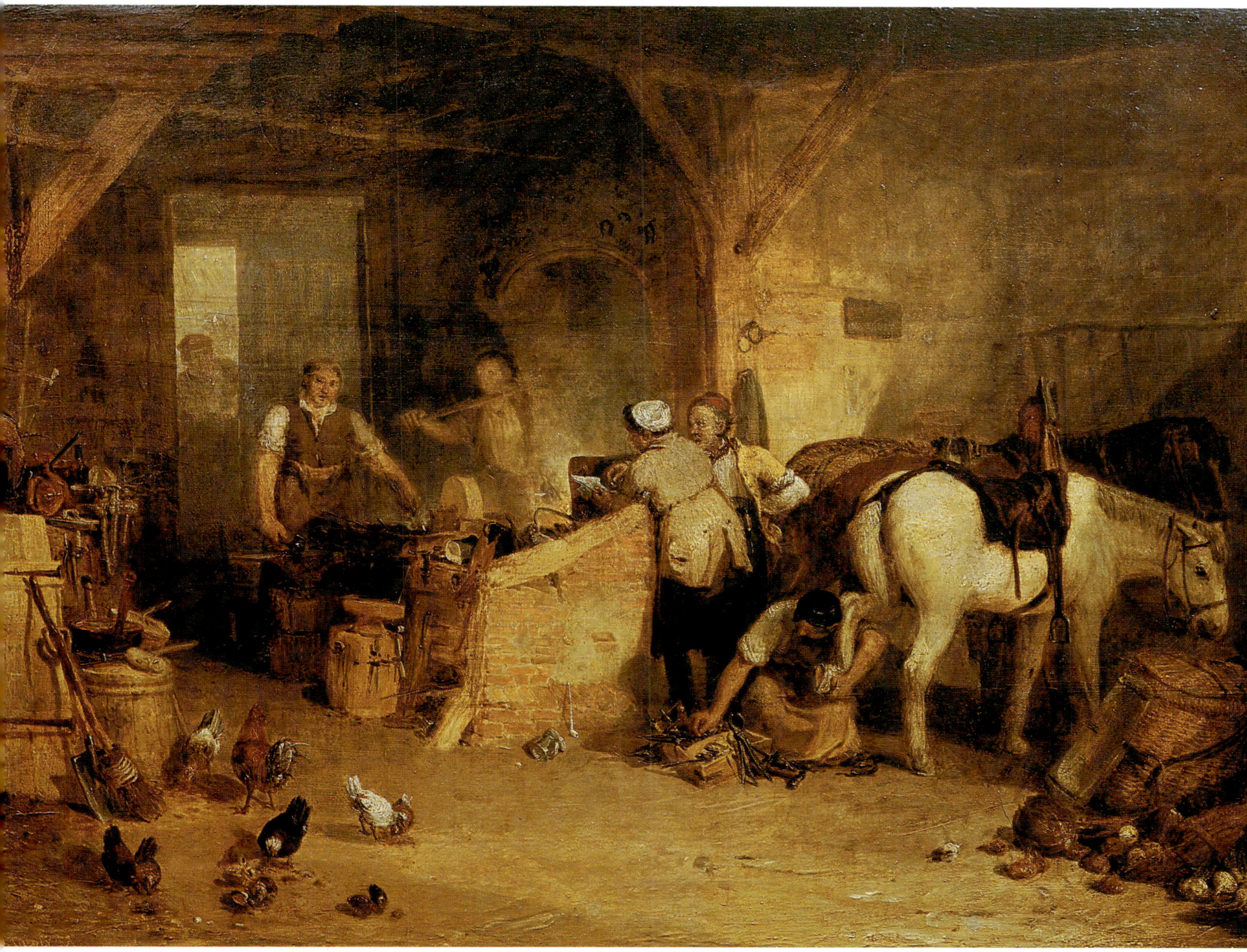

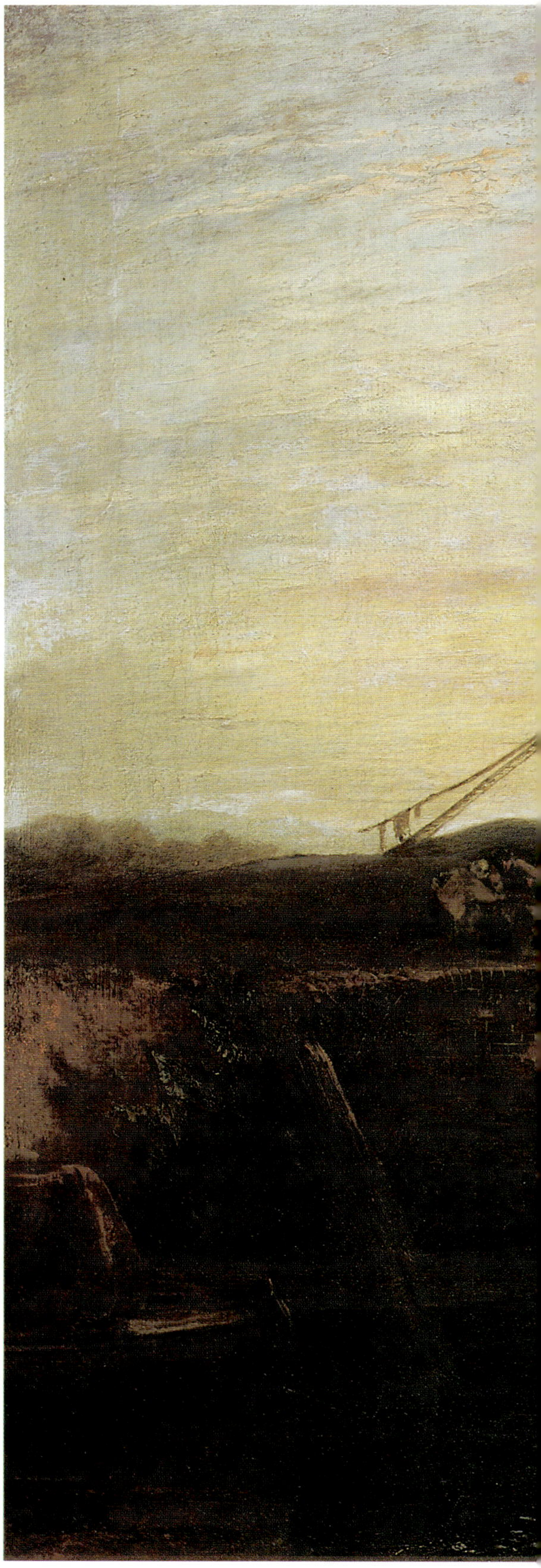

Grand Junction Canal at Southall Mill.
Windmill and Lock. 1810
(Turners Gallery)
Oil on canvas, 92 x 122 cm
Private collection

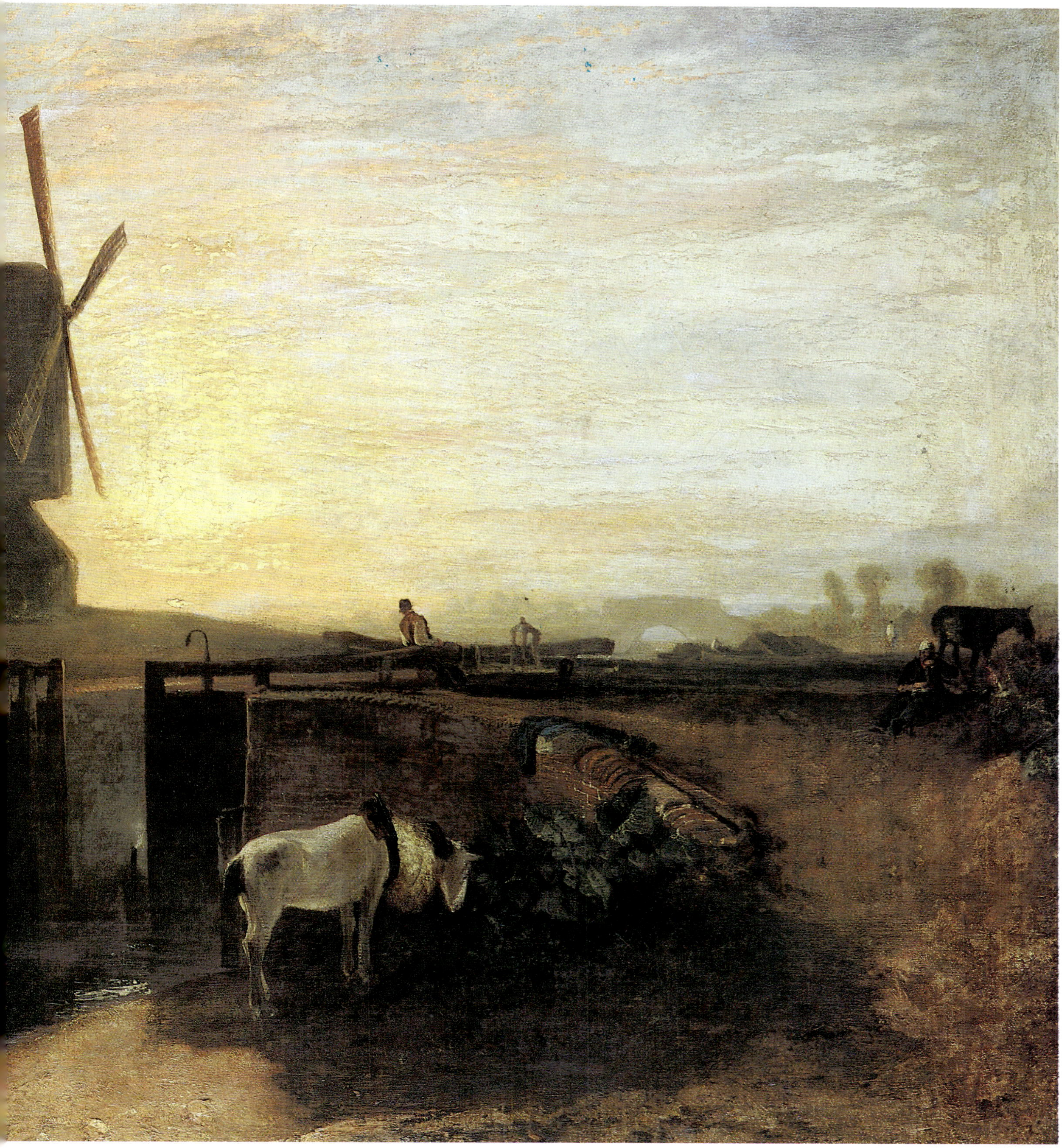

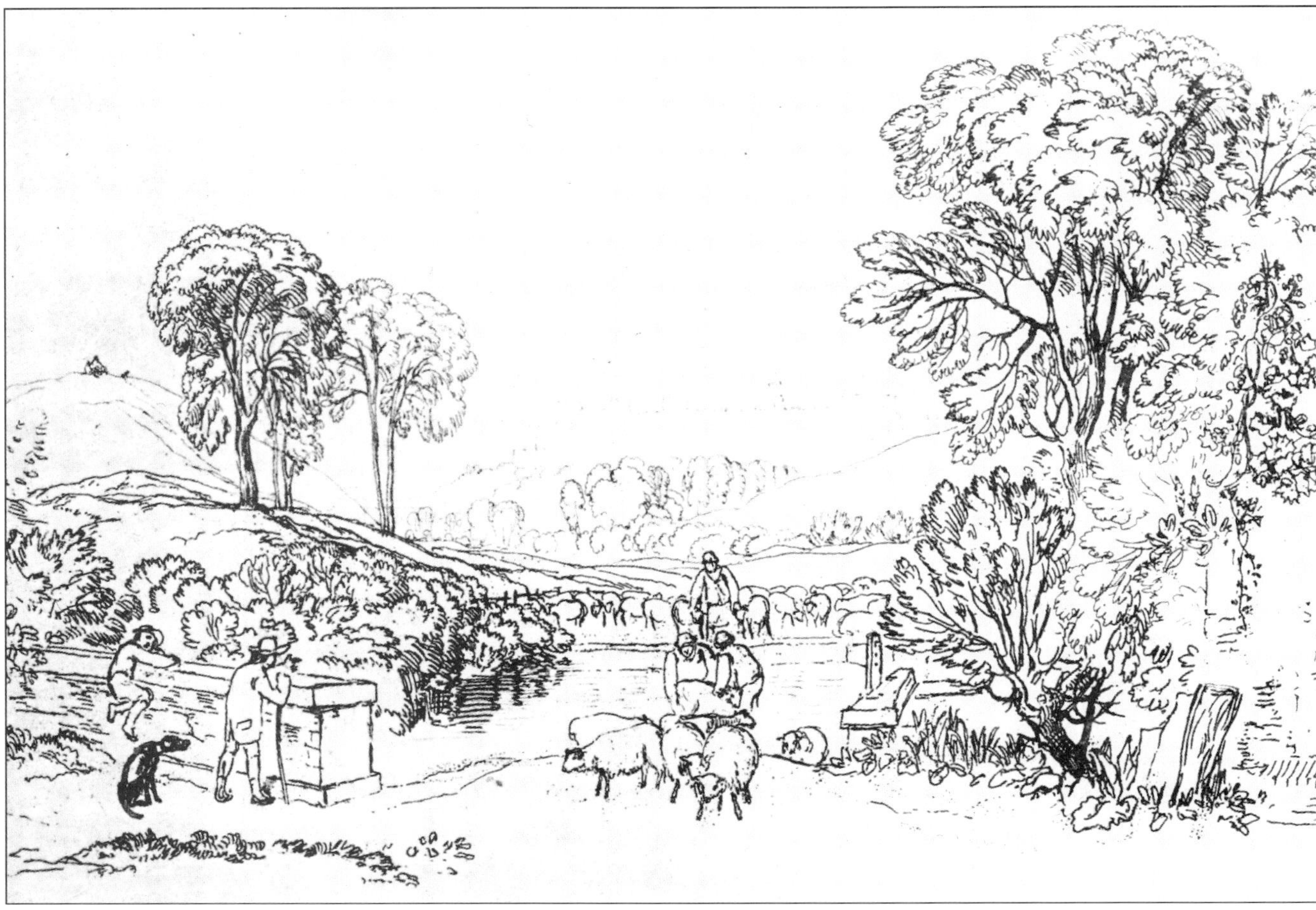

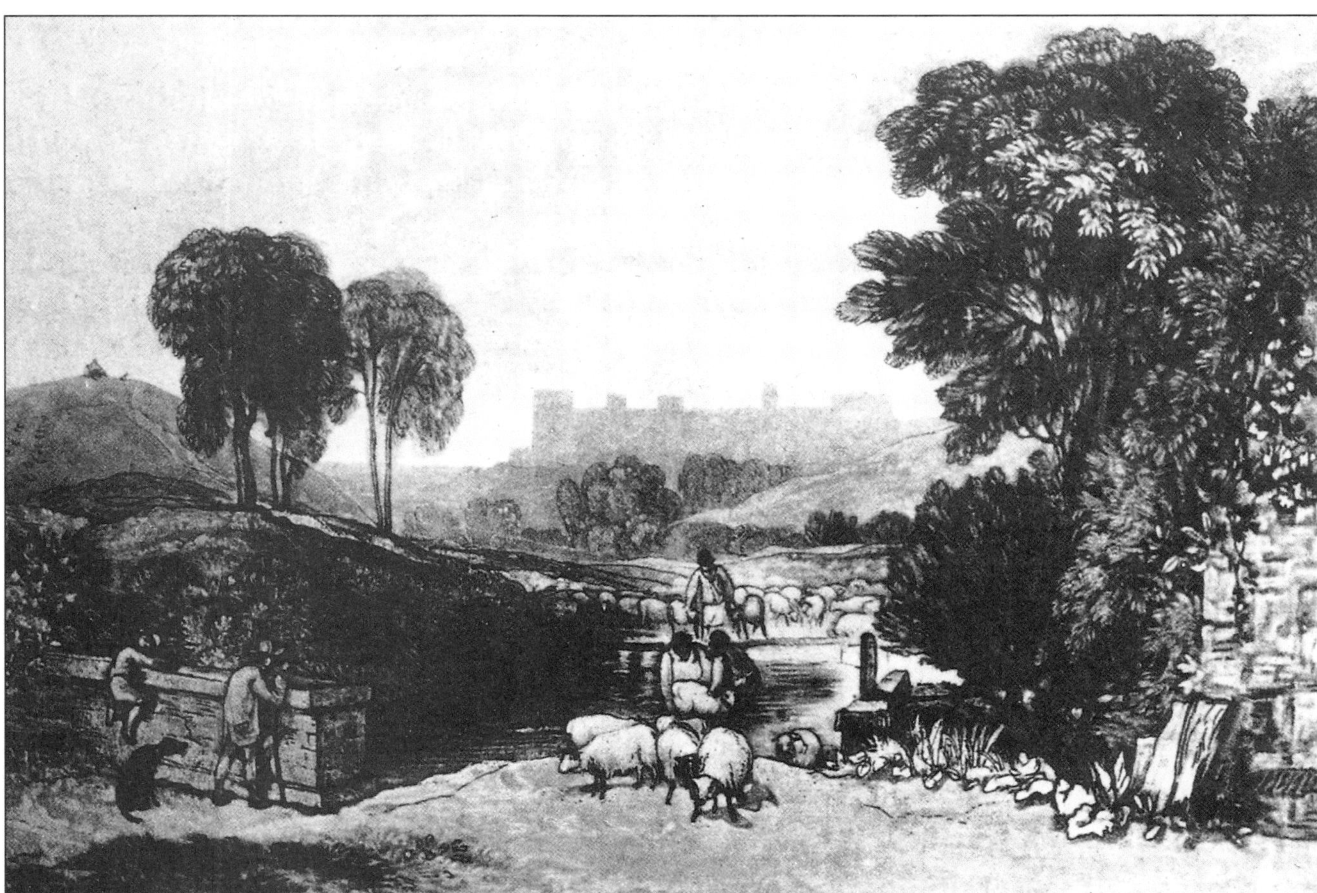

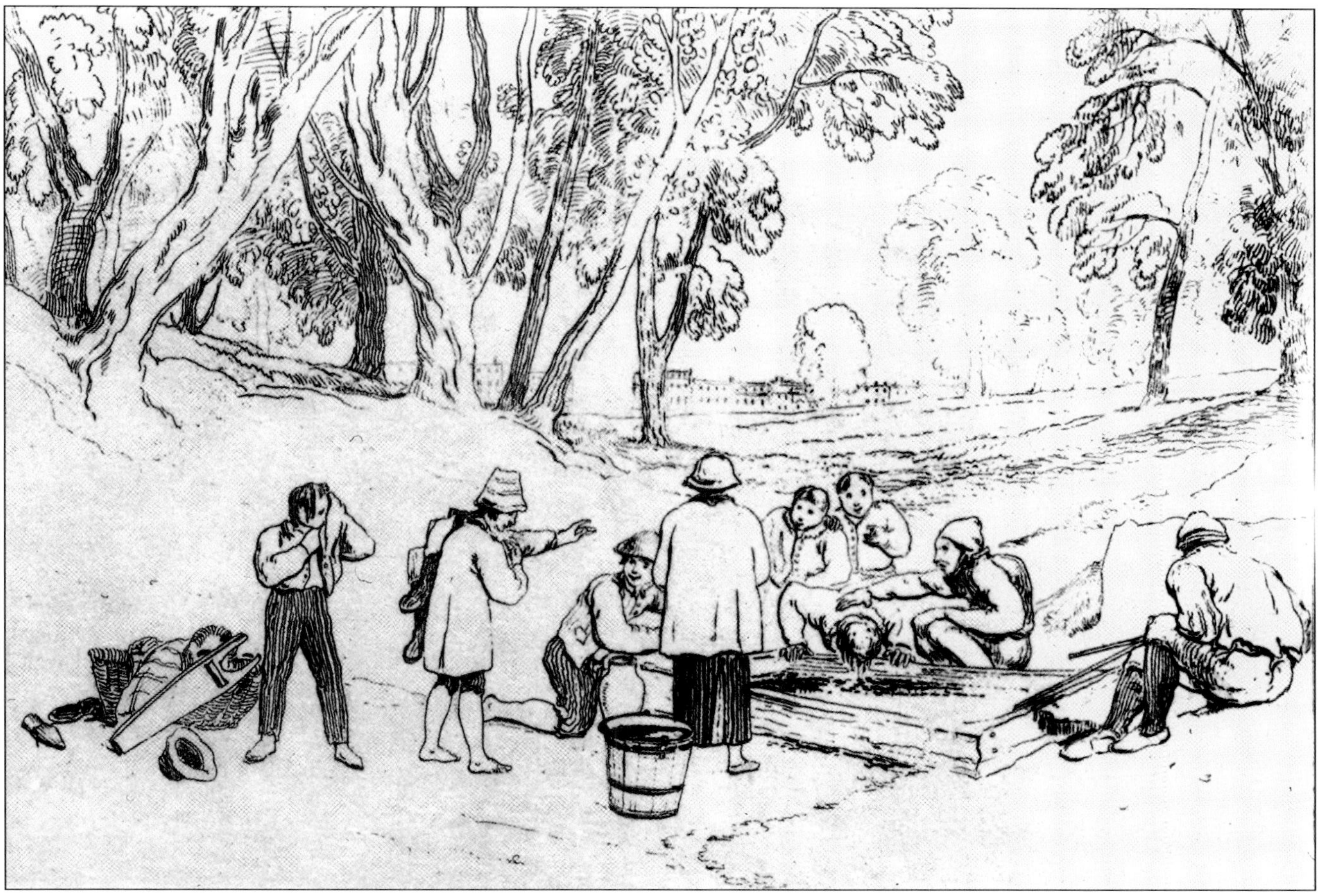

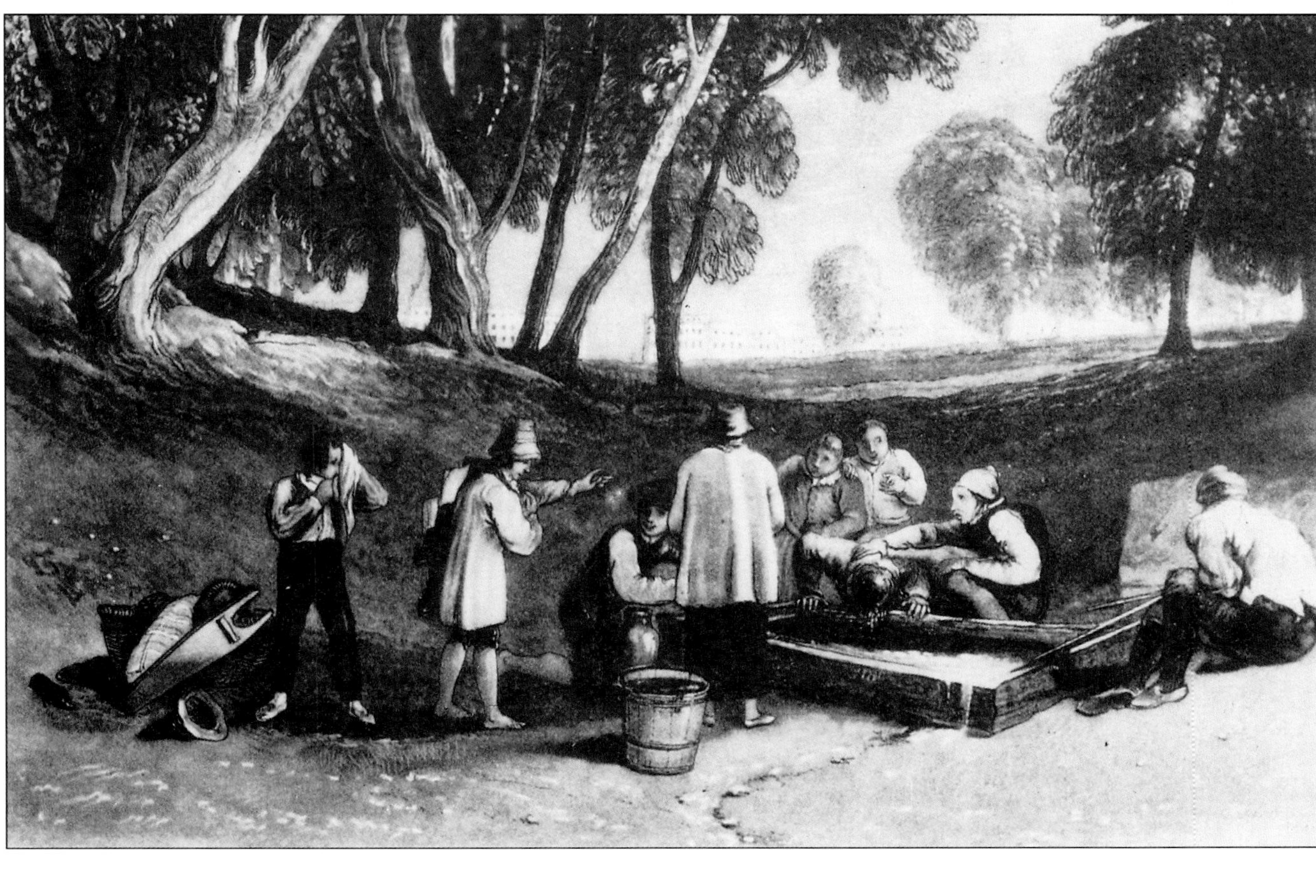

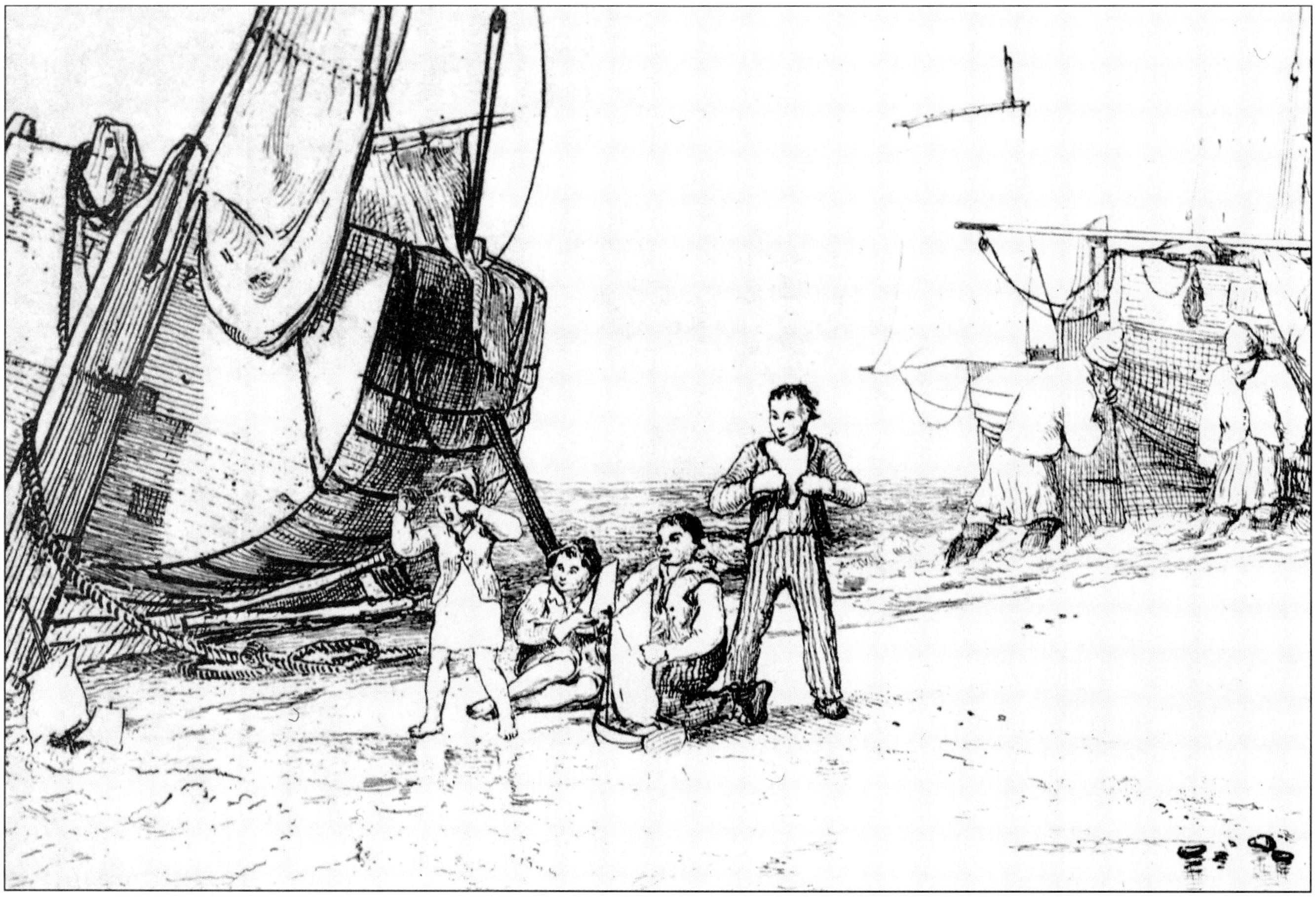

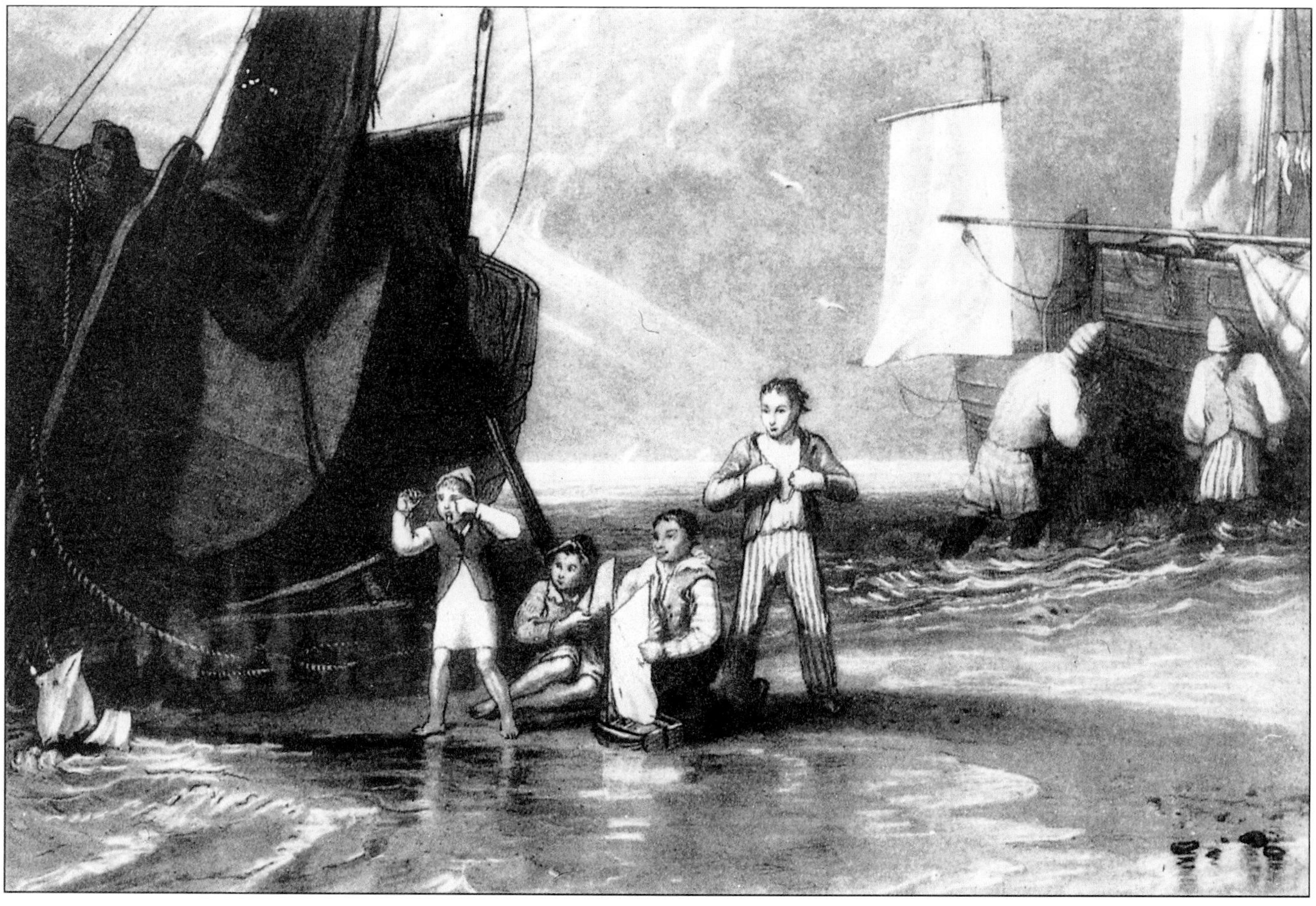

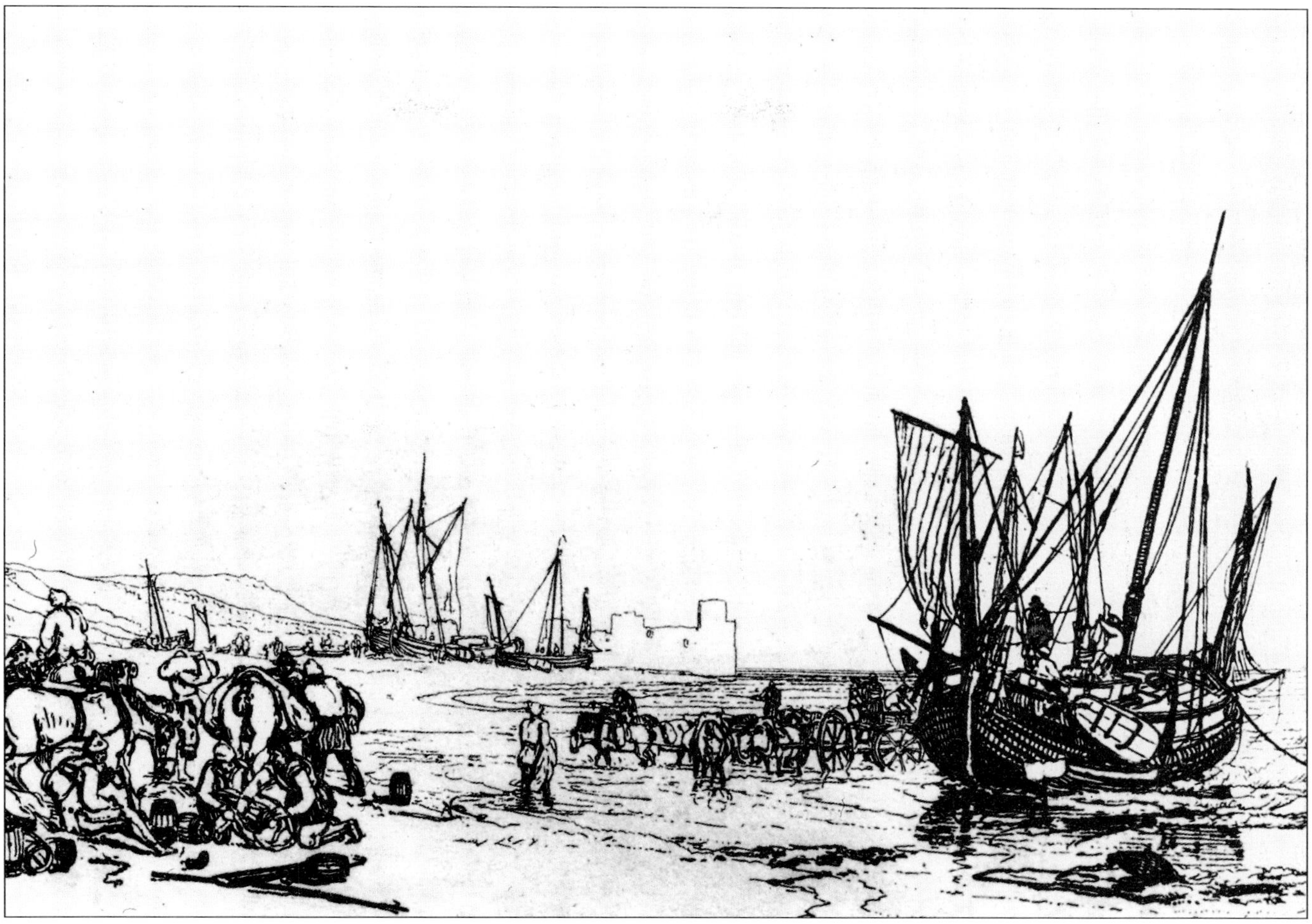

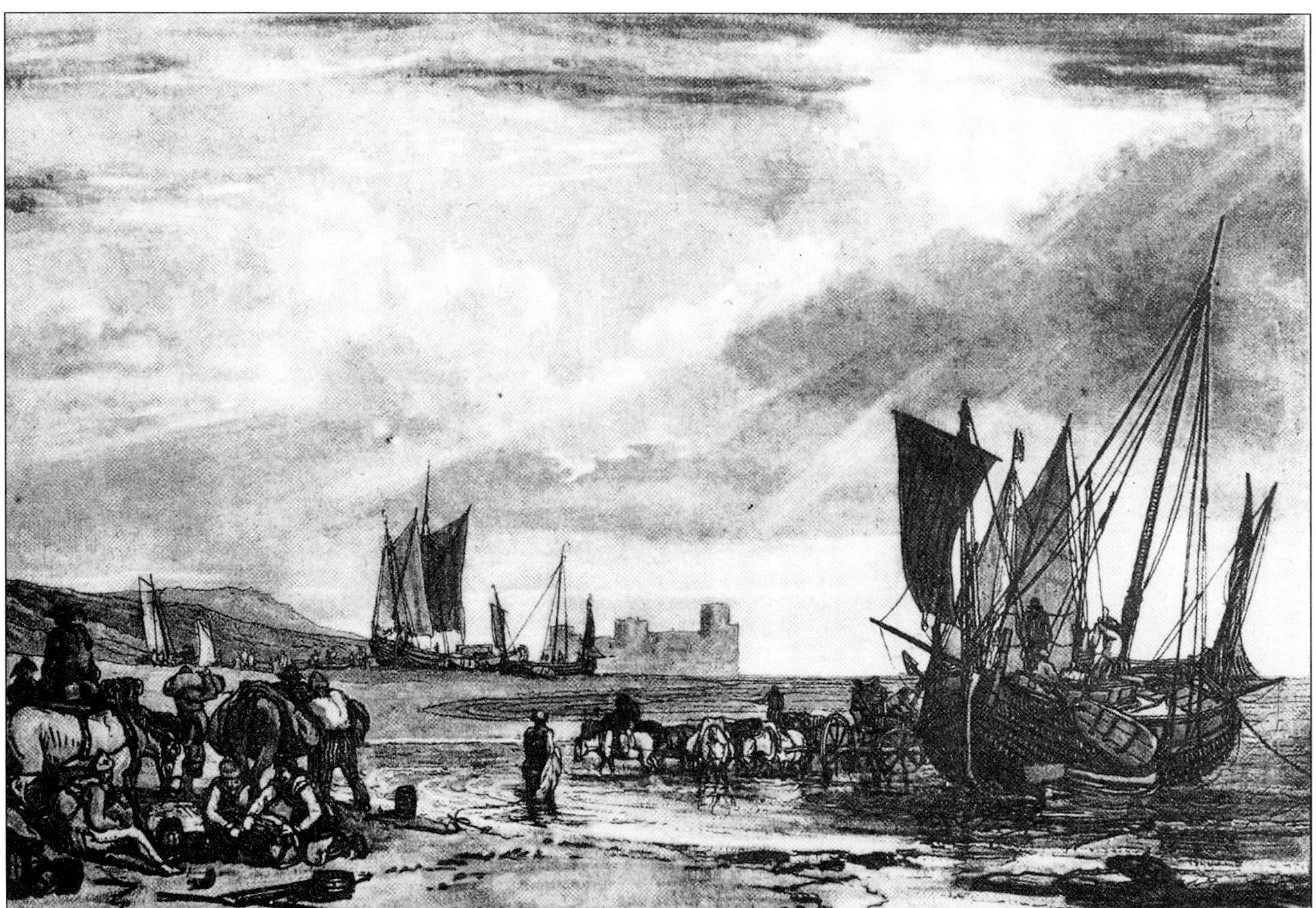

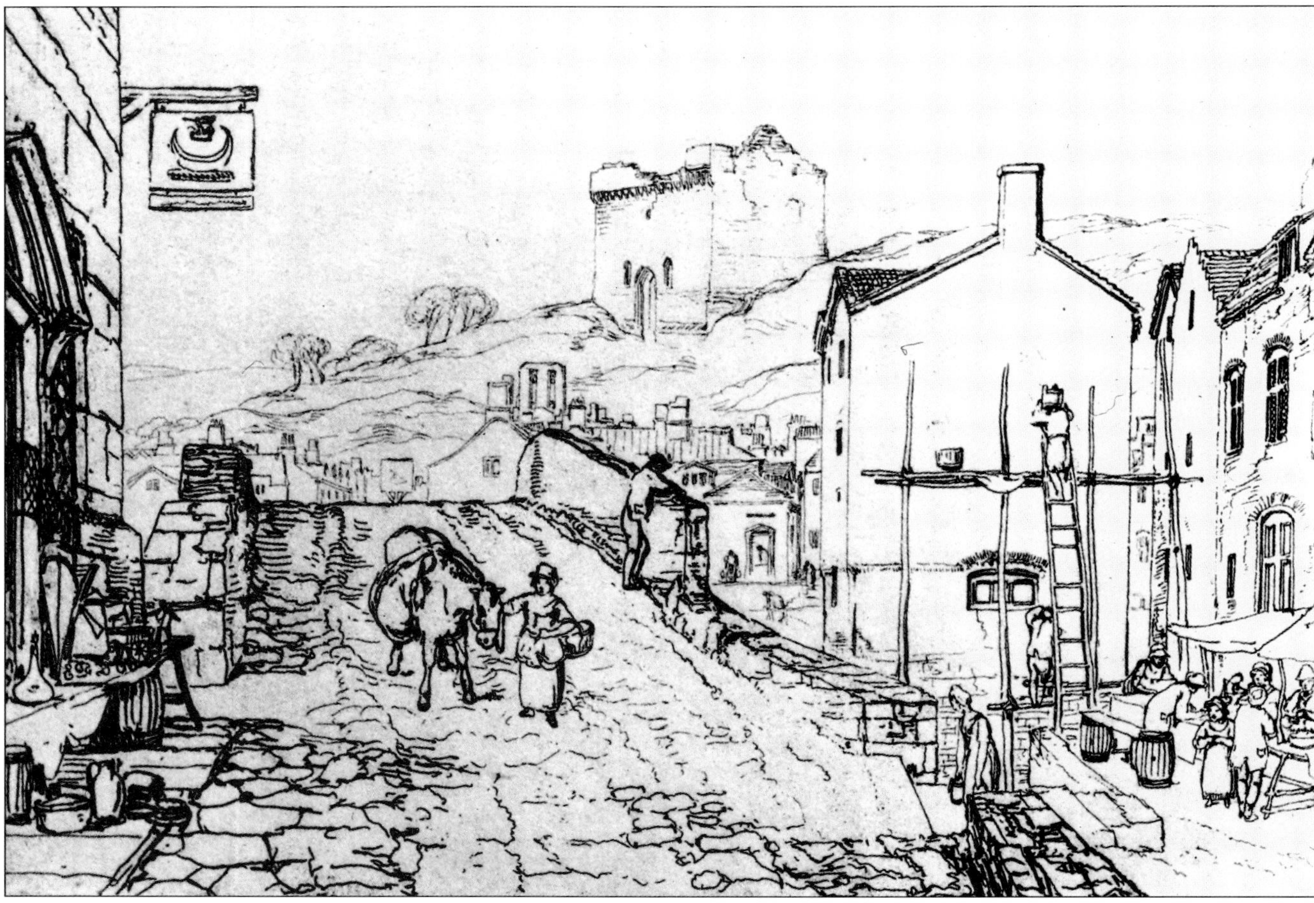

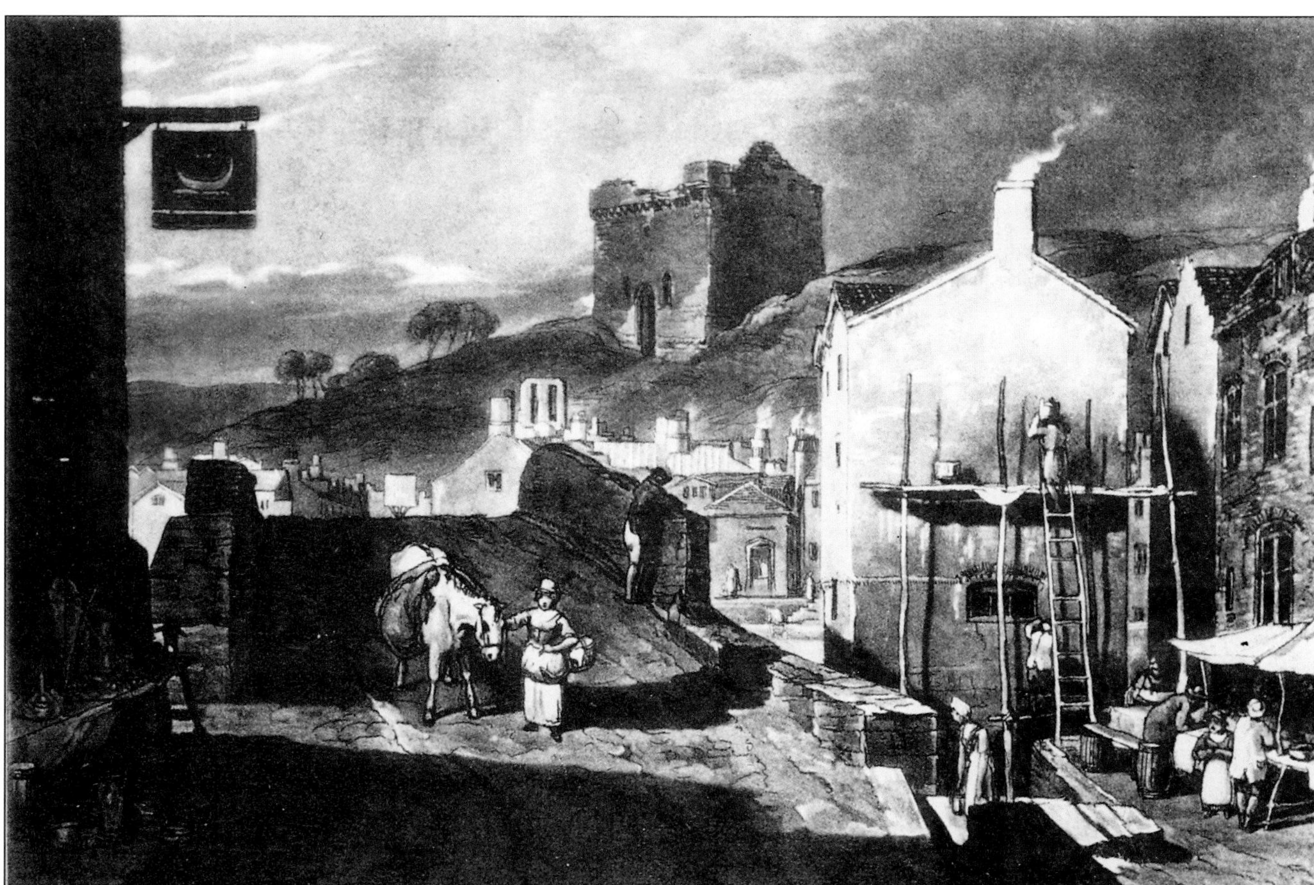

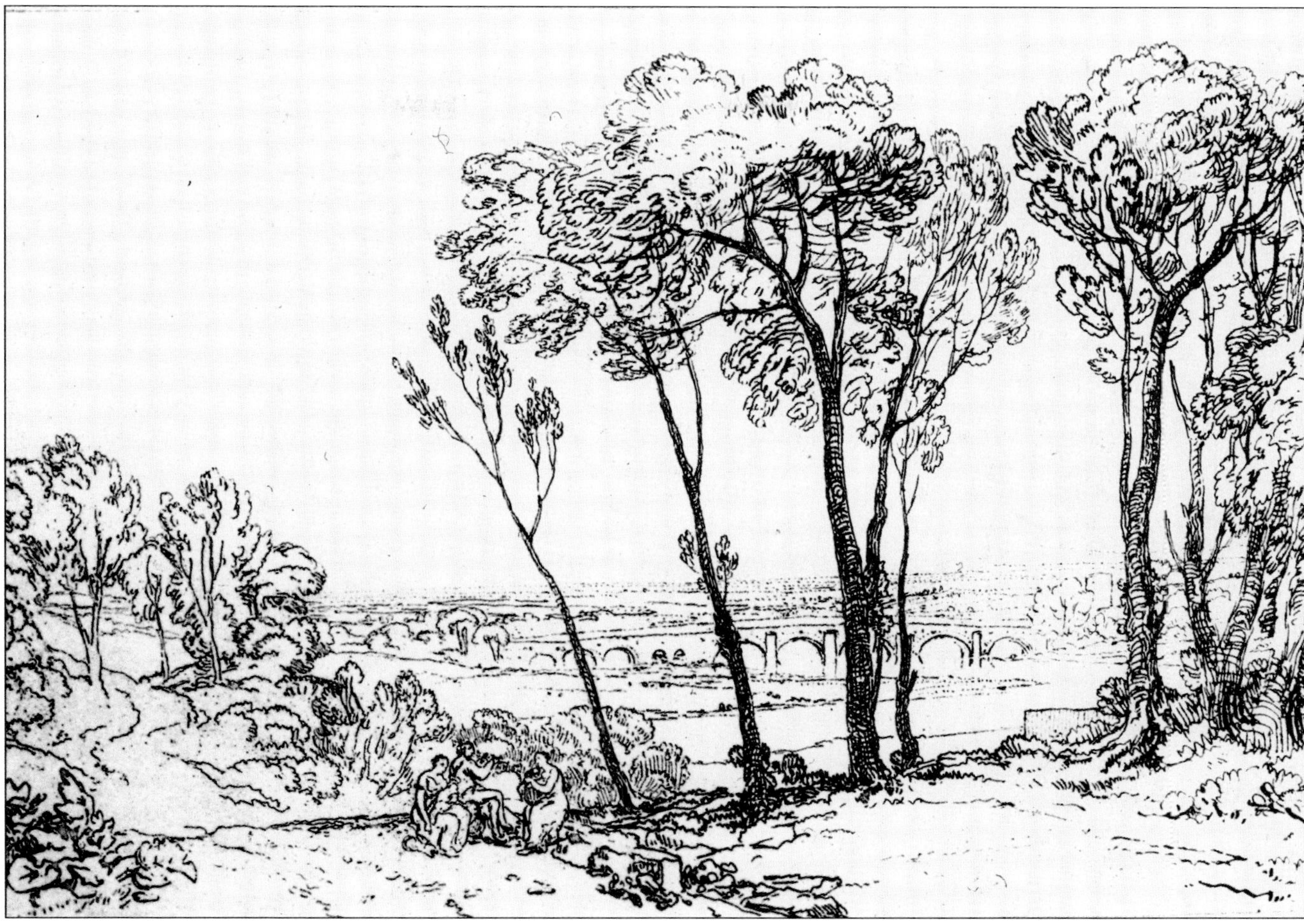

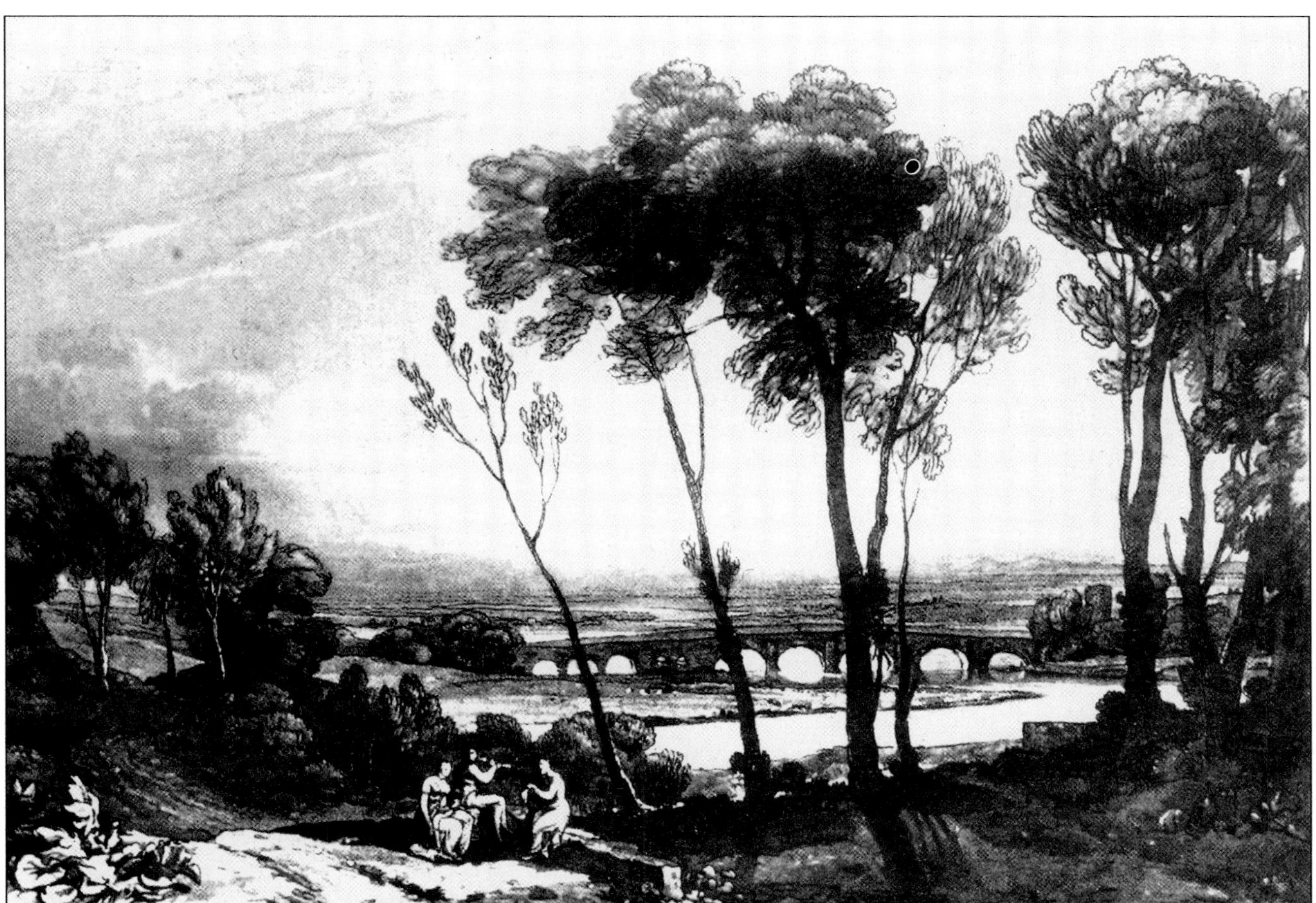

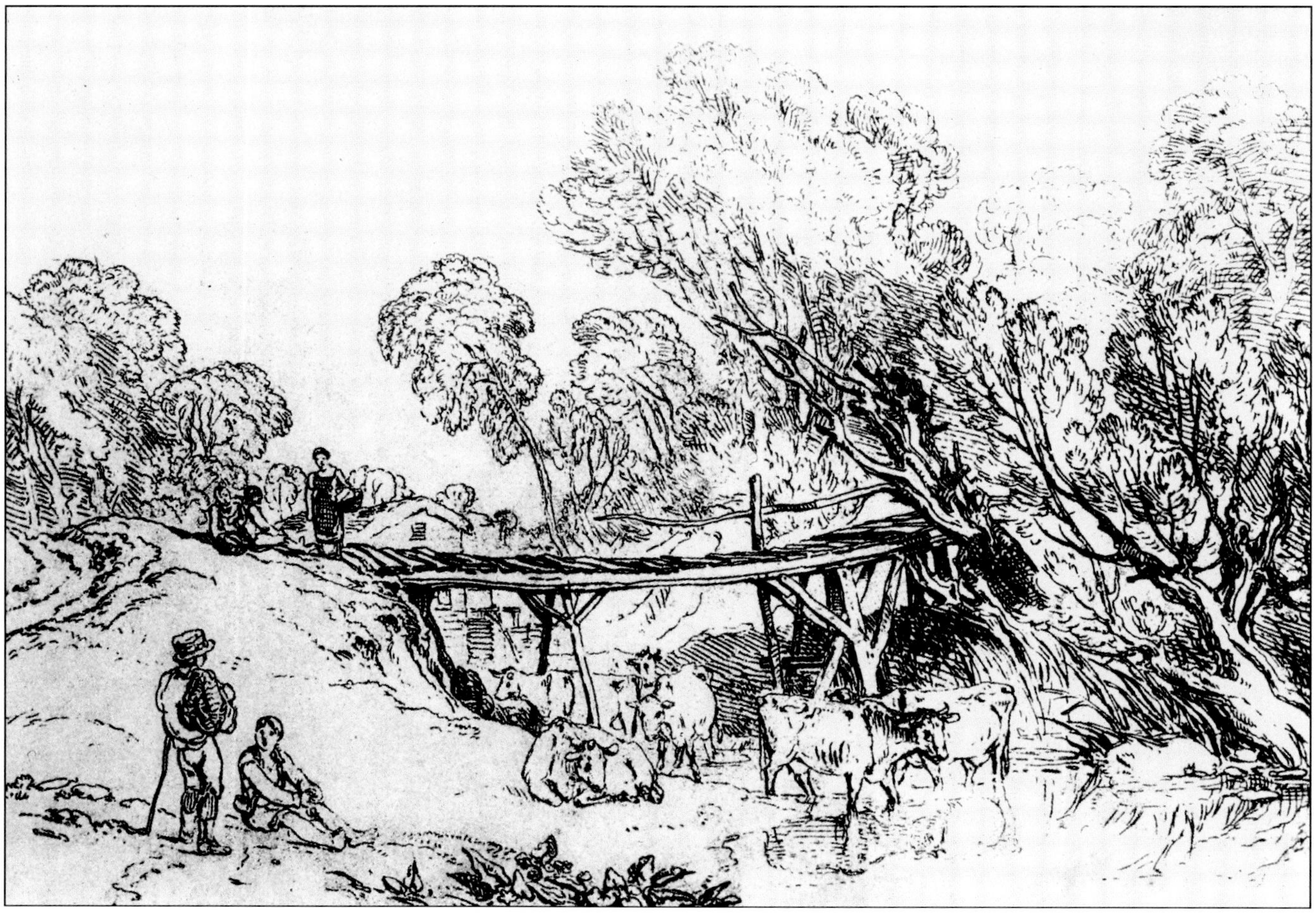

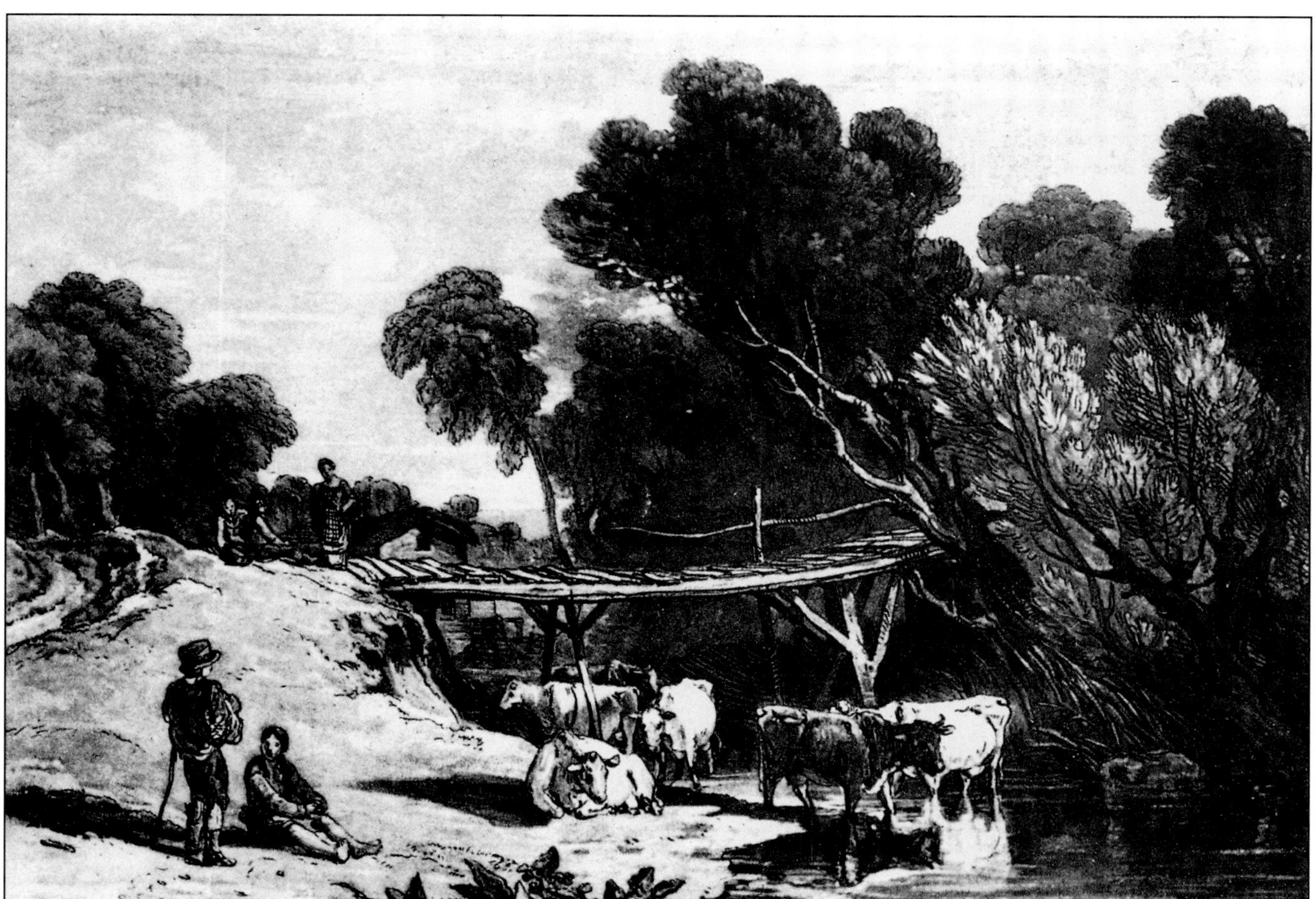

# TRAVELS IN ENGLAND

Bolton Abbey, Yorkshire. 1809
Watercolour, 27.8 x 39.5 cm
Trustees of the British Museum, London

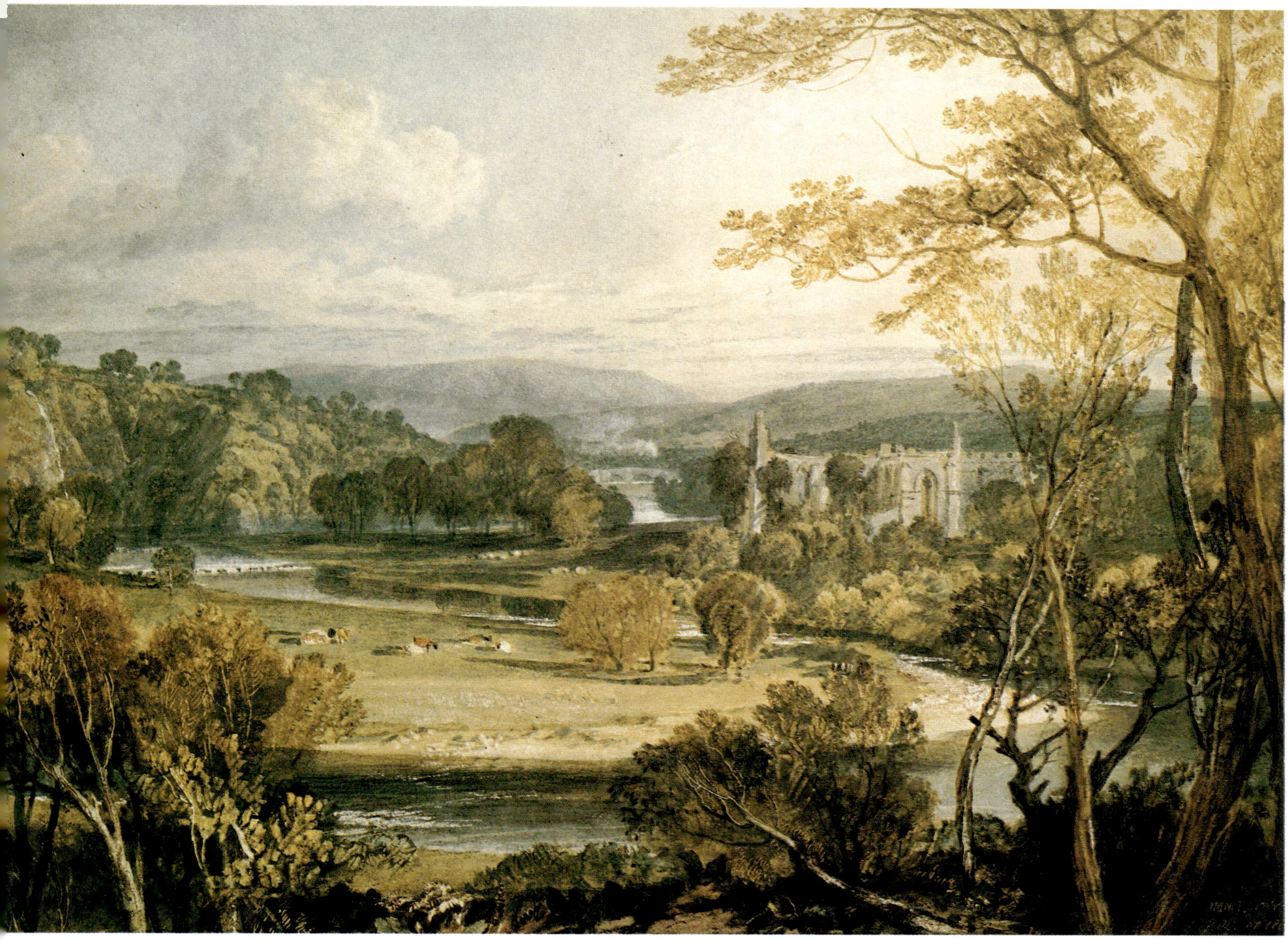

Fishing upon Blythe-sand,
tide setting in. 1809
(Turners Gallery)
Oil on canvas, 89 x 119.5 cm
The Tate Gallery, London

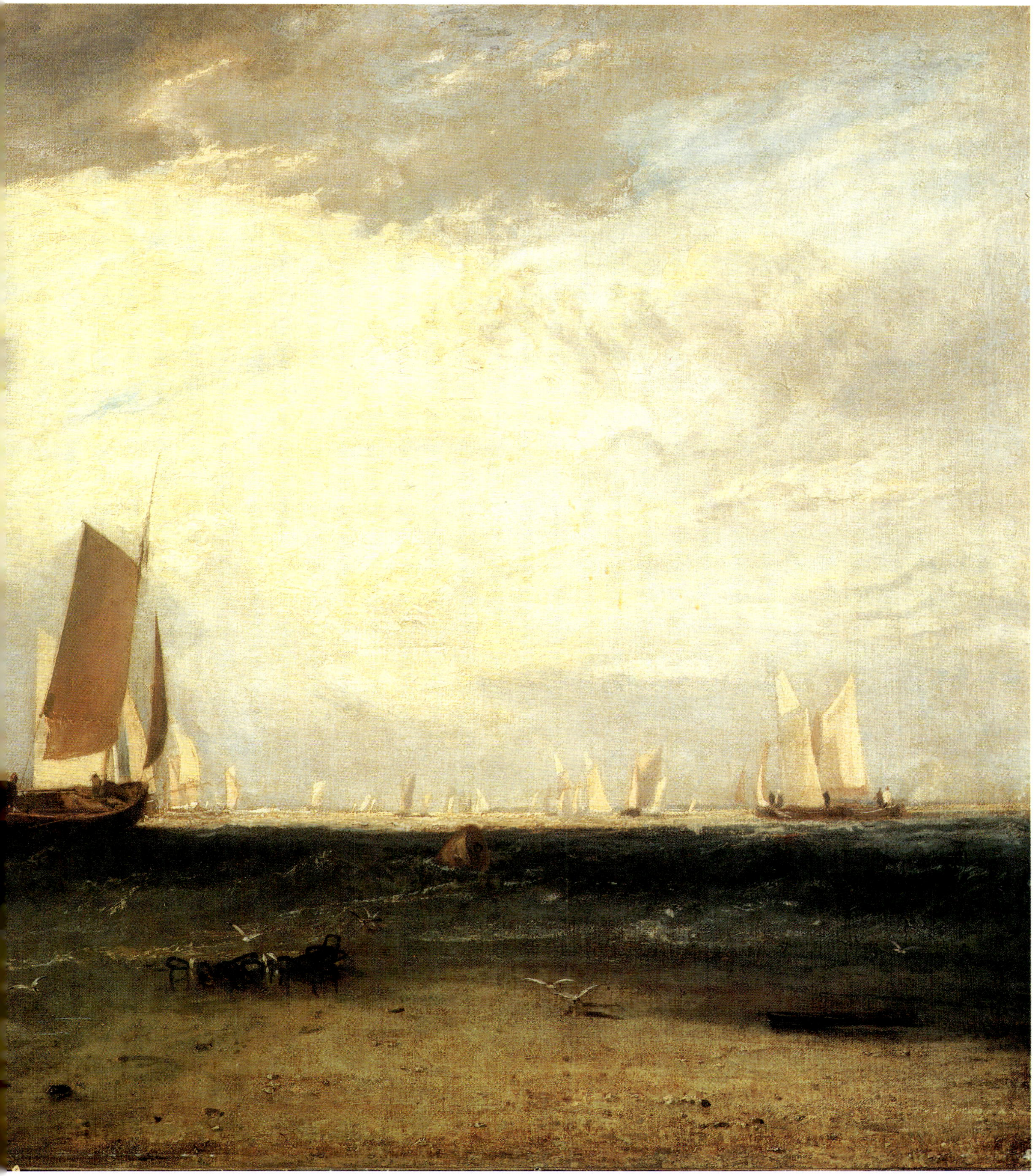

Crossing the brook. 1815
Oil on canvas, 193 x 165 cm
The Tate Gallery, London

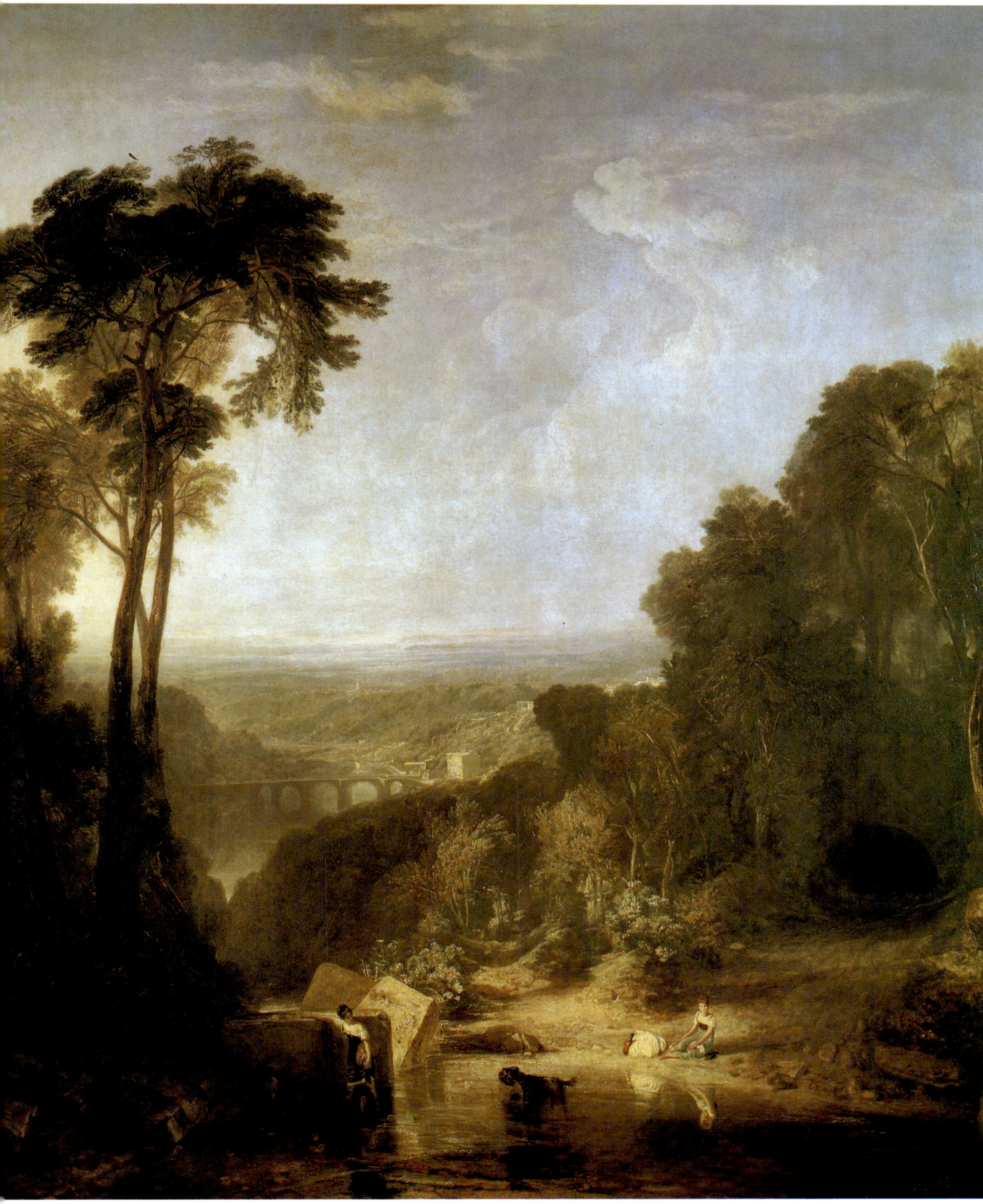

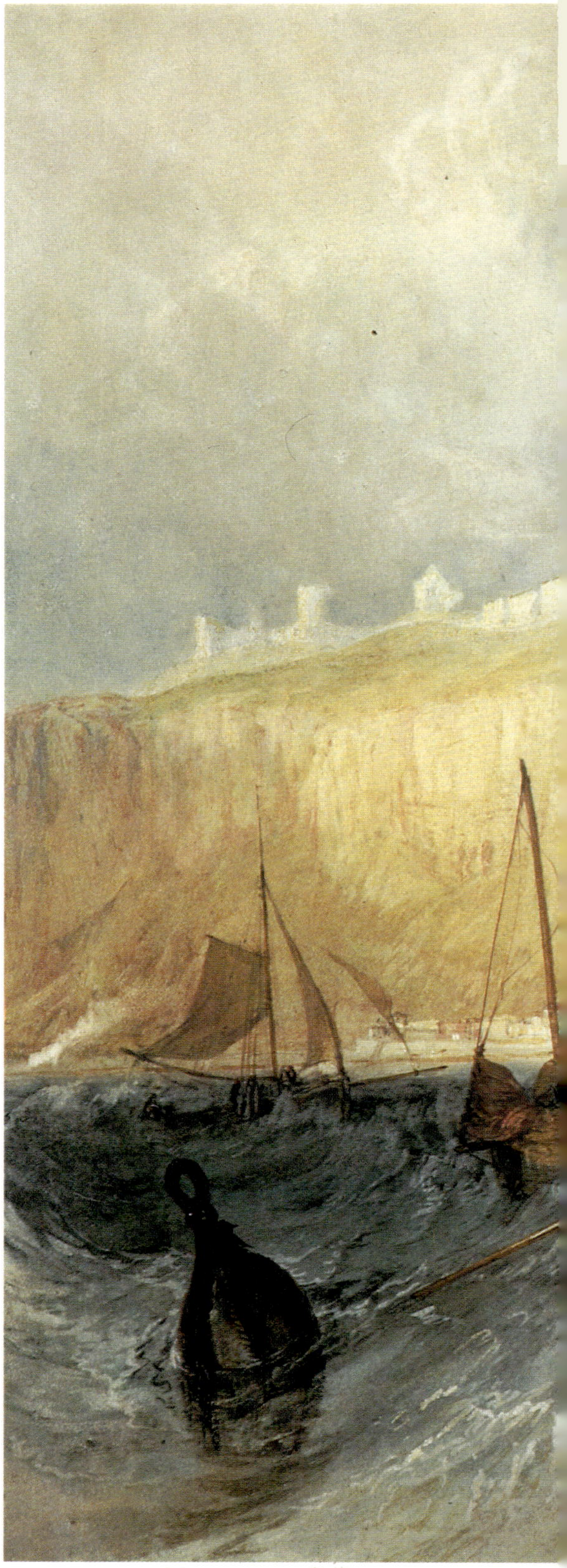

Hastings; deep-sea fishing. 1818
Watercolour, 39.8 x 59.1 cm
Trustees of the British Museum, London

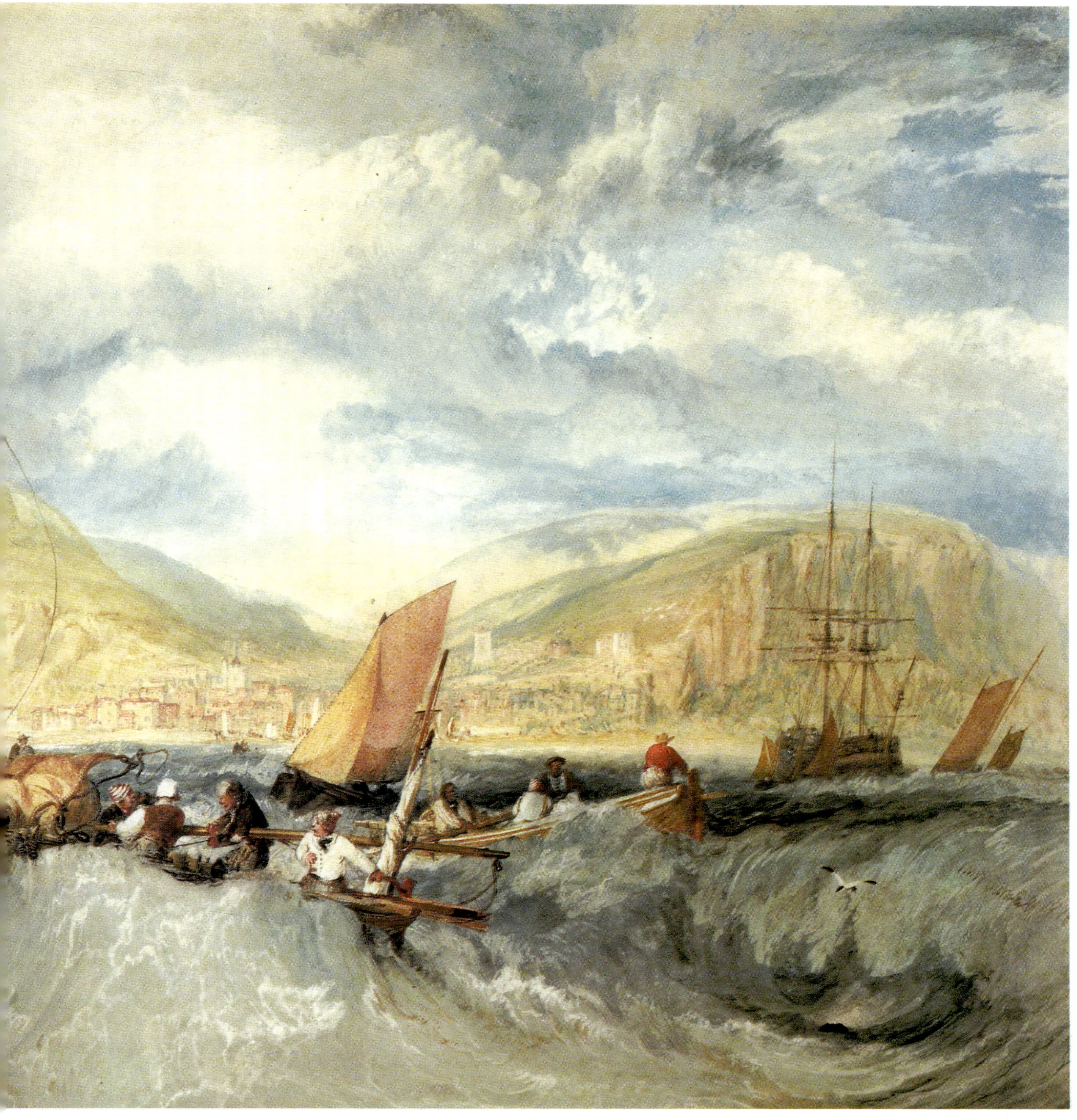

Saltash, Cornwall. 1825
Watercolour, 27 x 41 cm
Trustees of the British Museum, London

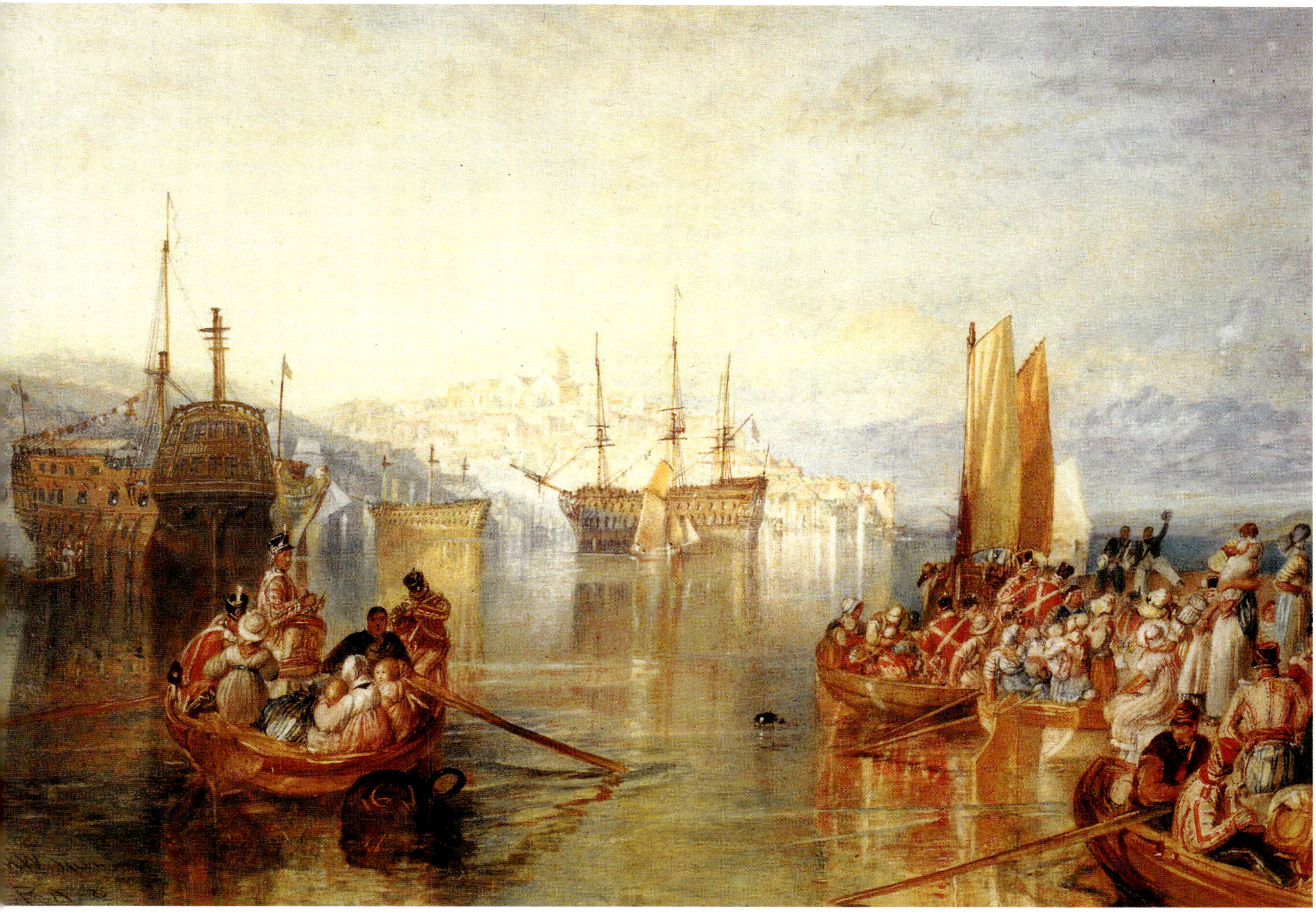

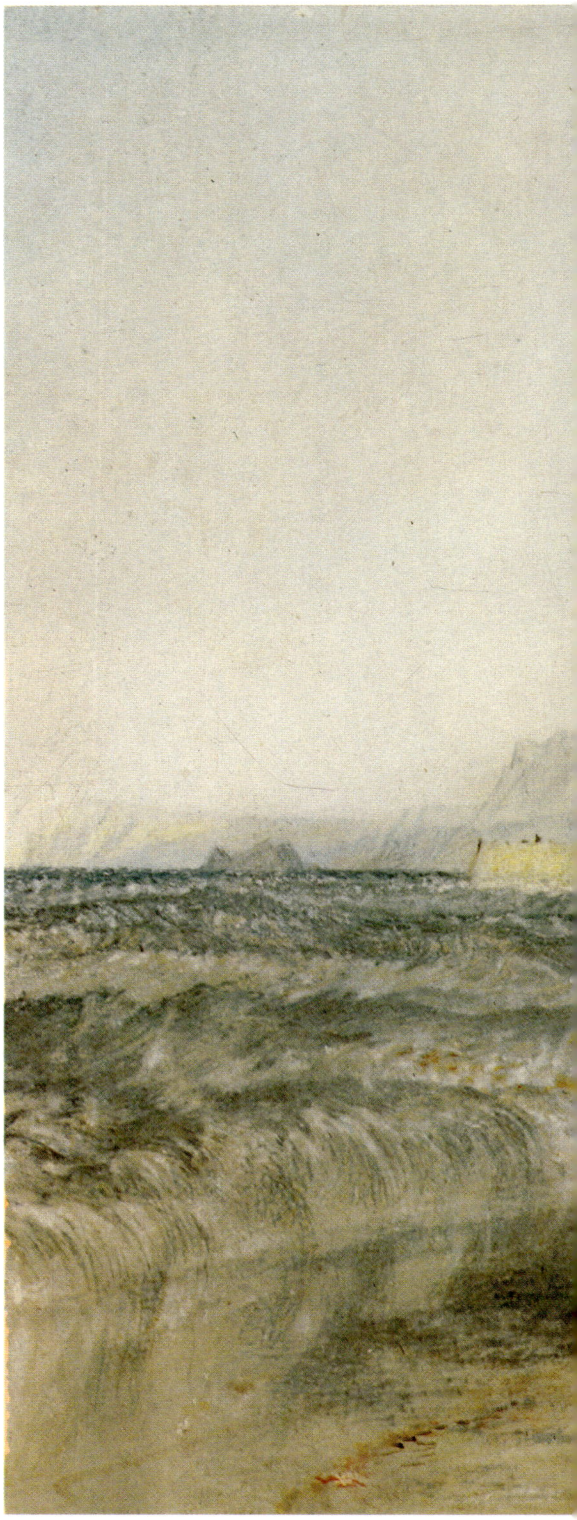

Whitby, Yorkshire. 1825–1830
Watercolour, 15.9 x 24.8 cm
Private collection

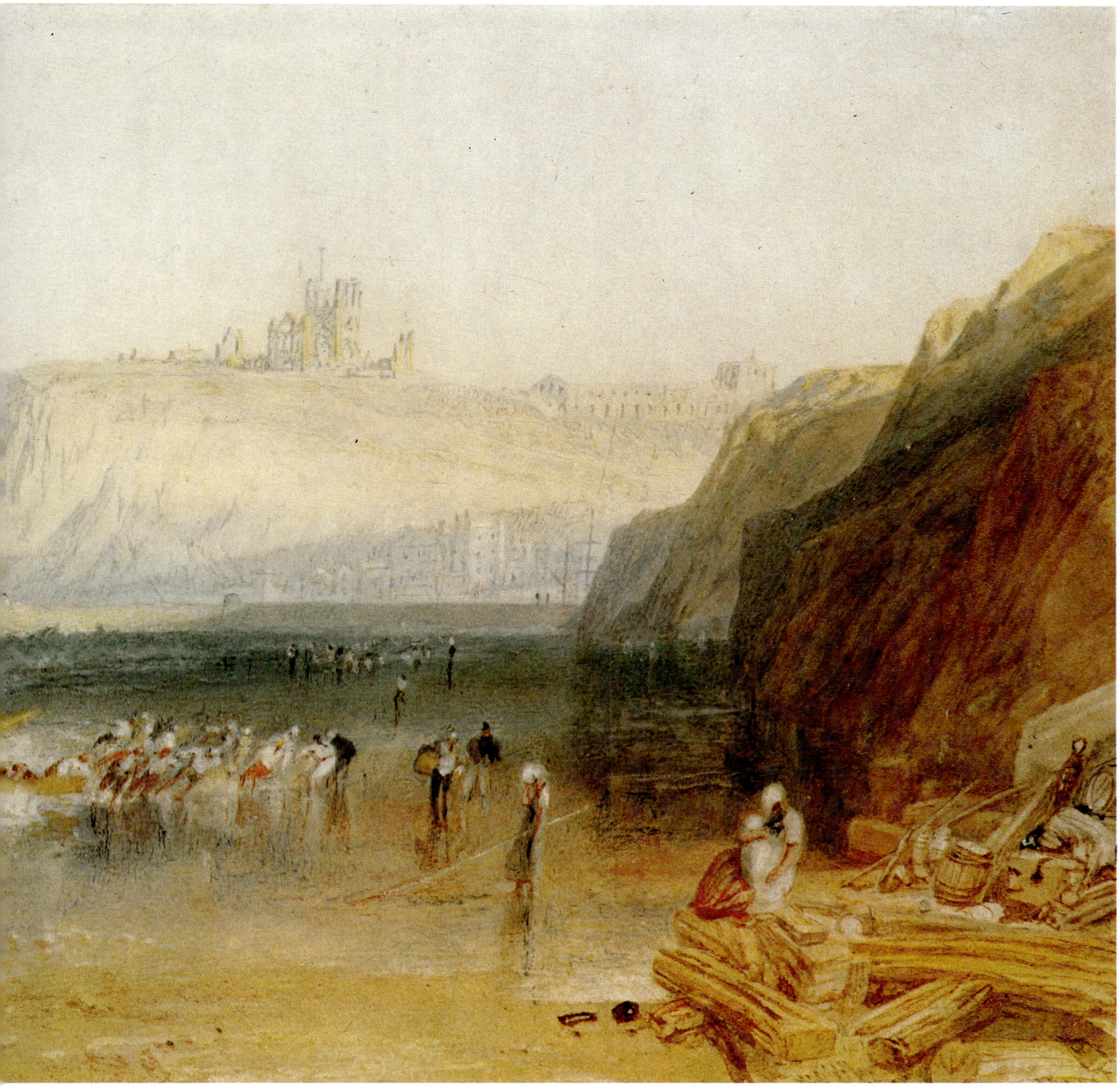

Prudhoe Castle, Northumberland
(detail). 1826

Watercolour, 29 x 41 cm
Trustees of the British Museum, London

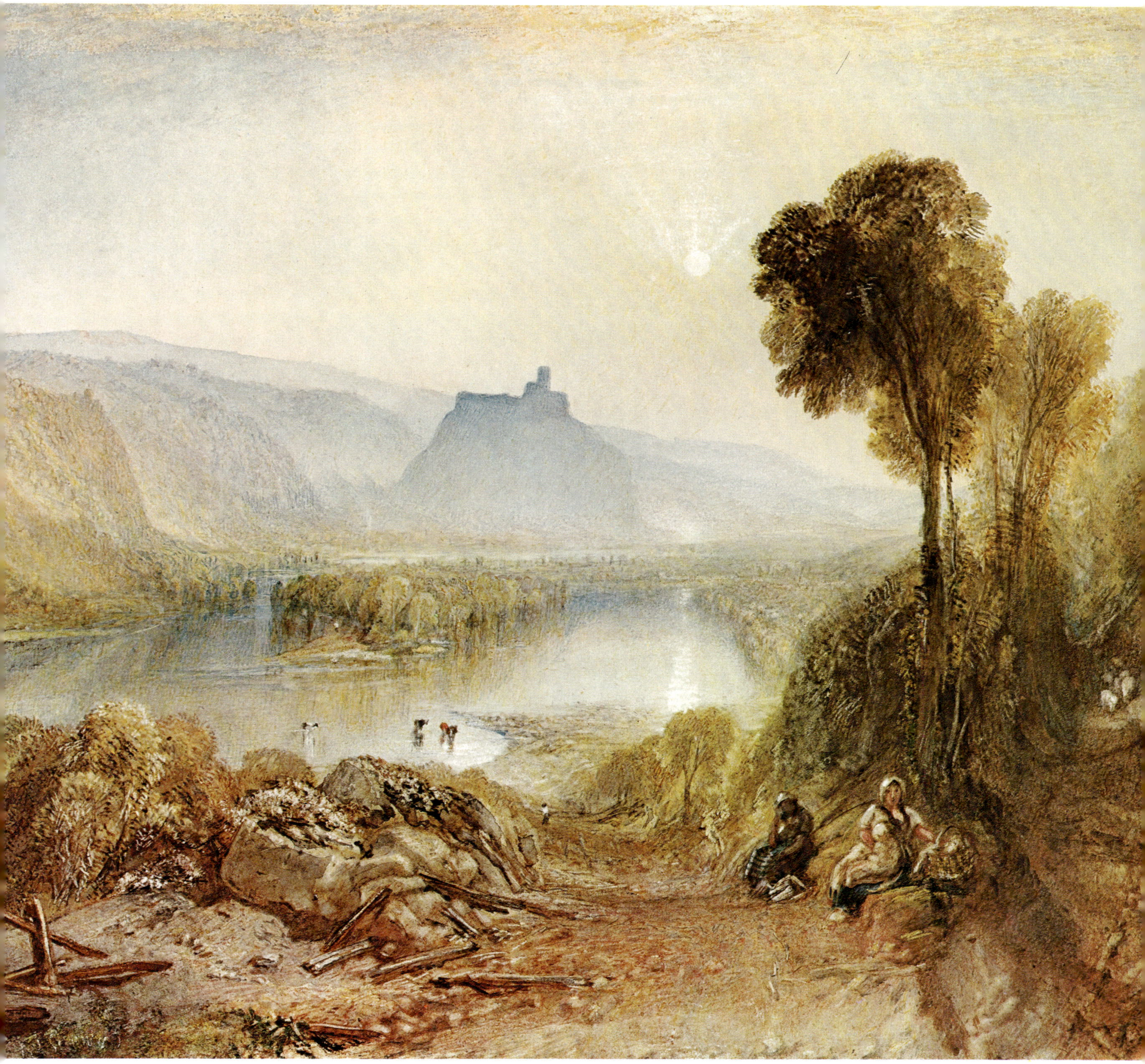

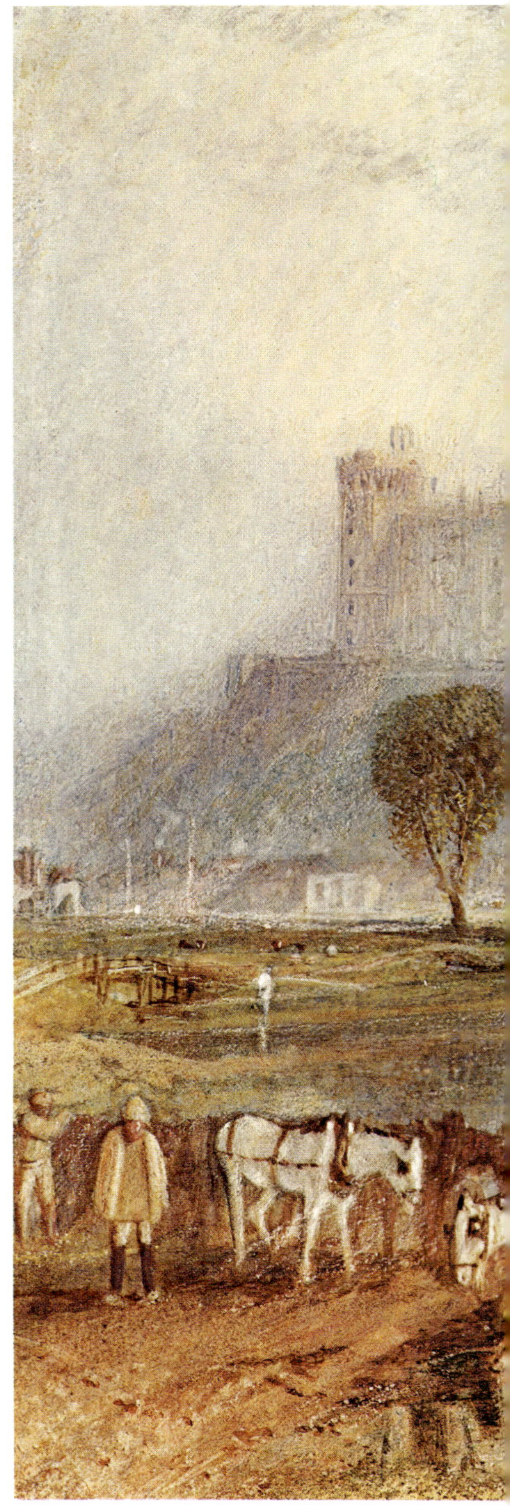

Windsor Castle, Berkshire. 1827—1829
Watercolour, 29 x 43 cm
Trustees of the British Museum, London

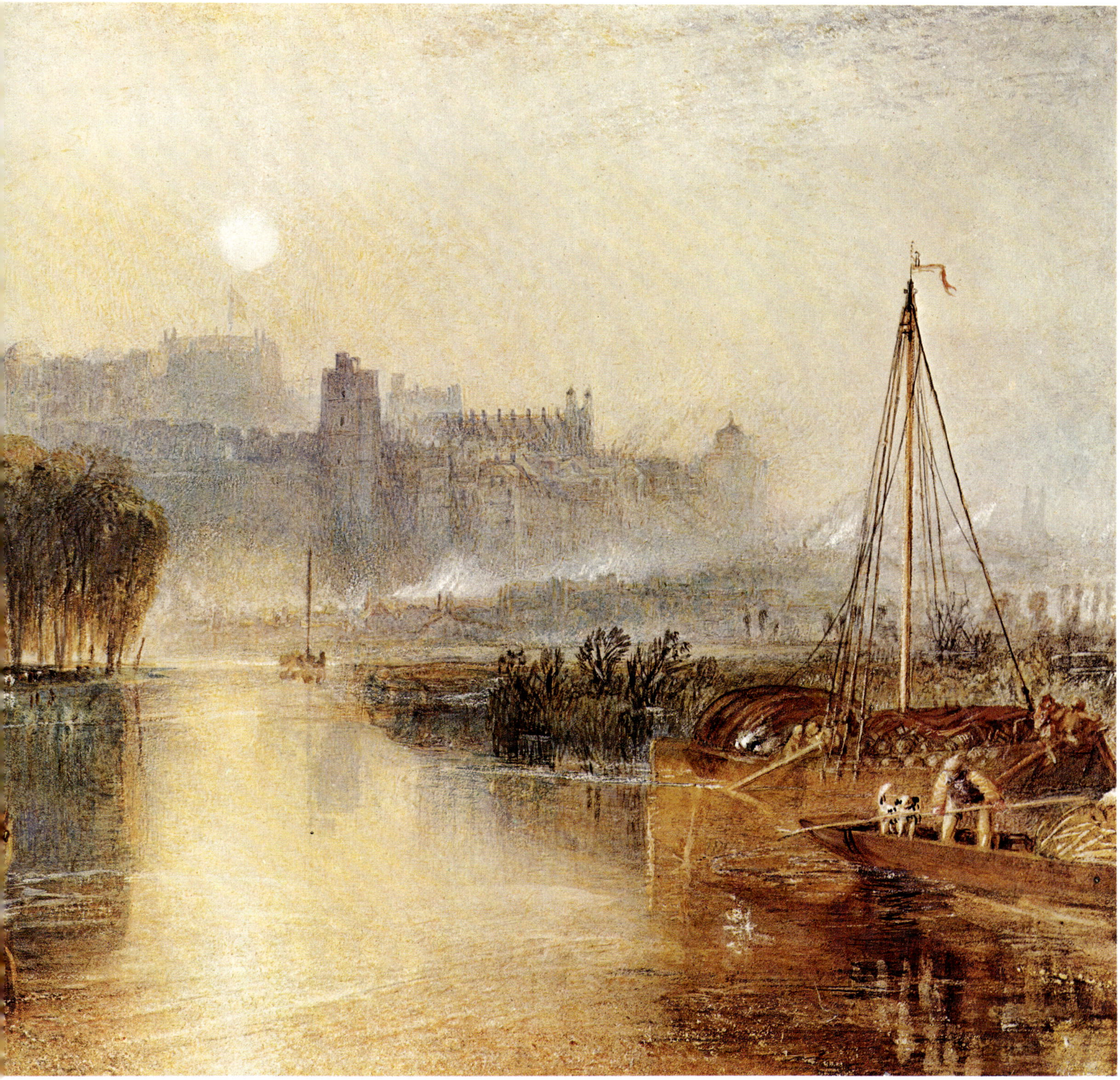

Shipping off East Cowes Headland,
(detail). 1827

Oil on canvas, 46 x 60 cm
The Tate Gallery, London

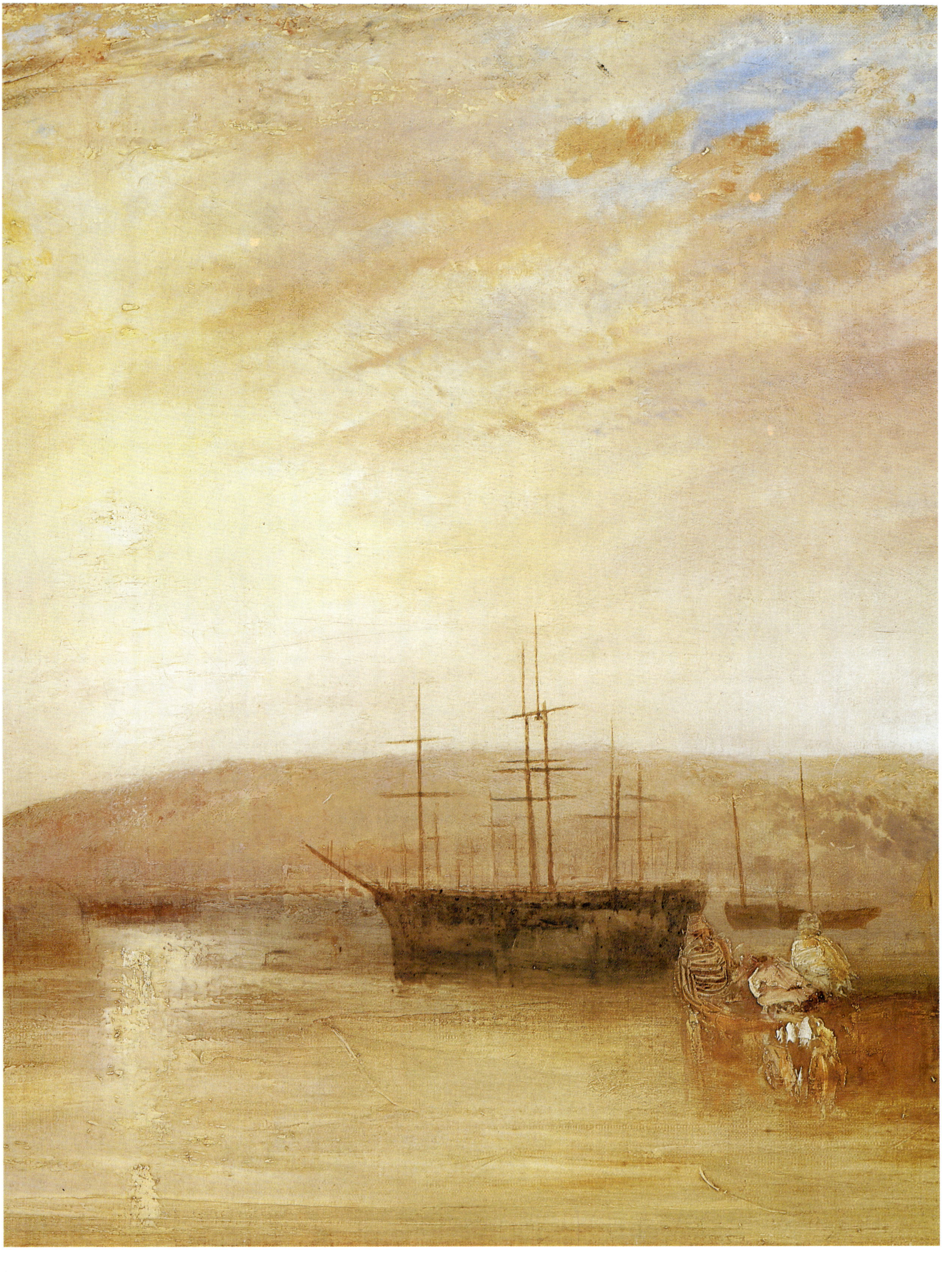

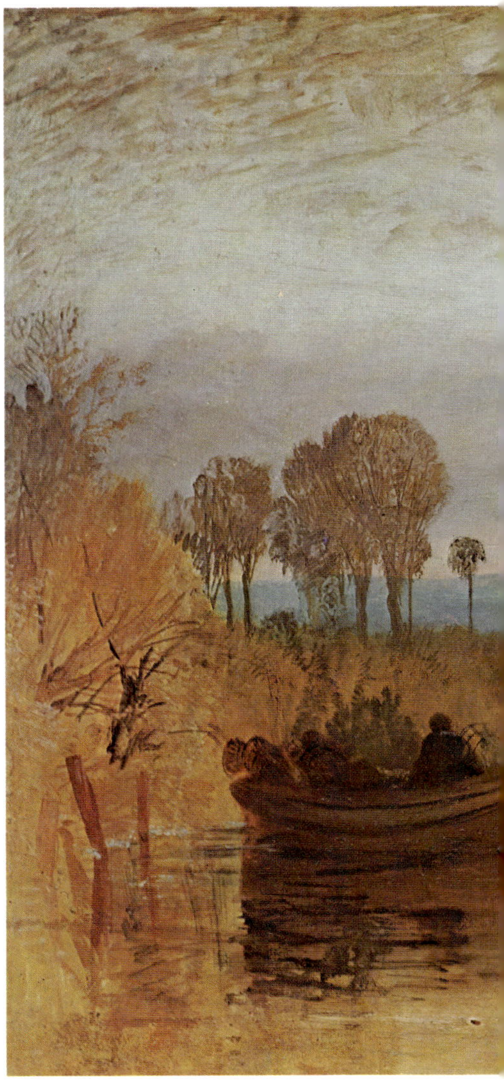

Petworth Park. Tillington Church
in the distance. Ca. 1828
Oil on canvas, 64.5 x 145.5 cm
The Tate Gallery, London

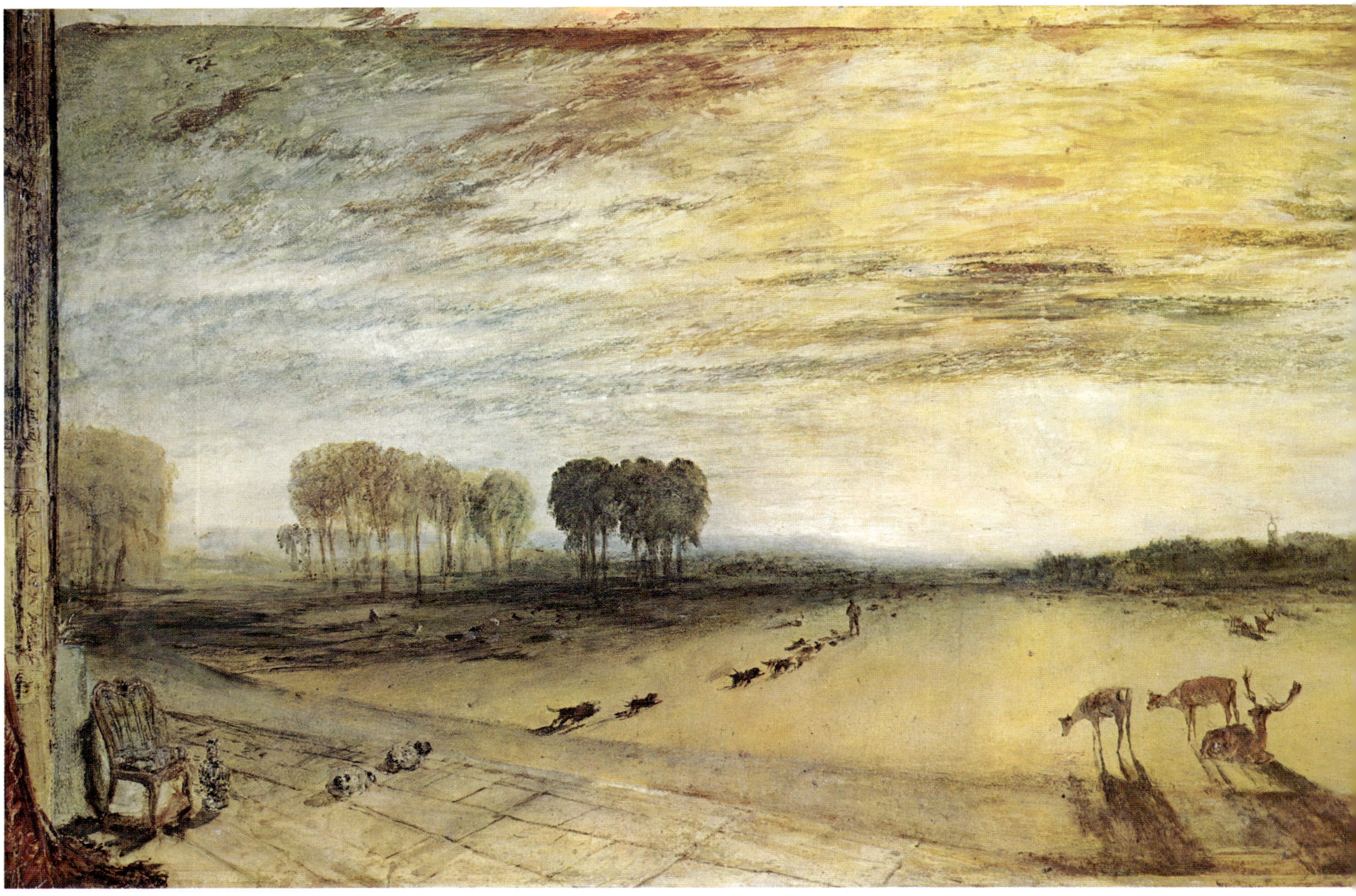

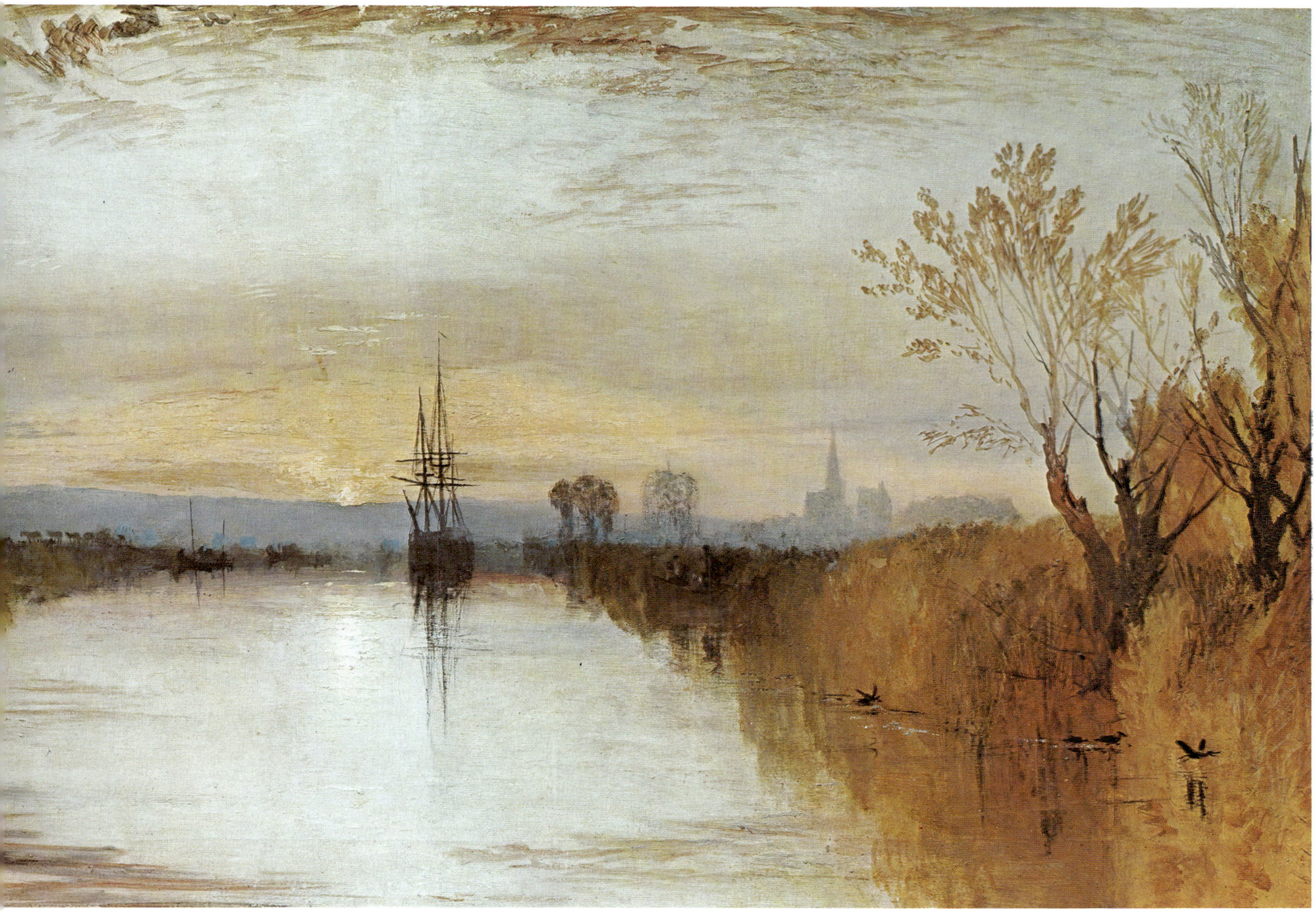

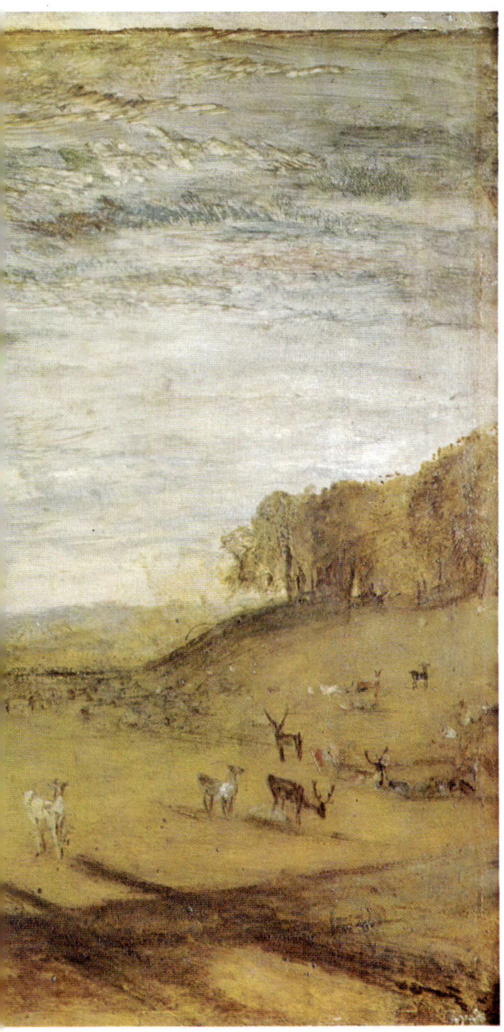

Chichester Canal. Ca. 1828
Oil on canvas, 65.5 x 134.5 cm
The Tate Gallery, London

Music party in Petworth. Ca. 1835
Oil on canvas, 121 x 90.5 cm
The Tate Gallery, London

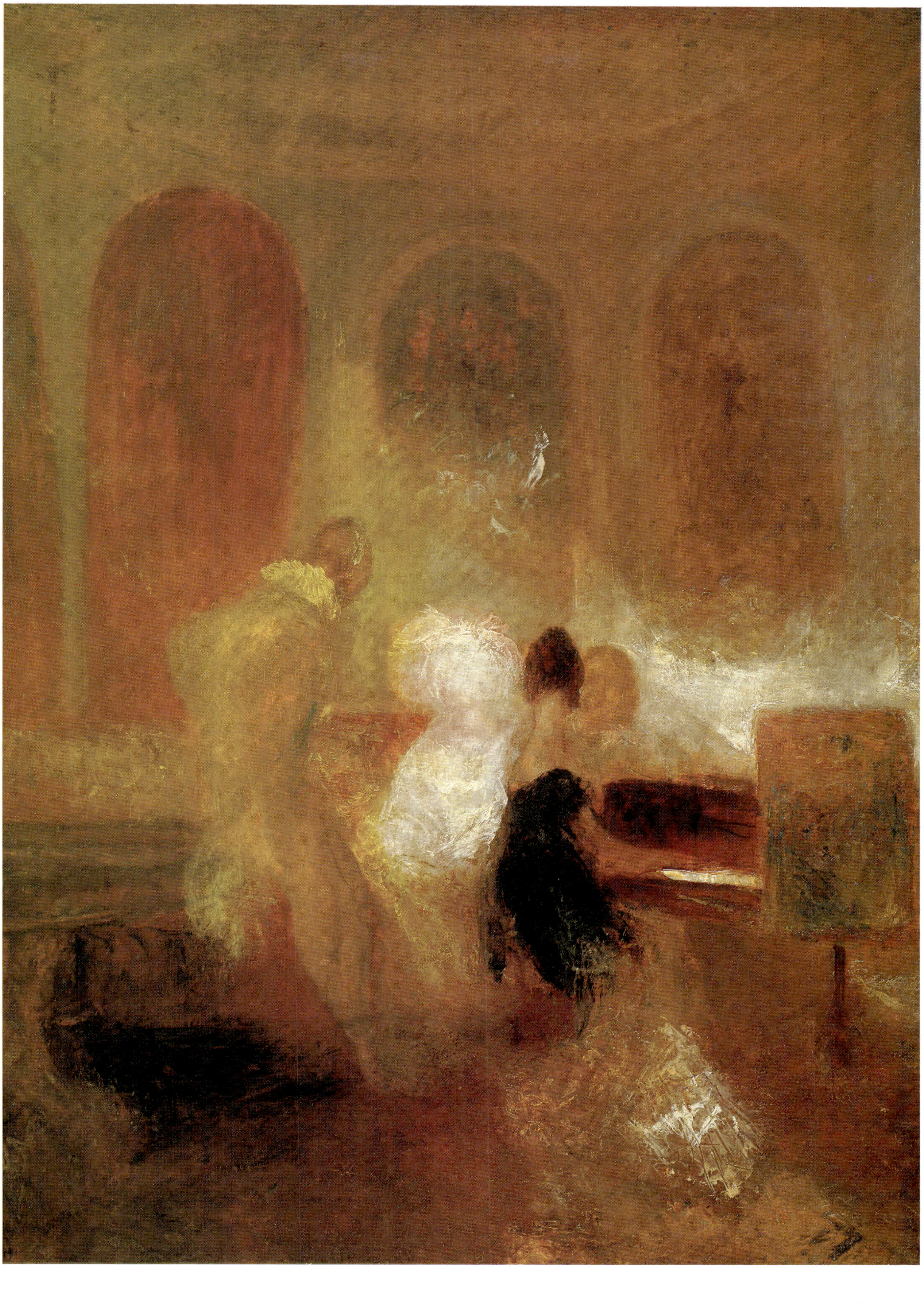

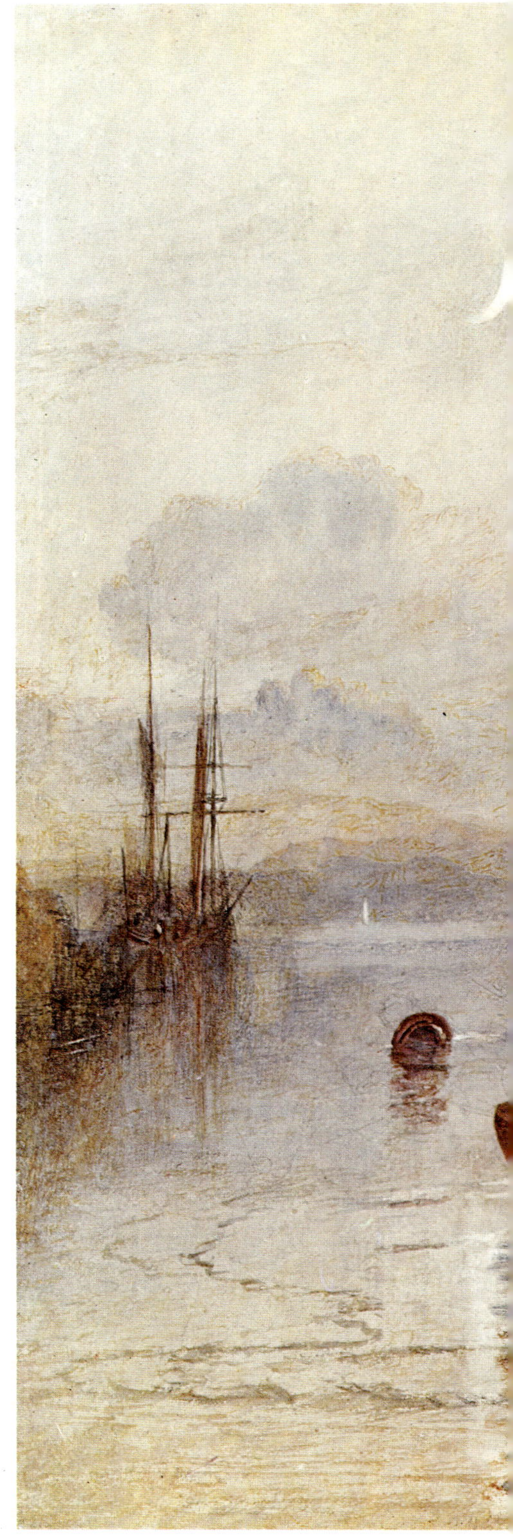

Caernarvon Castle, Wales. 1833—1834
Watercolour, 29 x 44 cm
Trustees of the British Museum, London

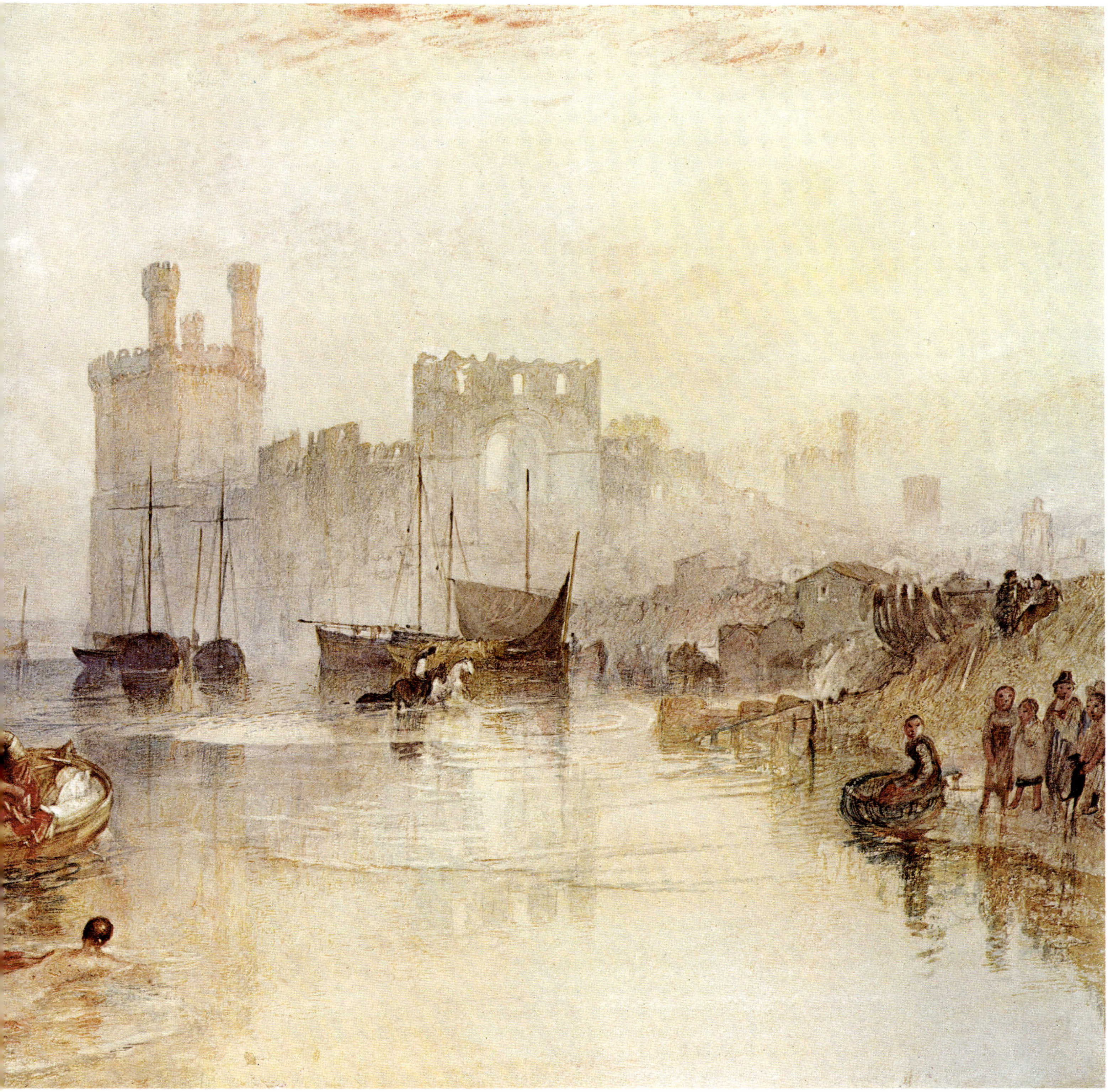

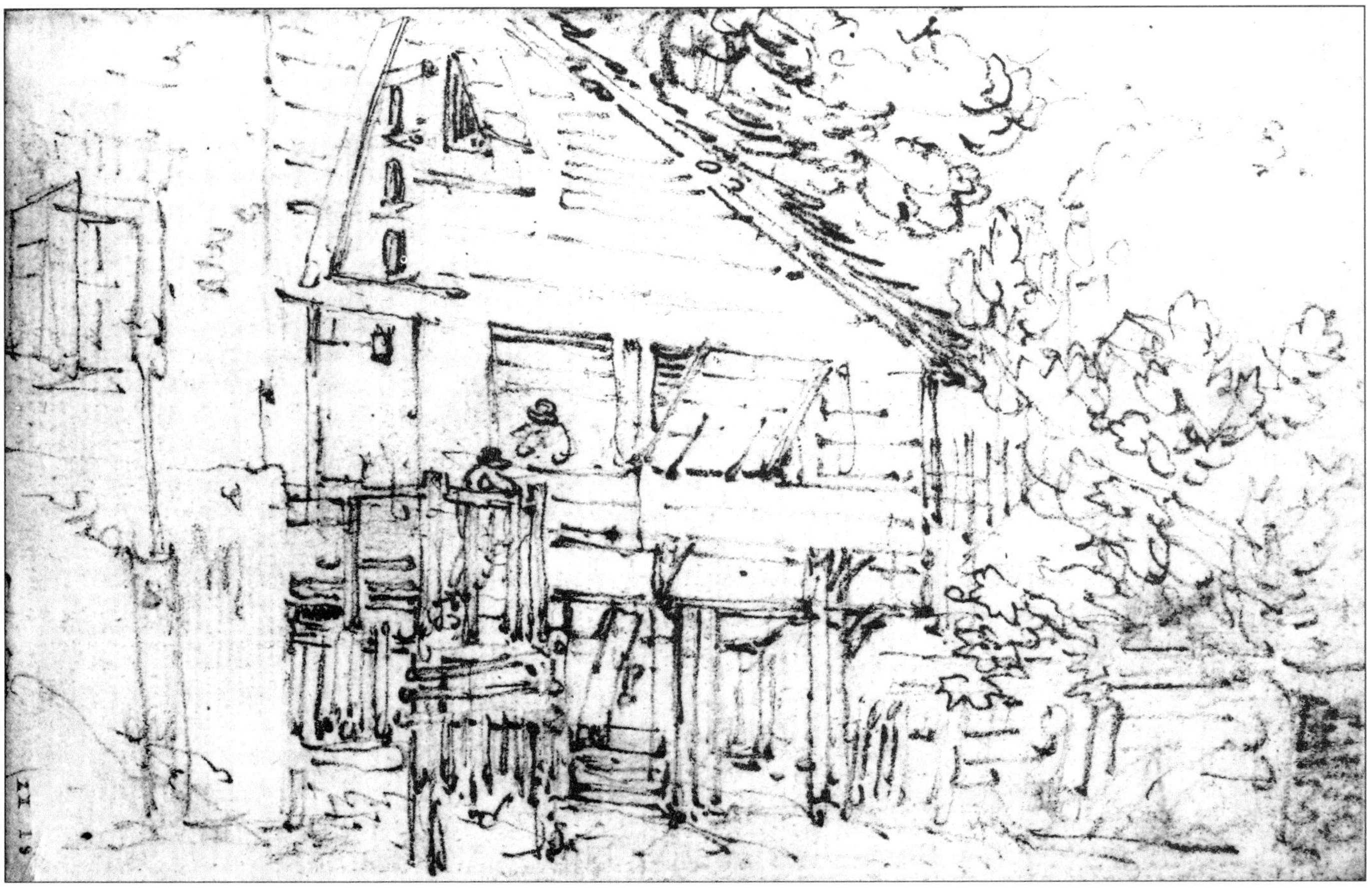

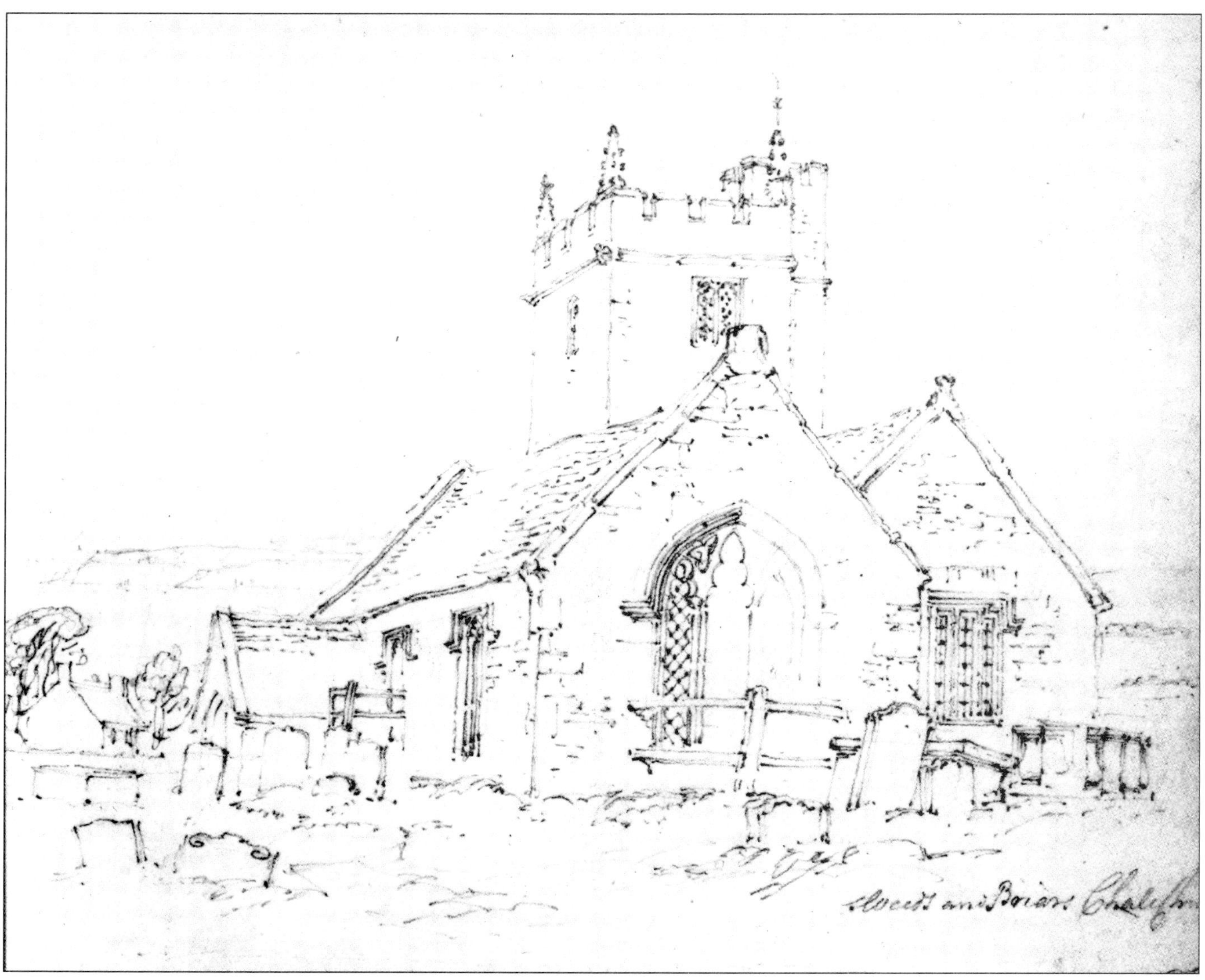

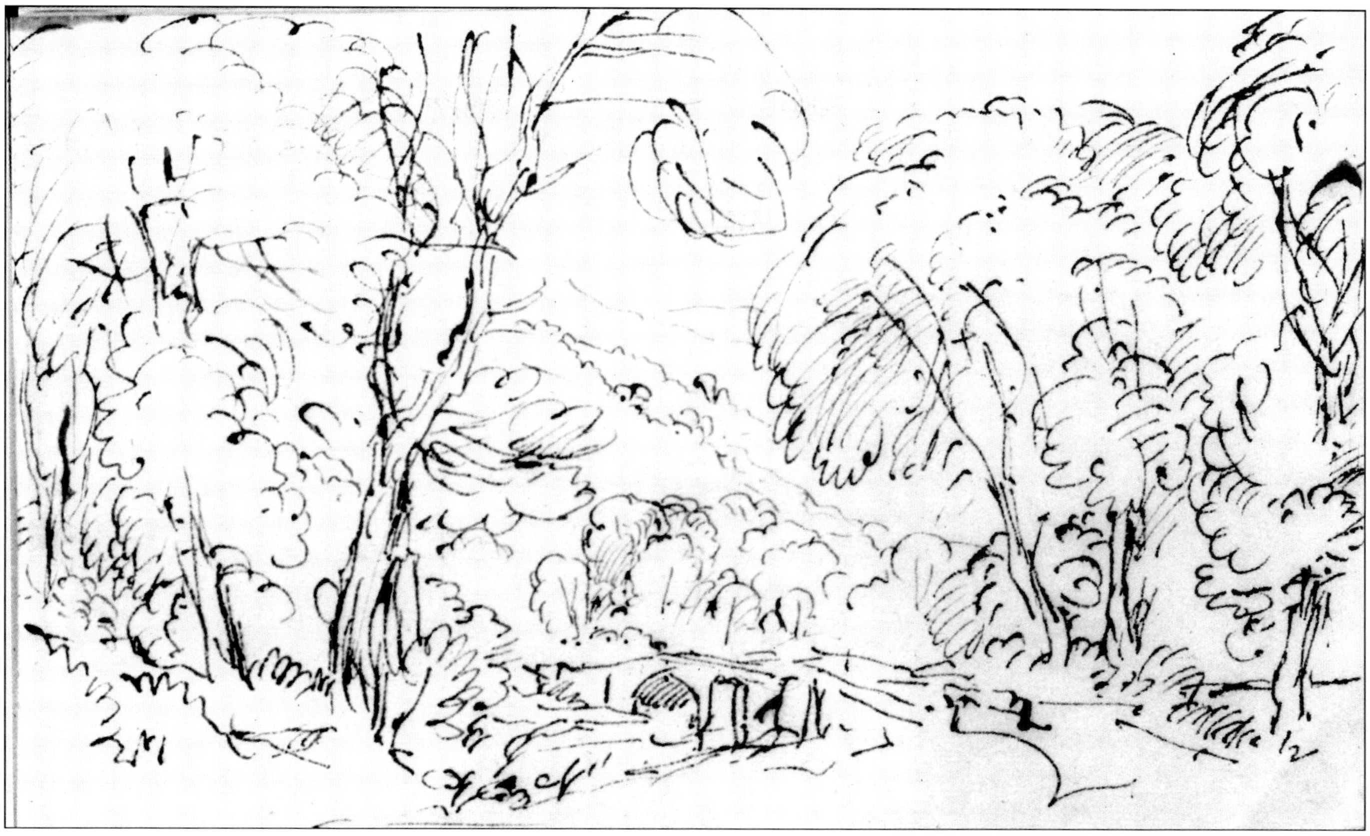

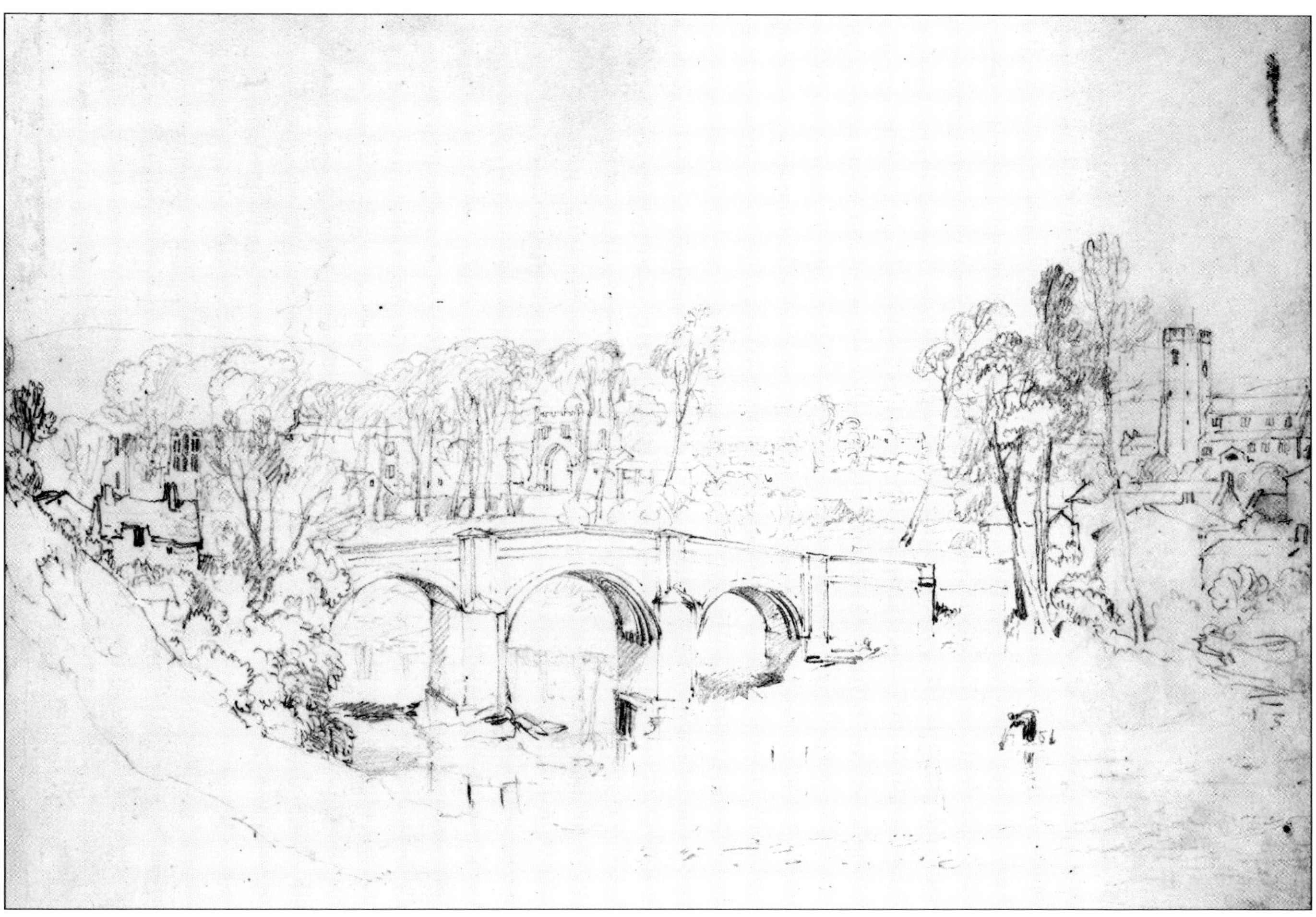

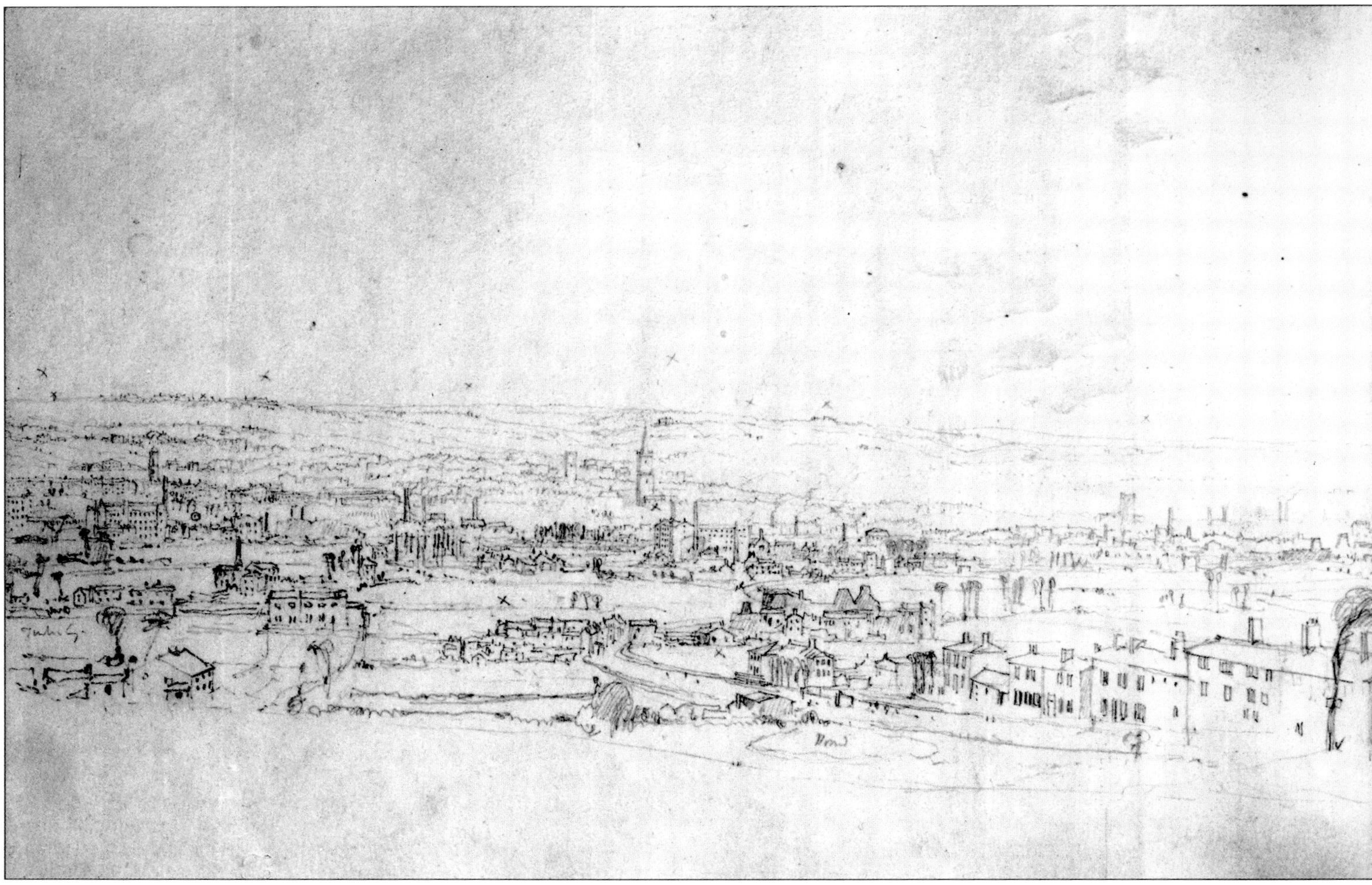

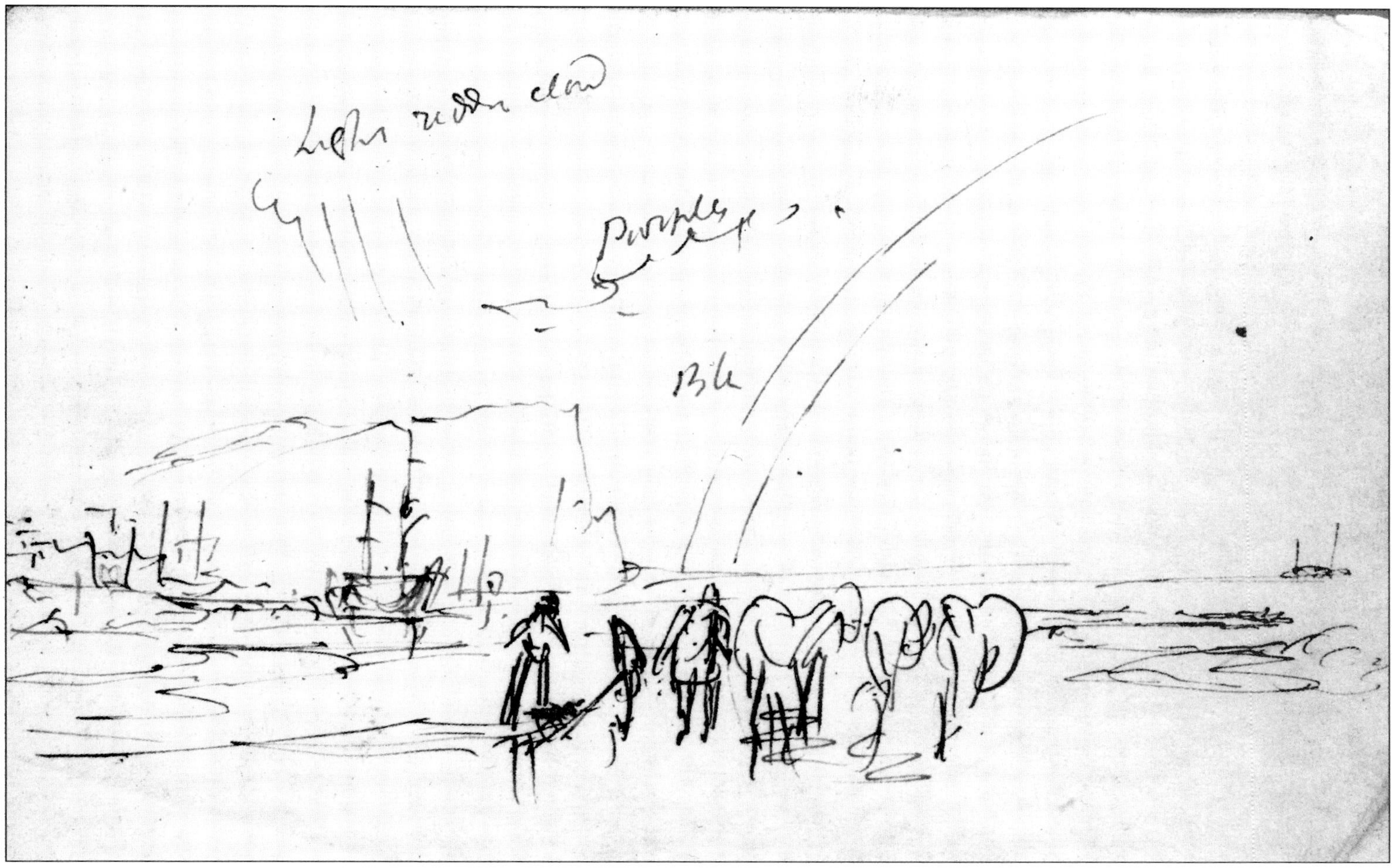

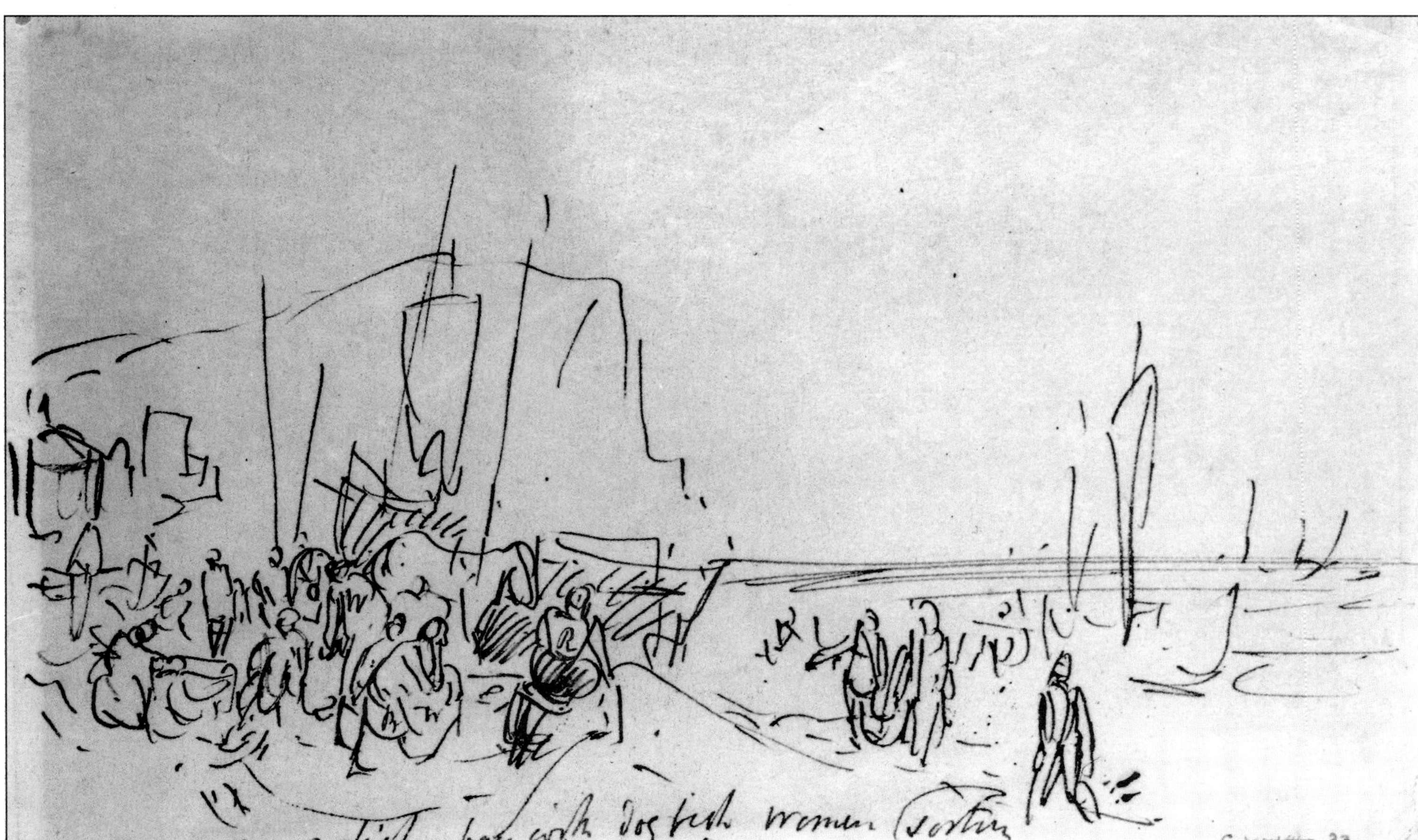
C CXXVII-33

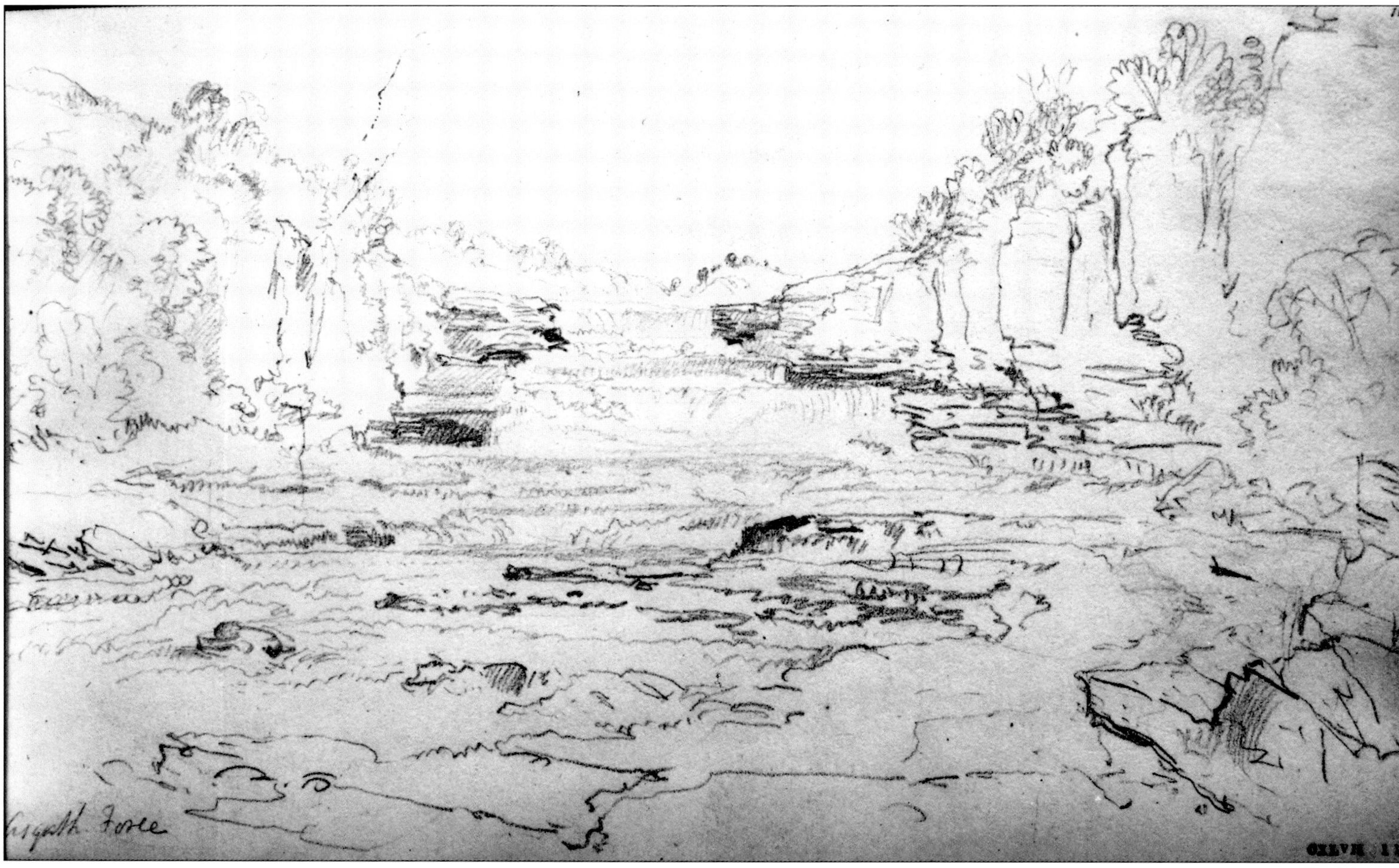

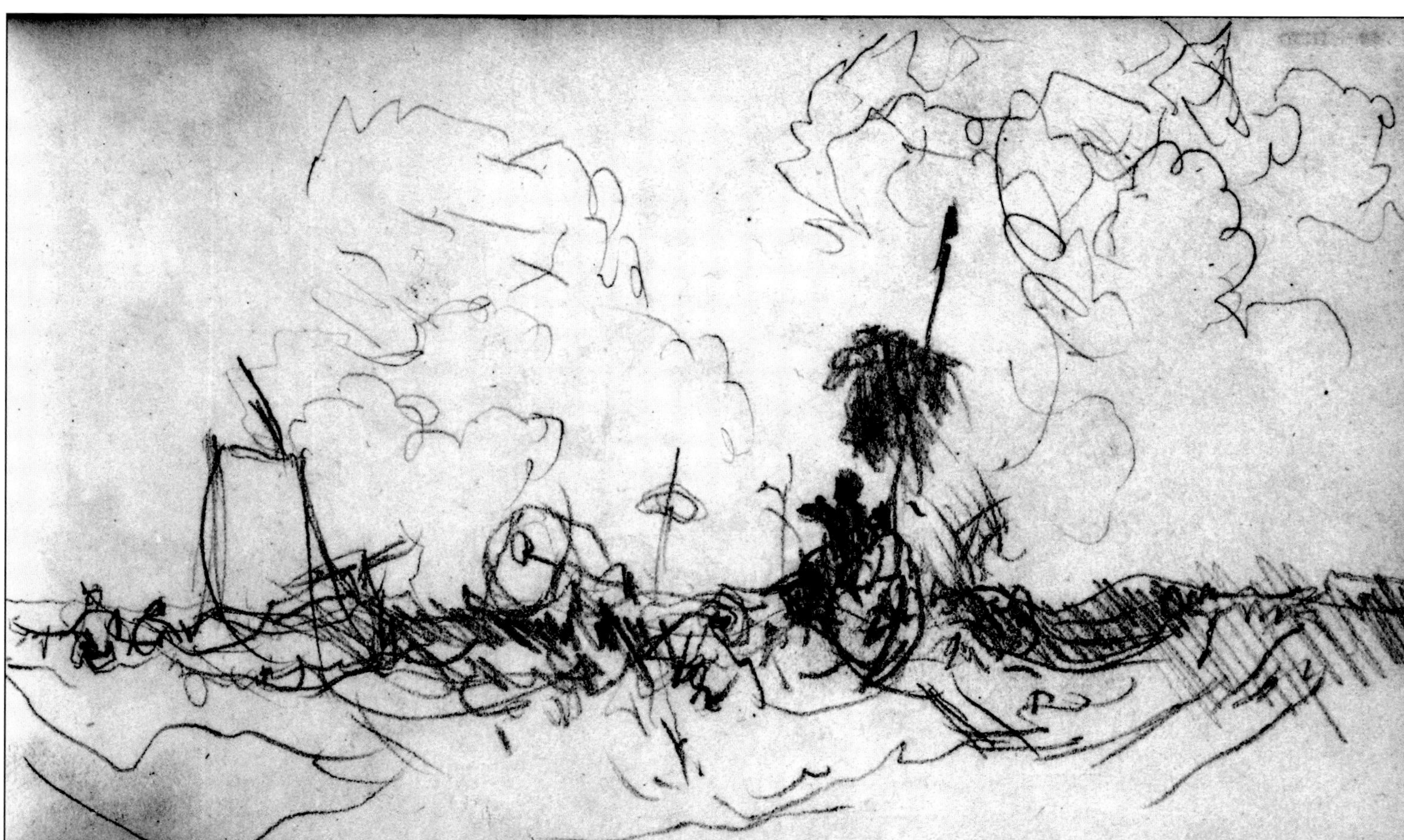

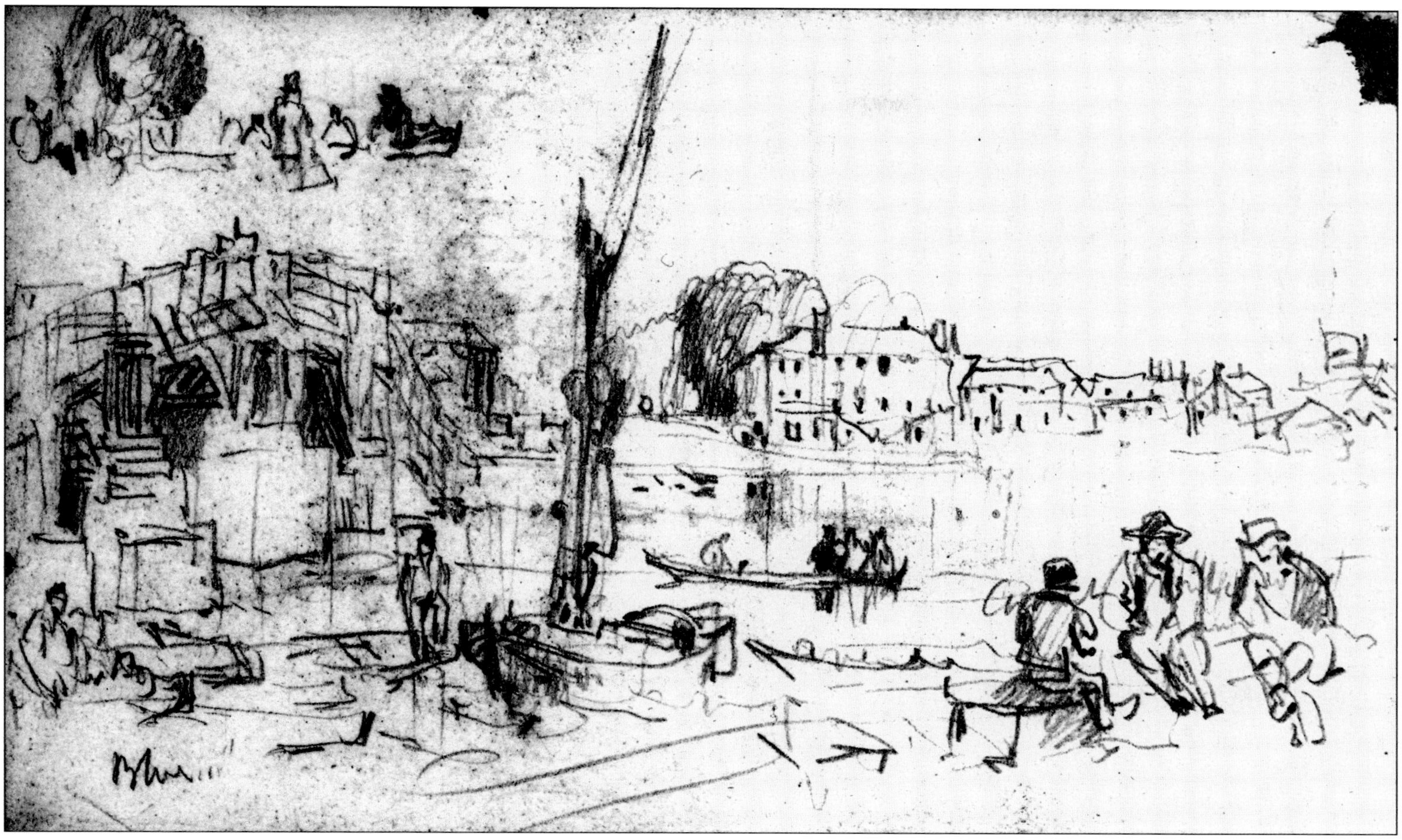

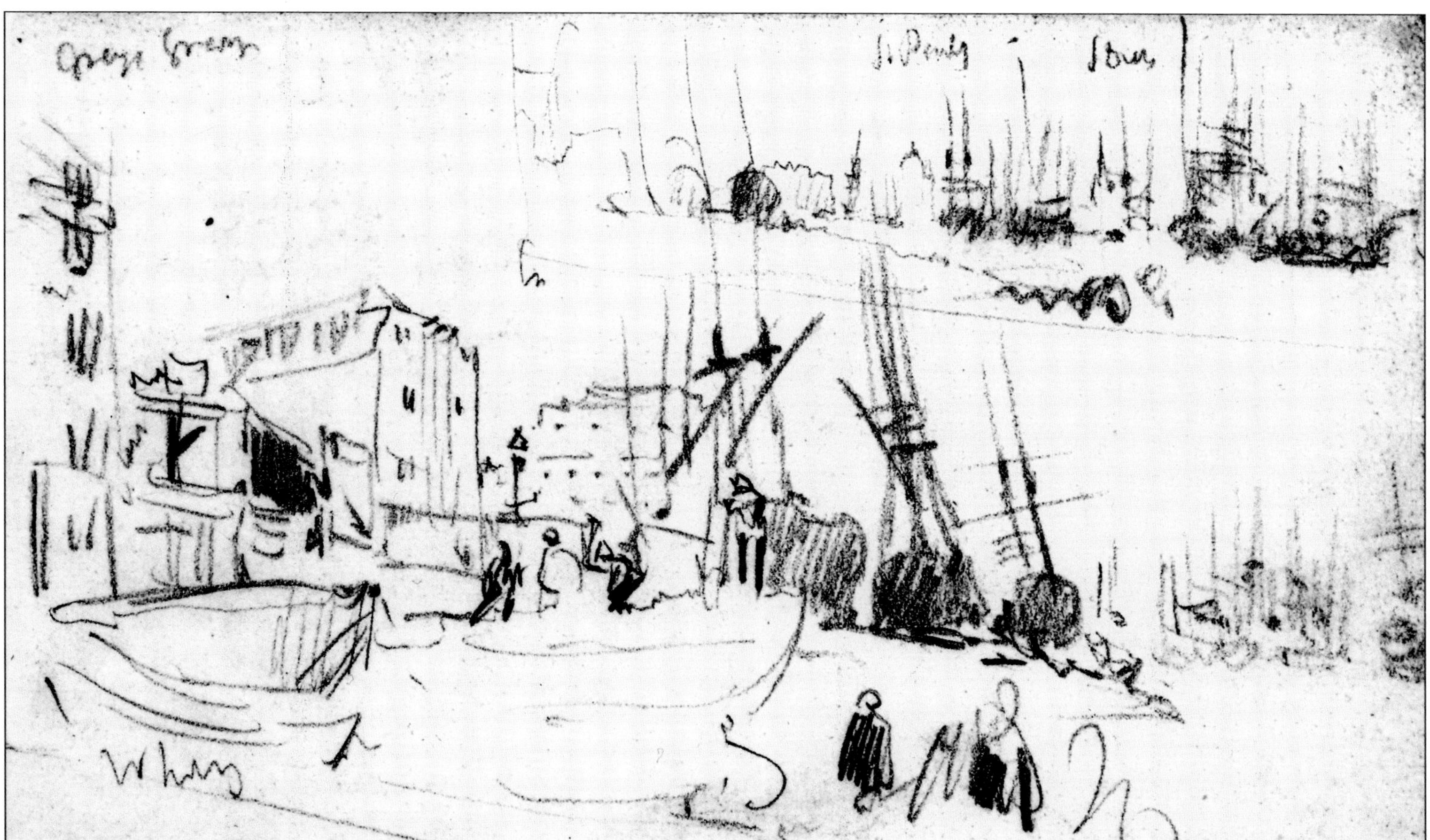

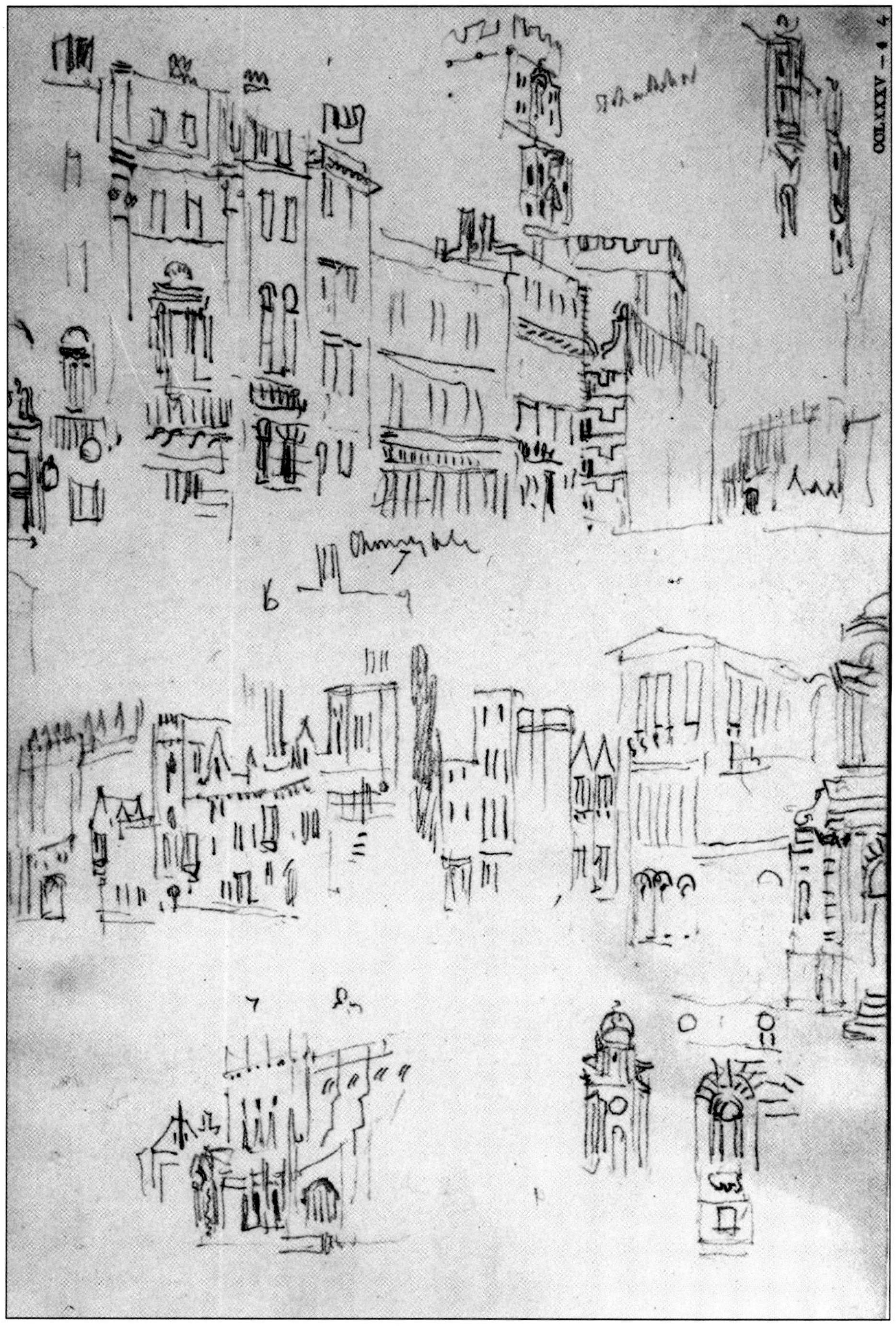

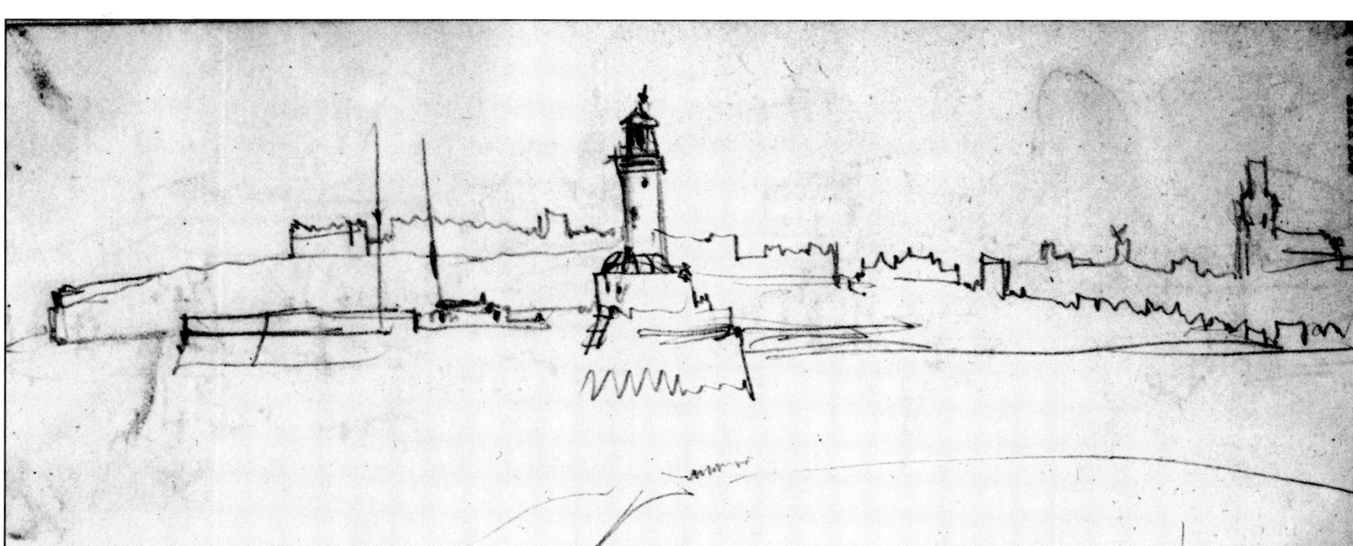

# TRAVELS ON THE CONTINENT

The passage of Mount St. Gothard, taken from the centre of the Teufels Broch, Swizterland. 1804 (Turners Gallery)

Watercolour, 98.5 x 68.5 cm
Abbot Hall Art Gallery, Kendal, Cumbria

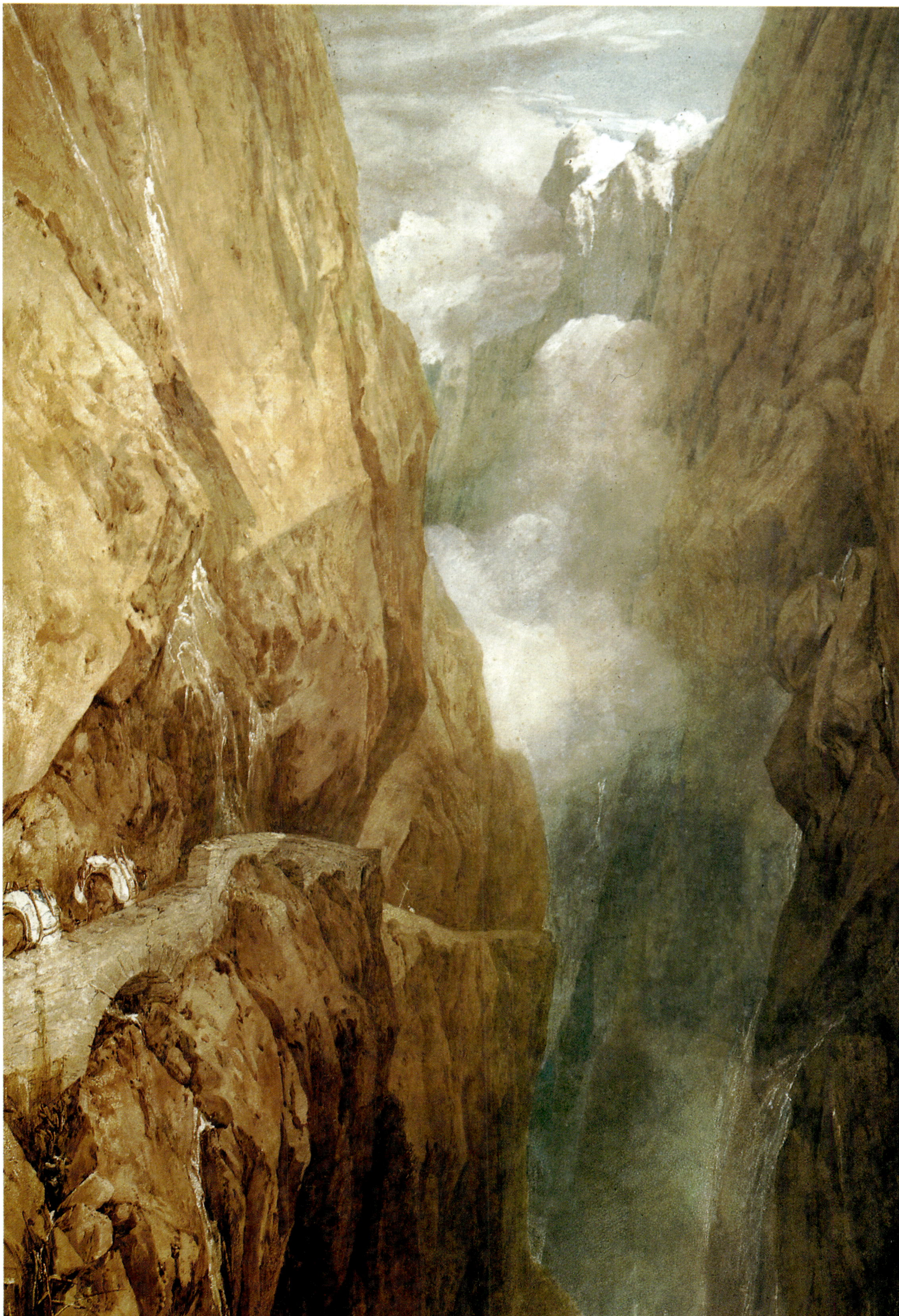

The fall of an Avalanche in the Grisons. 1810
(Turners Gallery)
Oil on canvas, 90 x 120 cm
The Tate Gallery, London

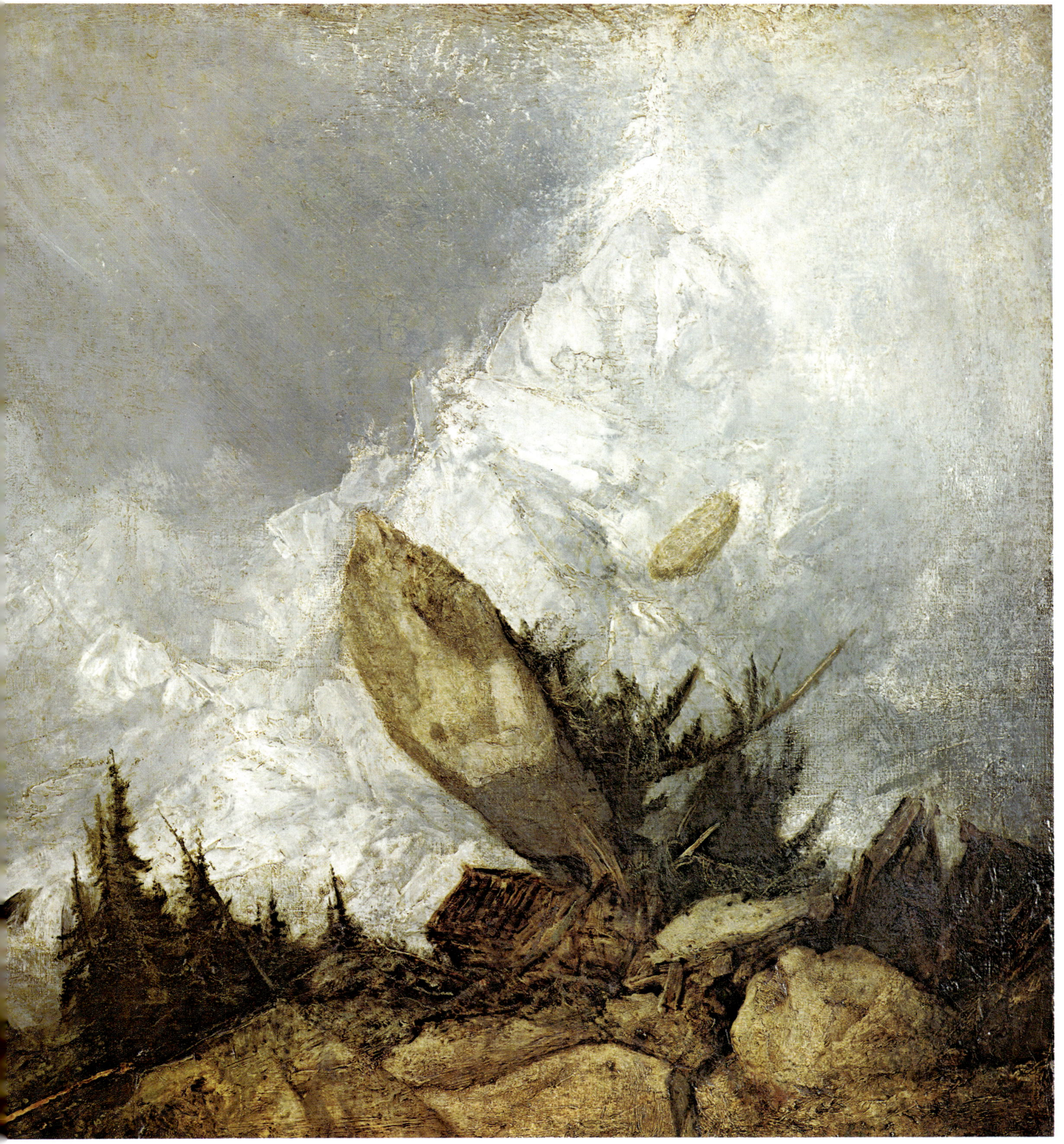

Cologne, the arrival of a packet boat;
Evening. 1826
Oil and maybe watercolour on canvas, 168.6 x 224.1 cm
Frick Collection, New York

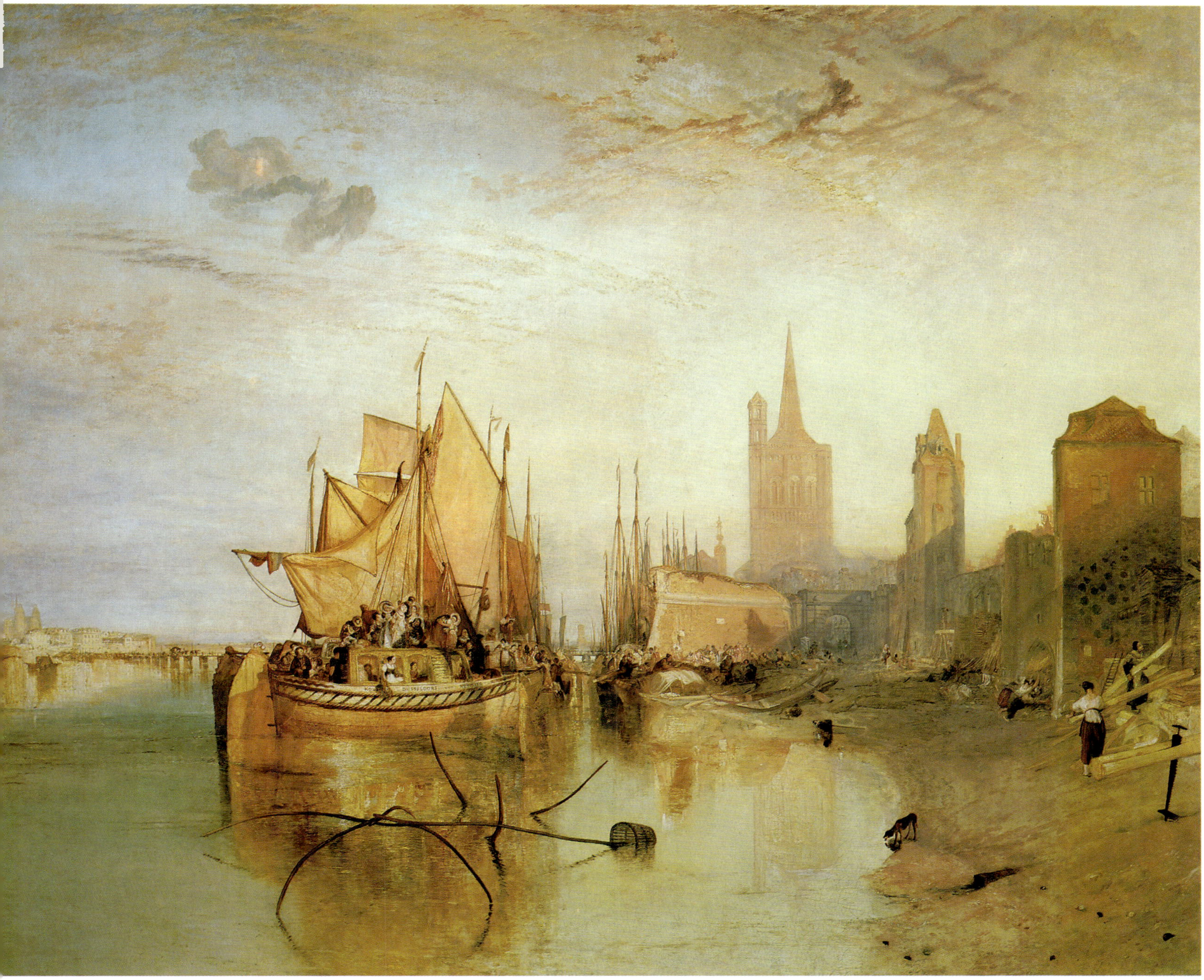

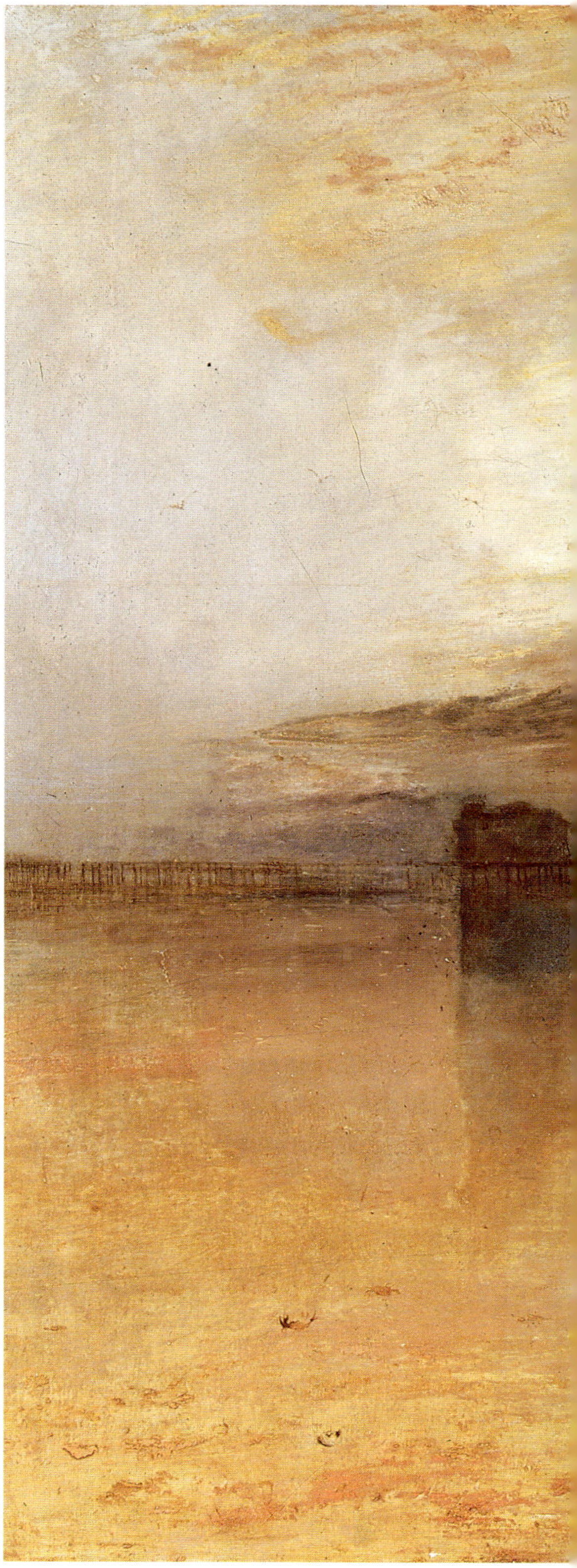

Calais sands, low water,
Poissards collecting bait. 1830
Oil on canvas, 73 x 107 cm
Bury Art Gallery, Lancashire

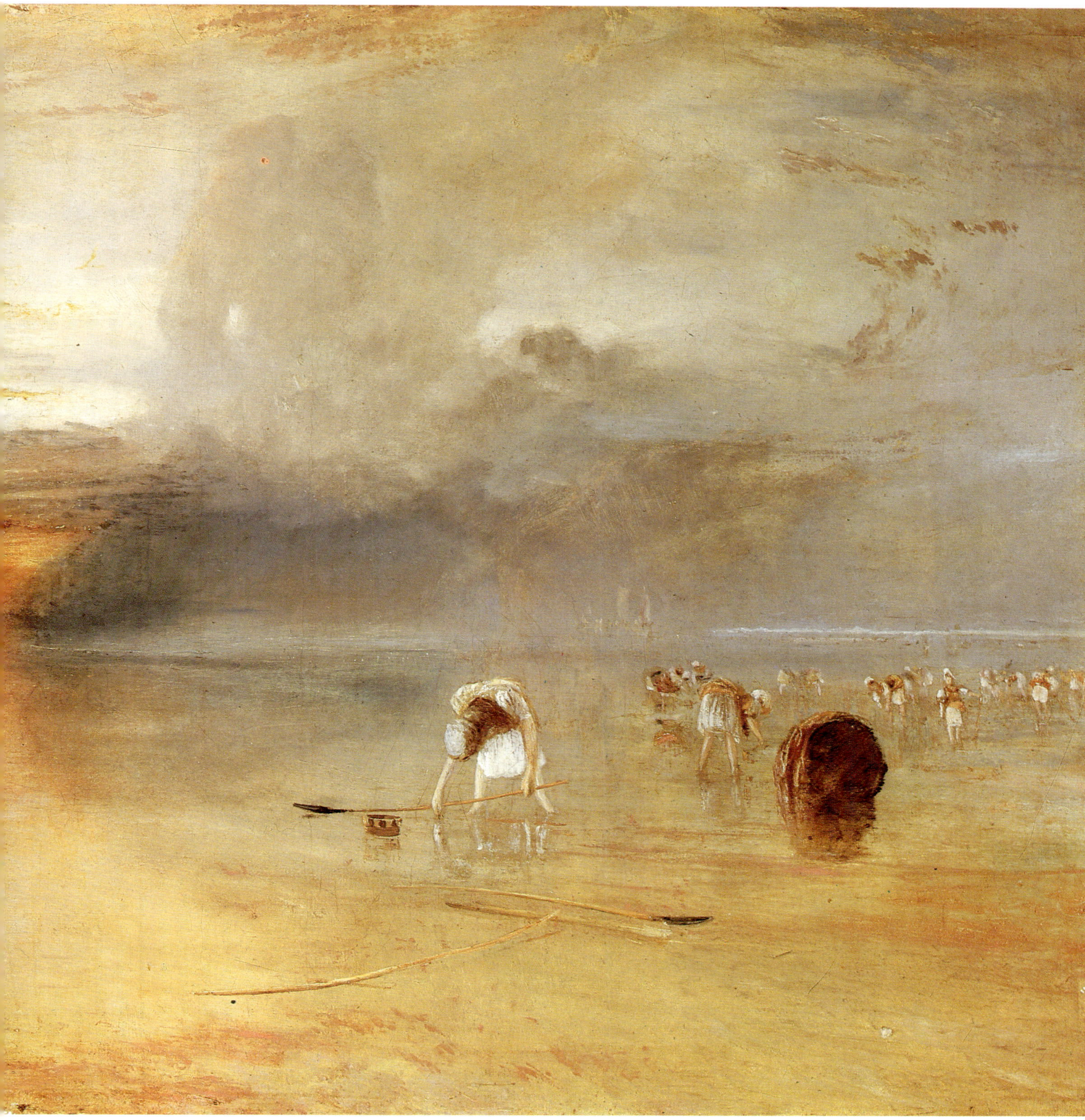

Rouen, looking up the Seine. Ca. 1832
Watercolour and pen on blue paper, 14.1 x 19.2 cm
Trustees of the British Museum, London

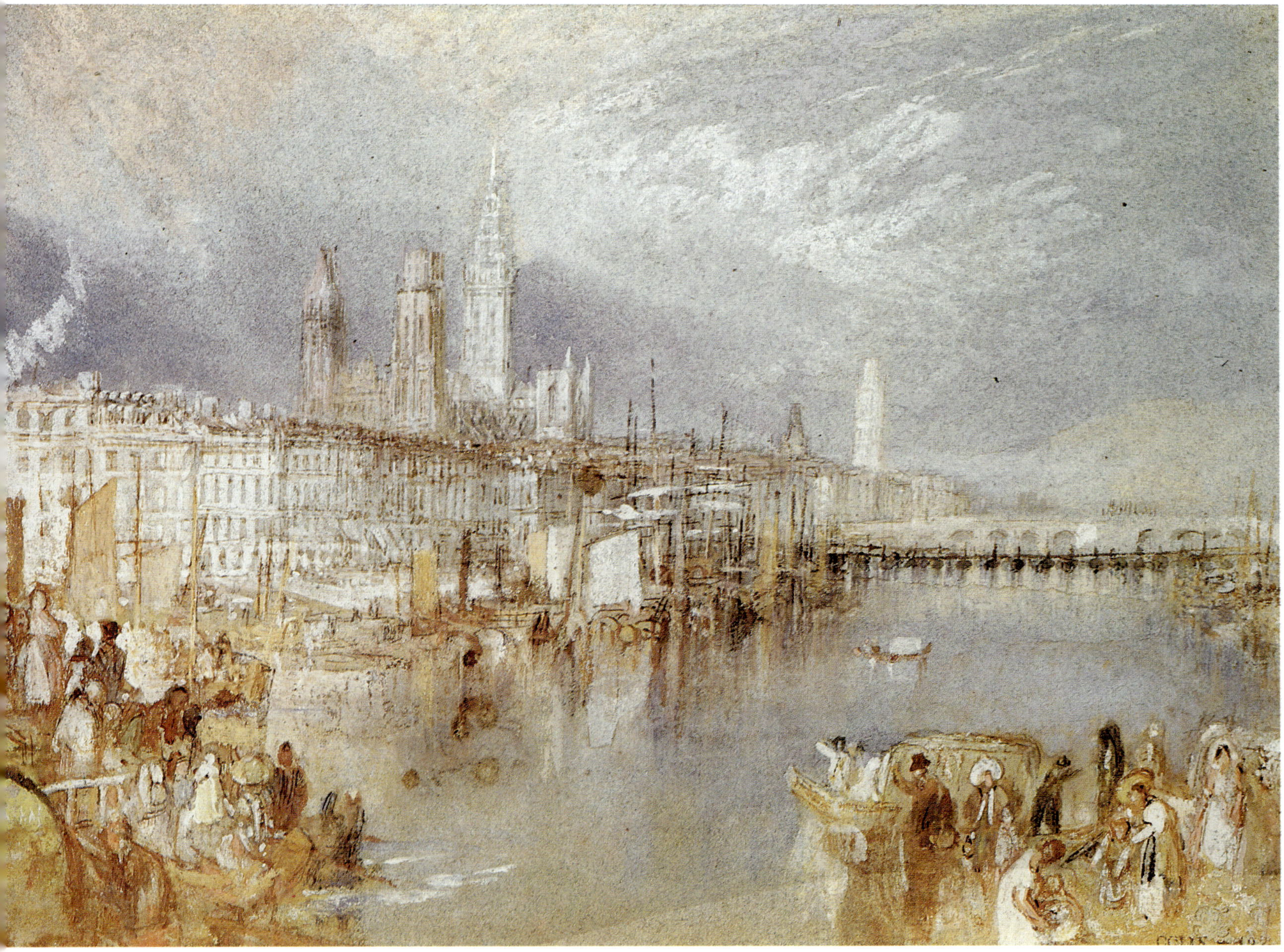

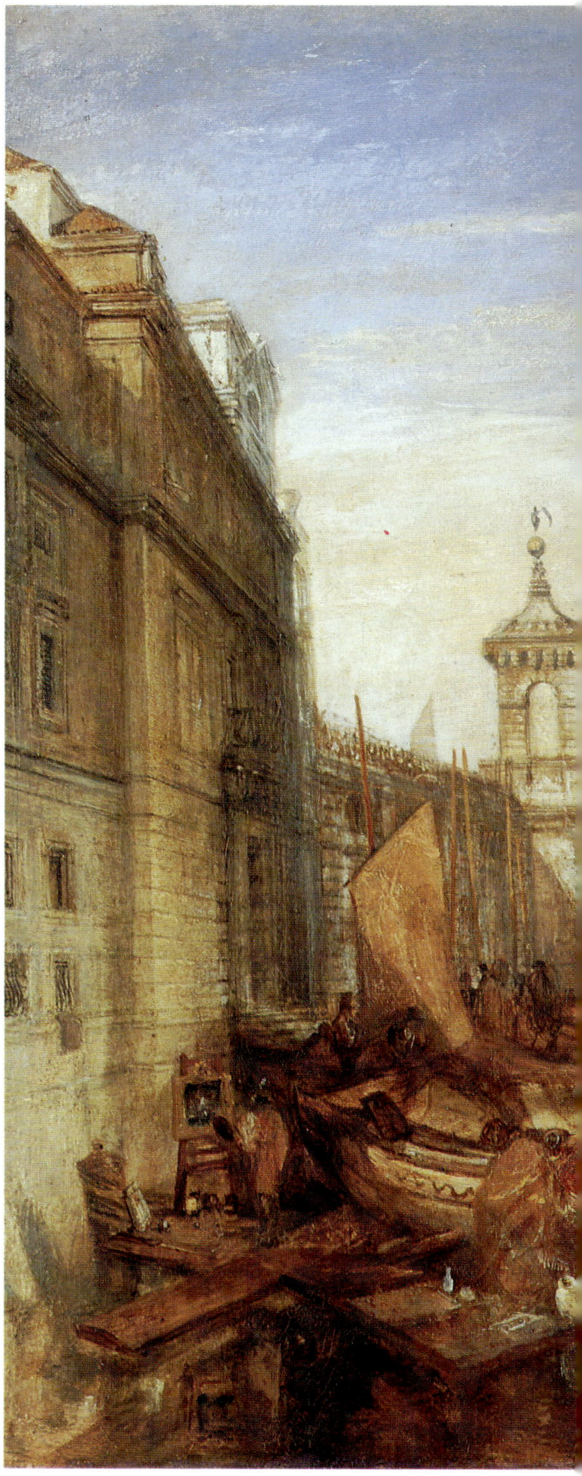

Bridge of Sighs, Ducal Palace and Custom-house
Venice, Canaletto painting. 1833
Oil on mahogany, 51 x 82.5 cm
The Tate Gallery, London

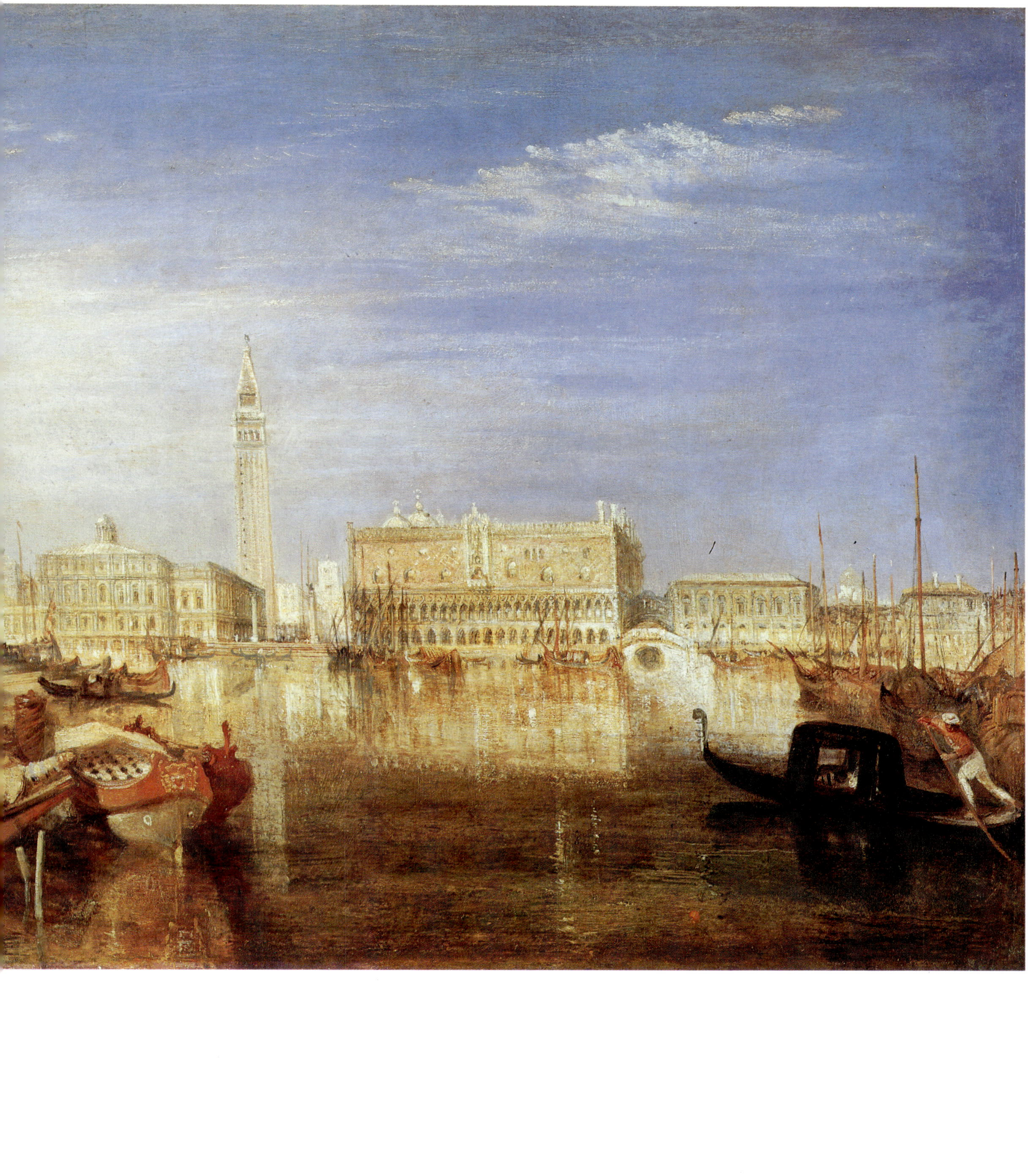

Venice, from the Lagoon. 1840
Watercolour and pen, 23 x 30.5 cm
Fitzwilliam Museum, Cambridge

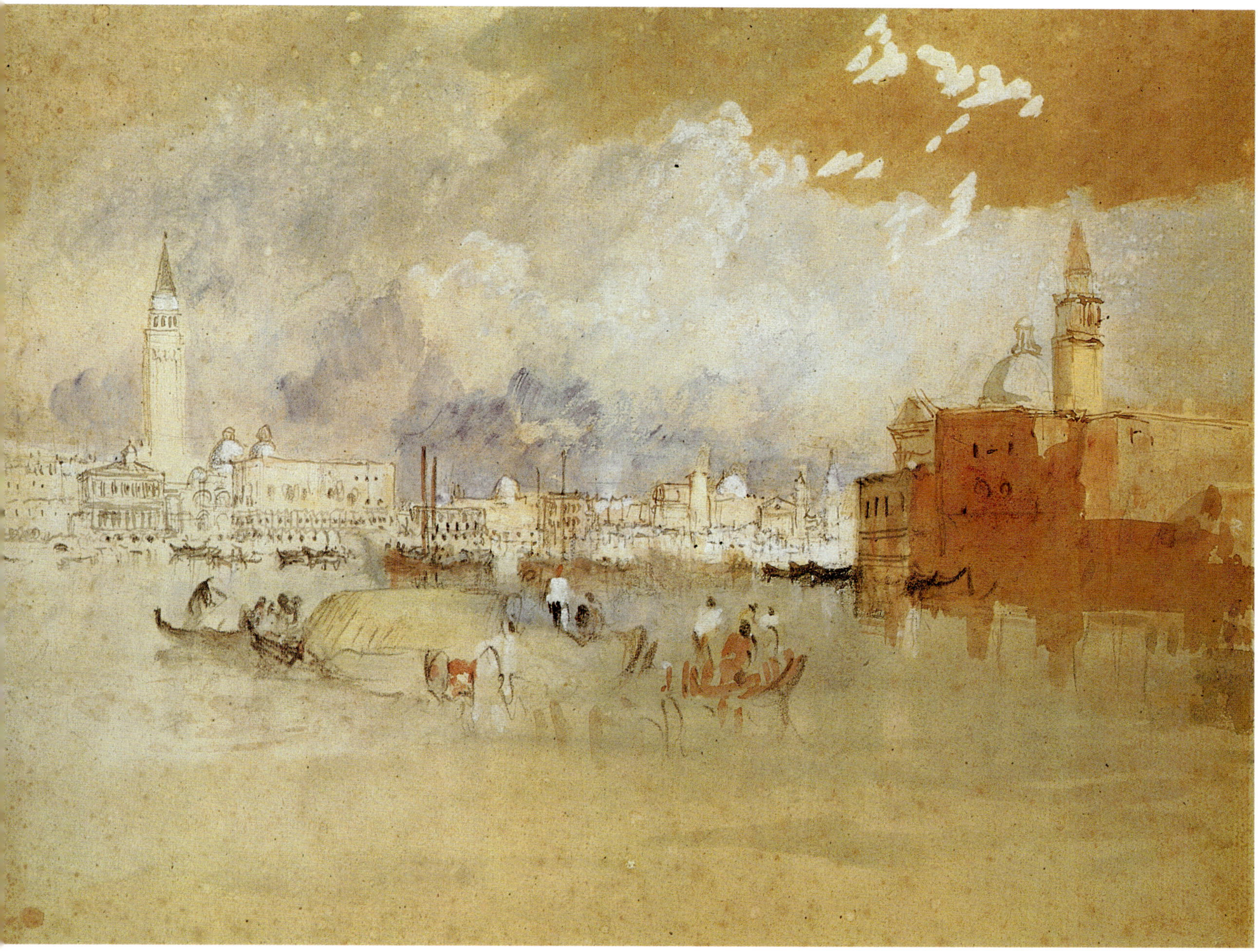

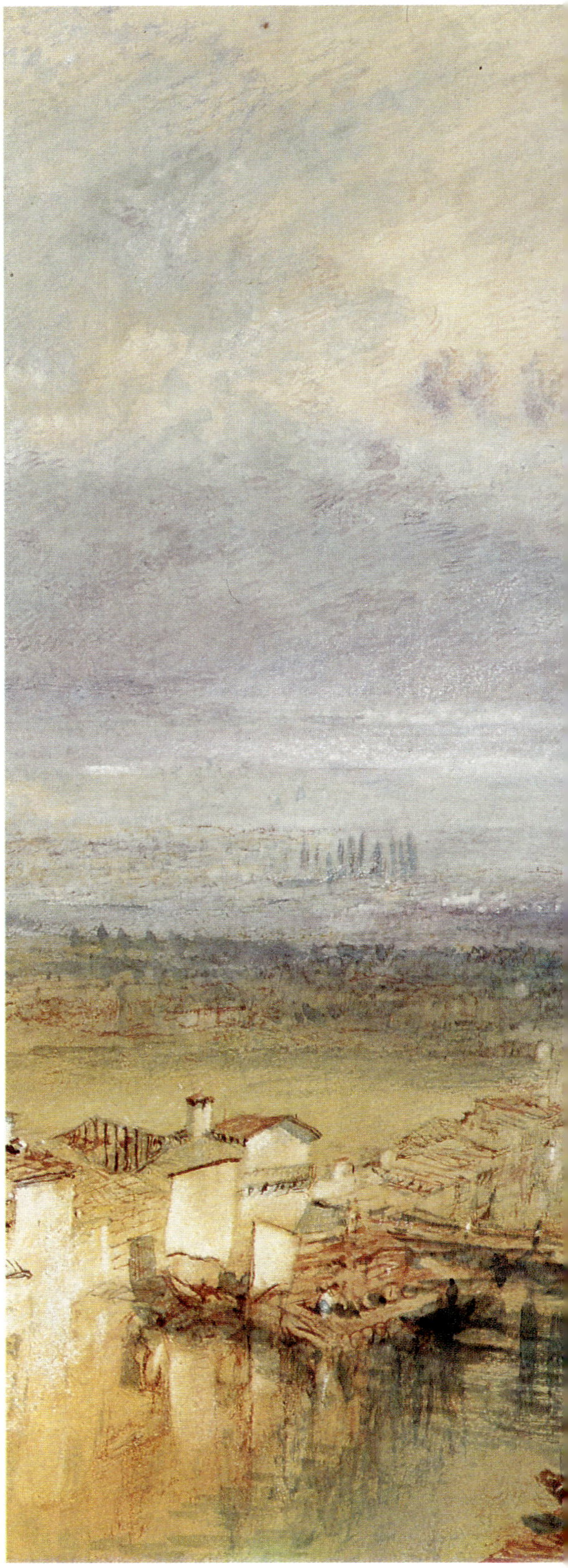

Constance. 1842
Watercolour, 30.4 x 45.4 cm
Private collection

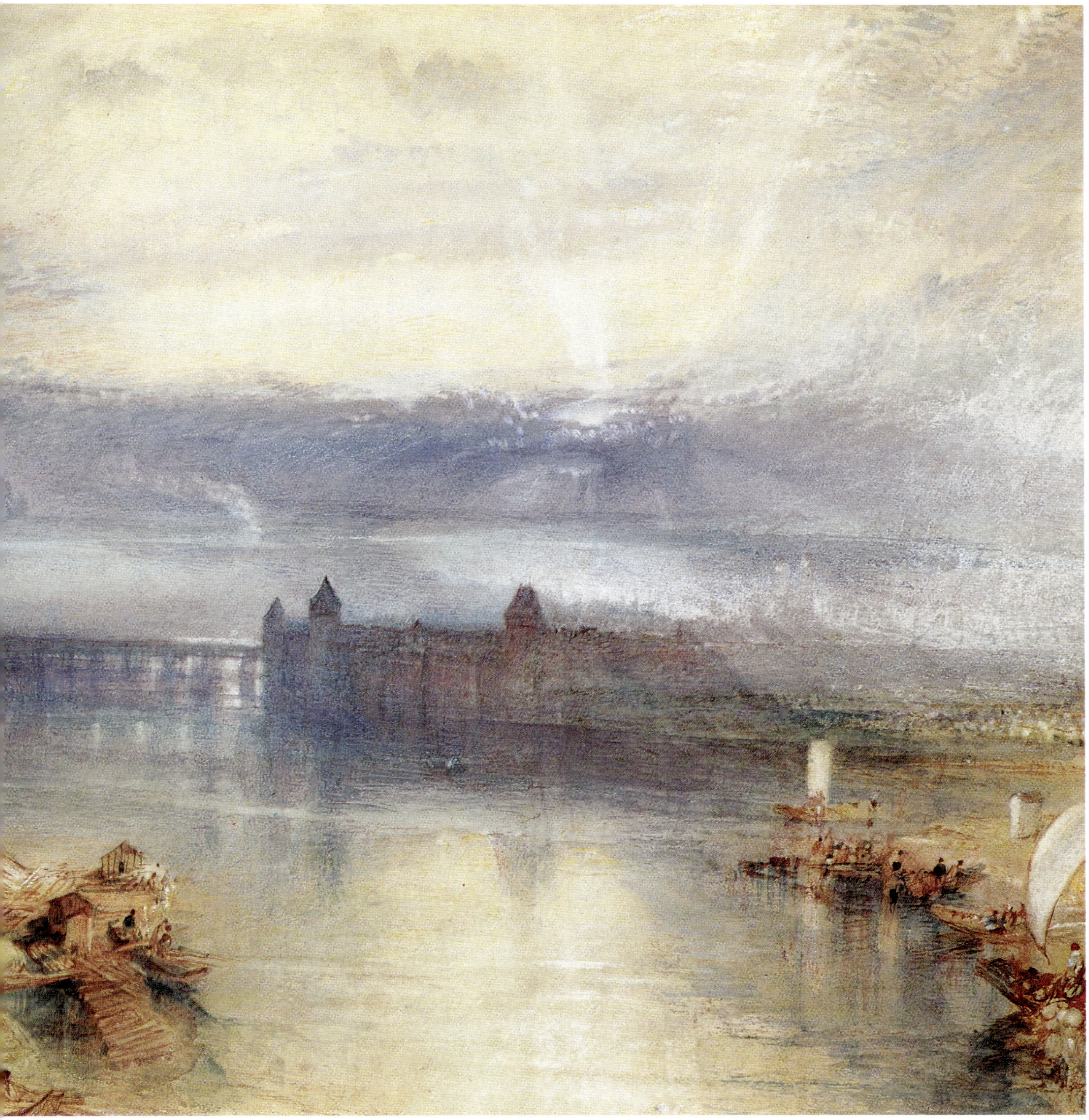

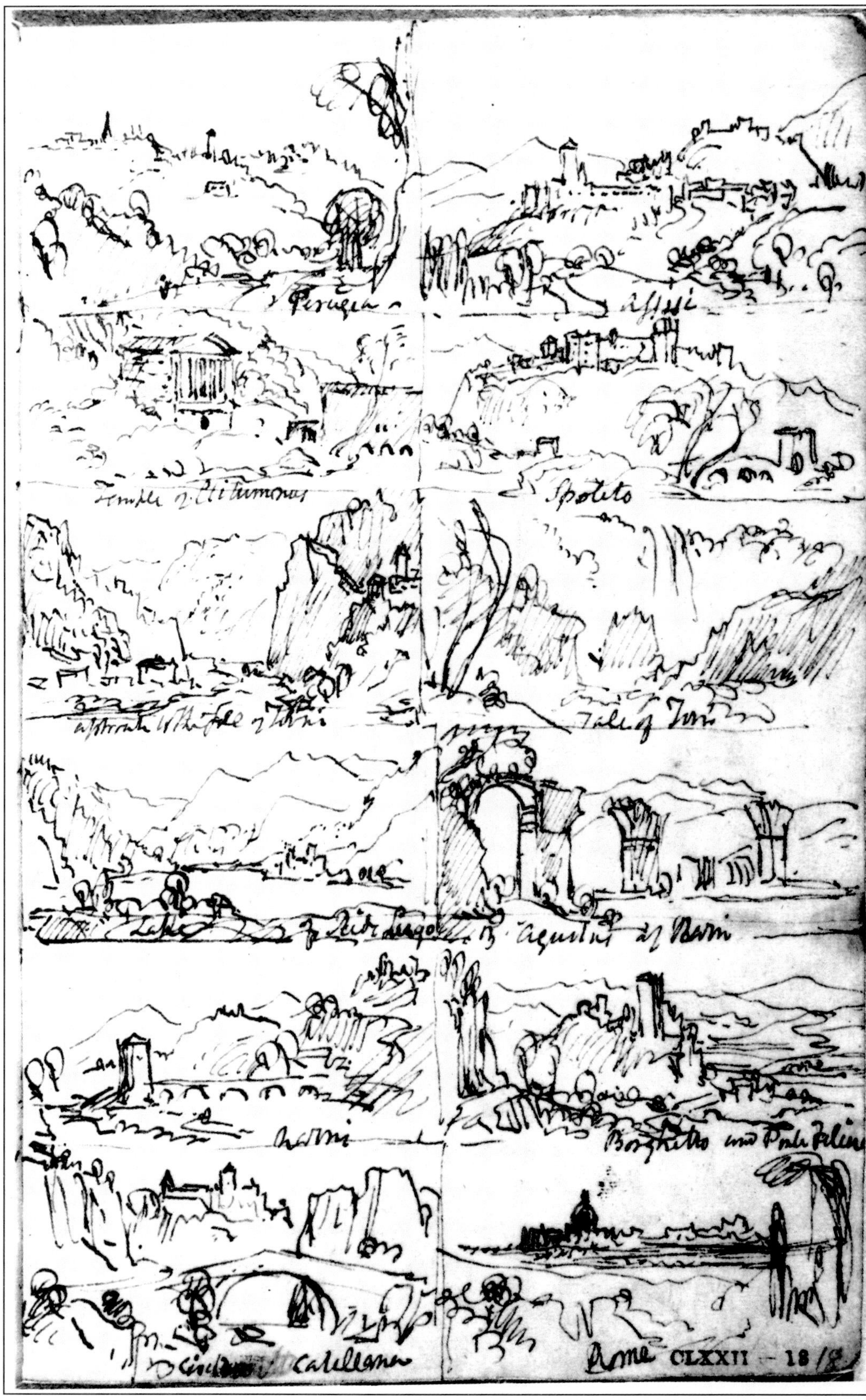
Perugia
Assisi
Spoleto
Narni
Rome
CLXXII

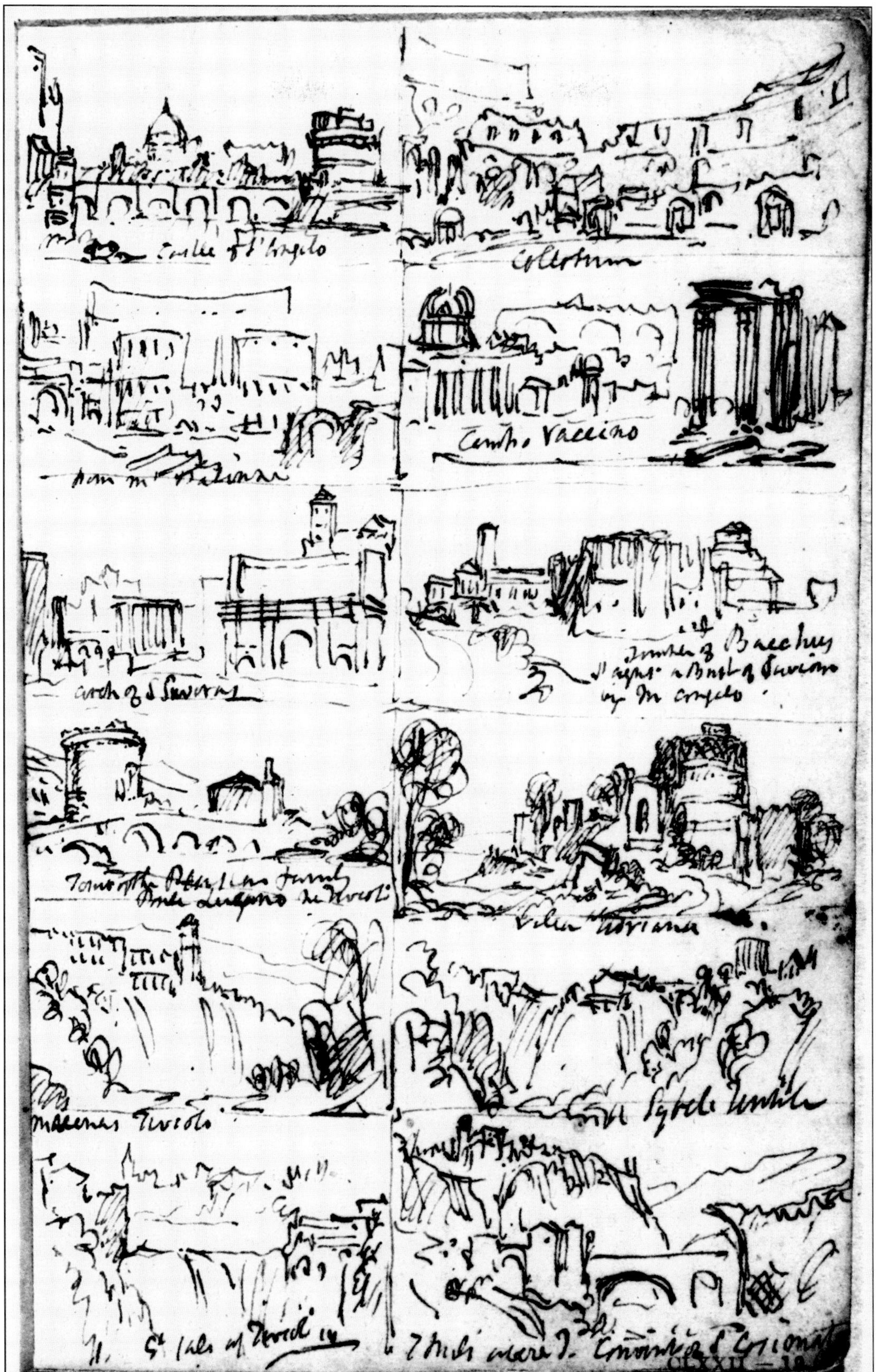
Tempio Vaccino
Villa Adriana

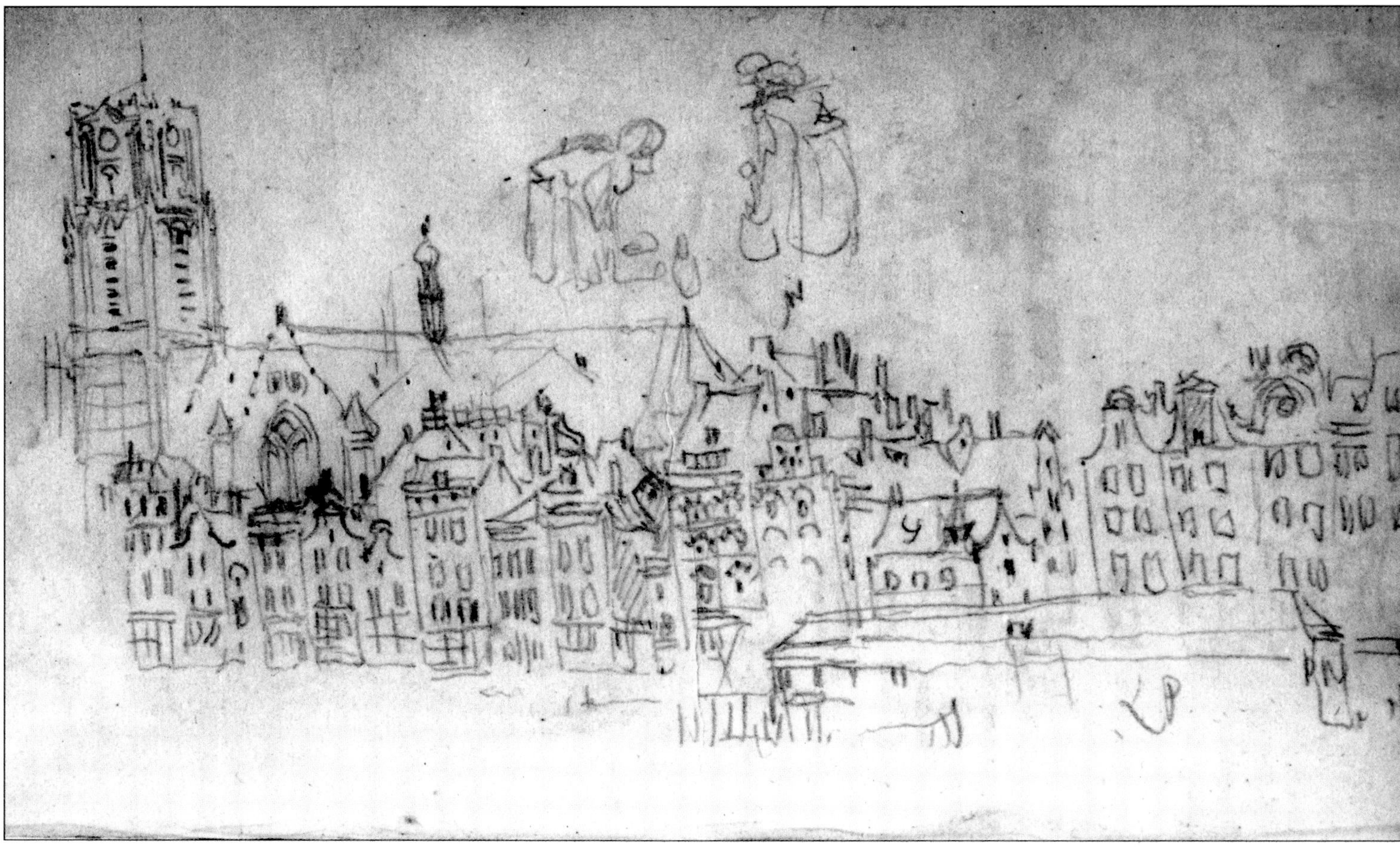

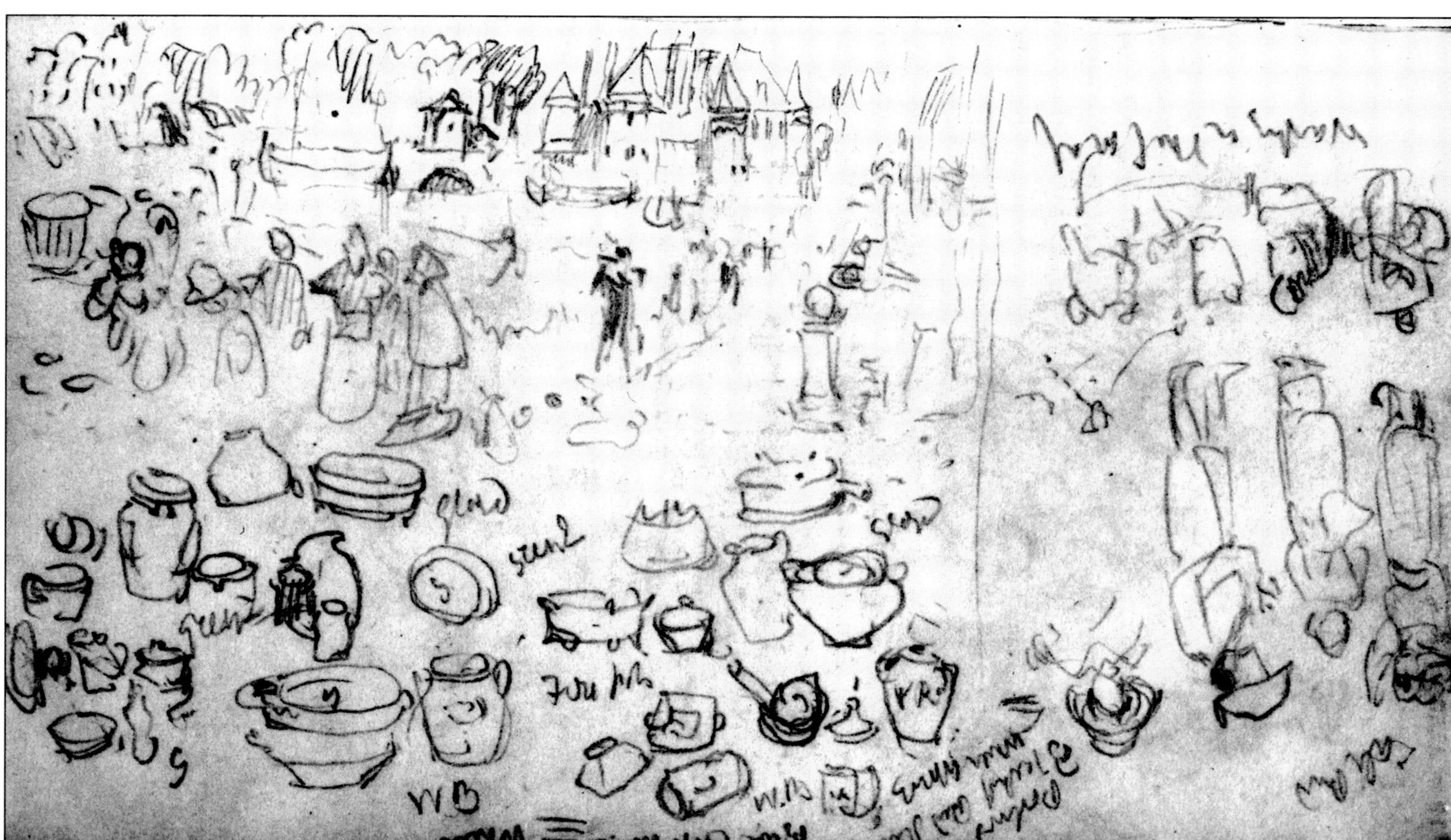

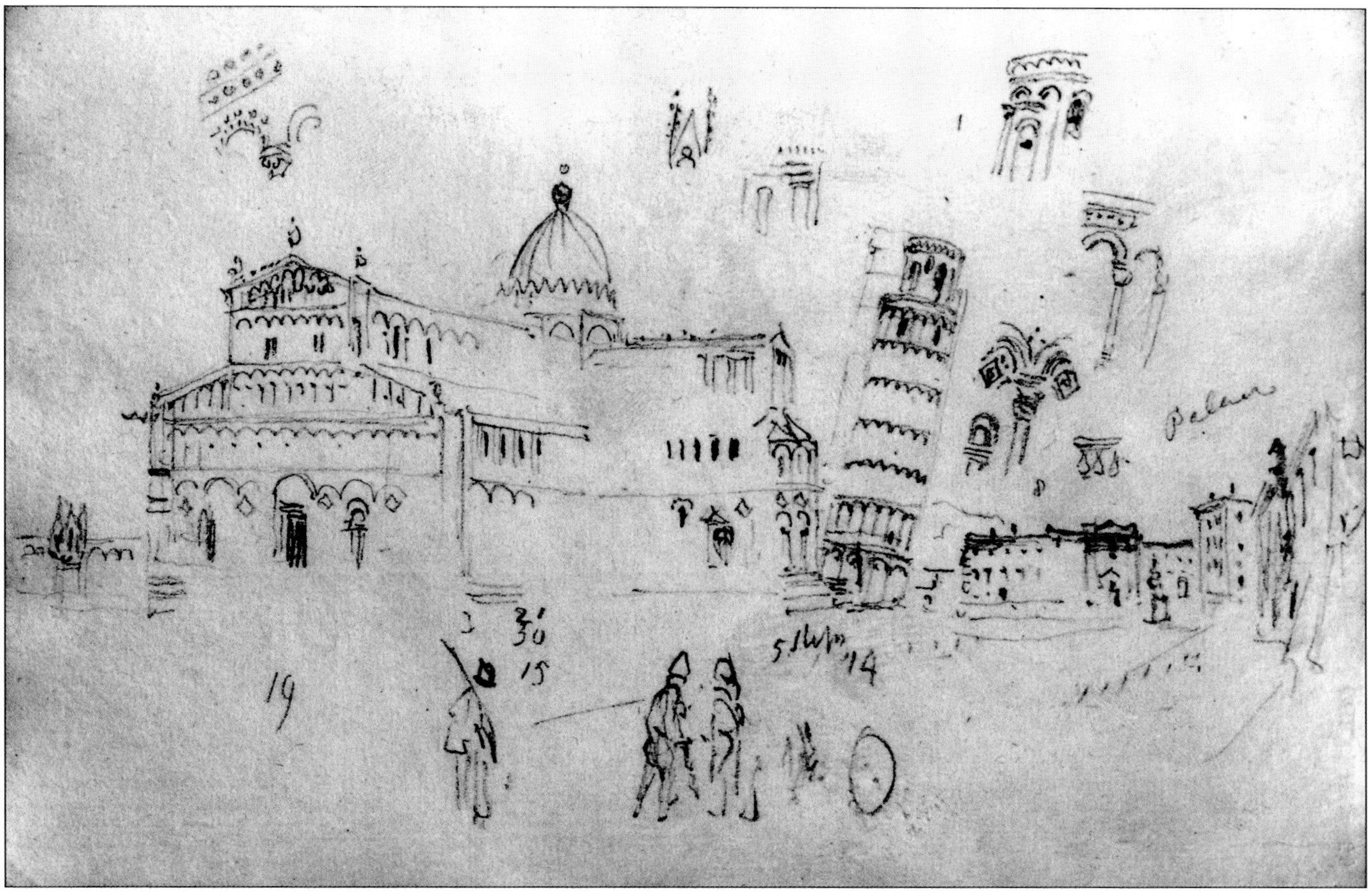

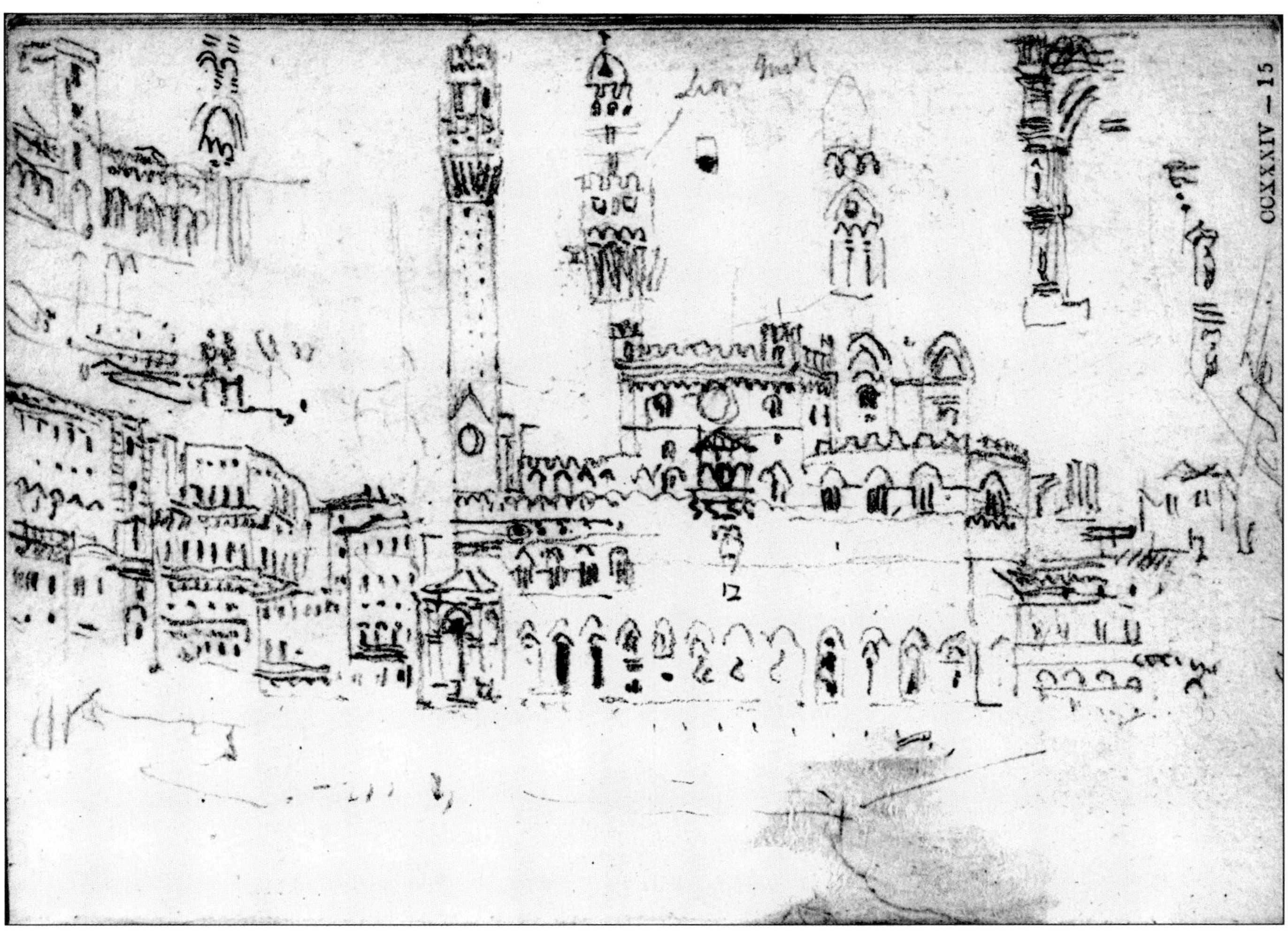
CCXXXIV – 15

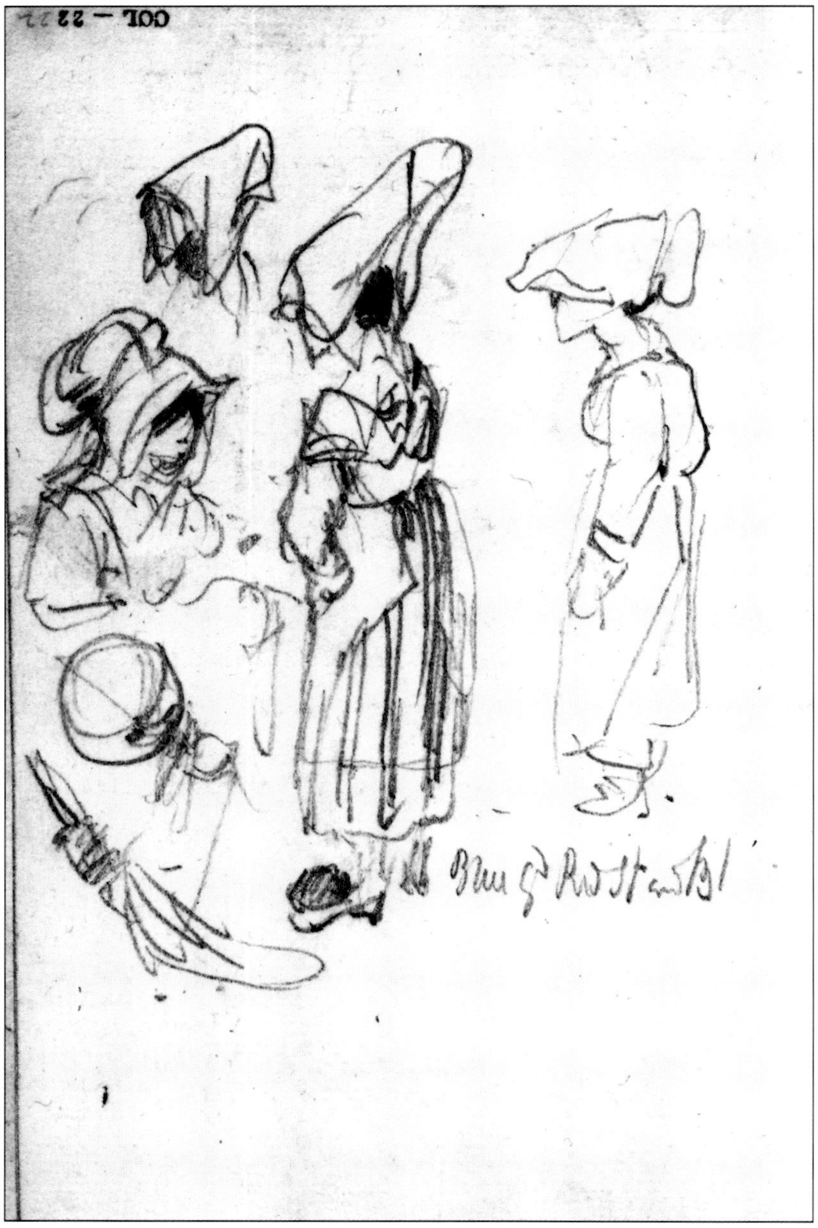

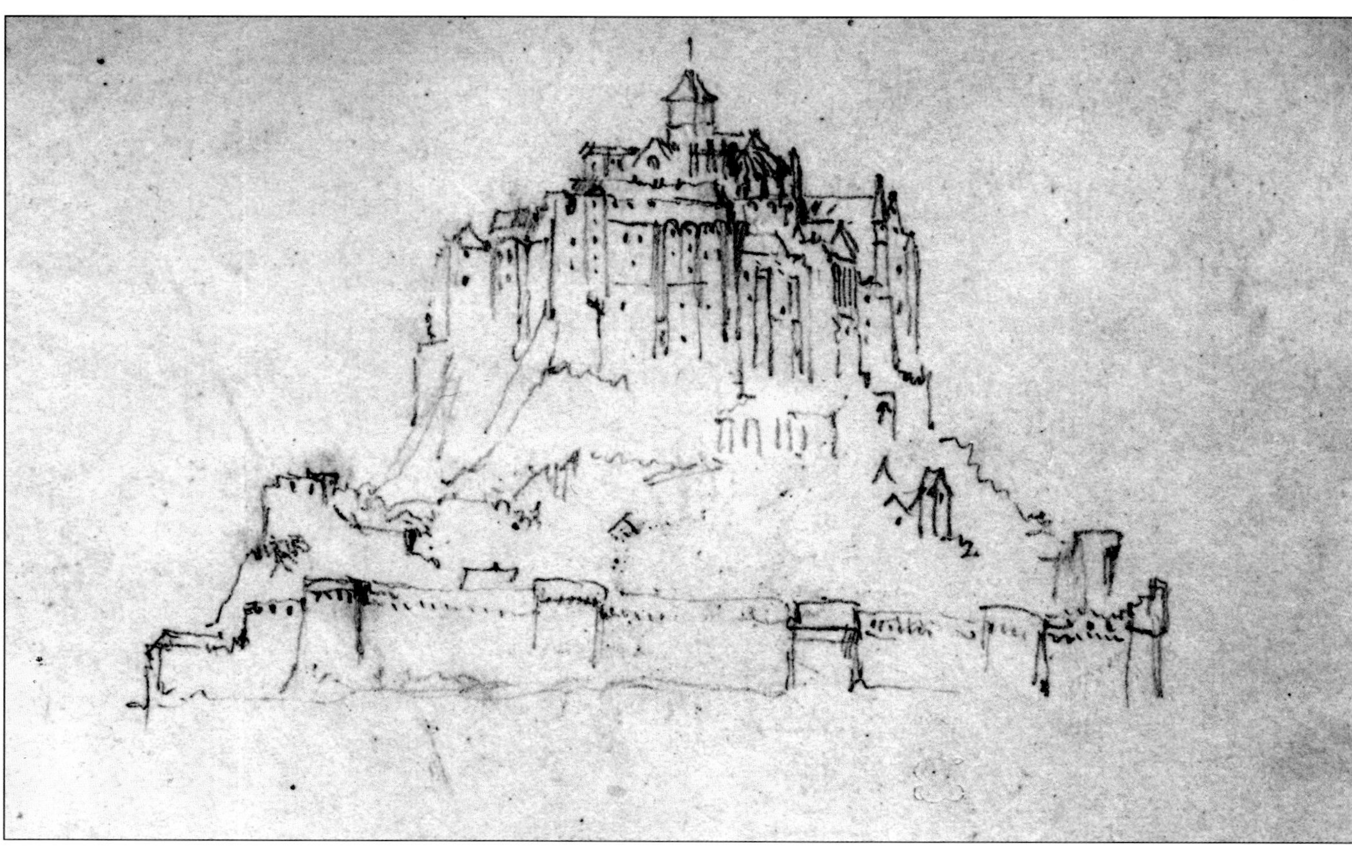

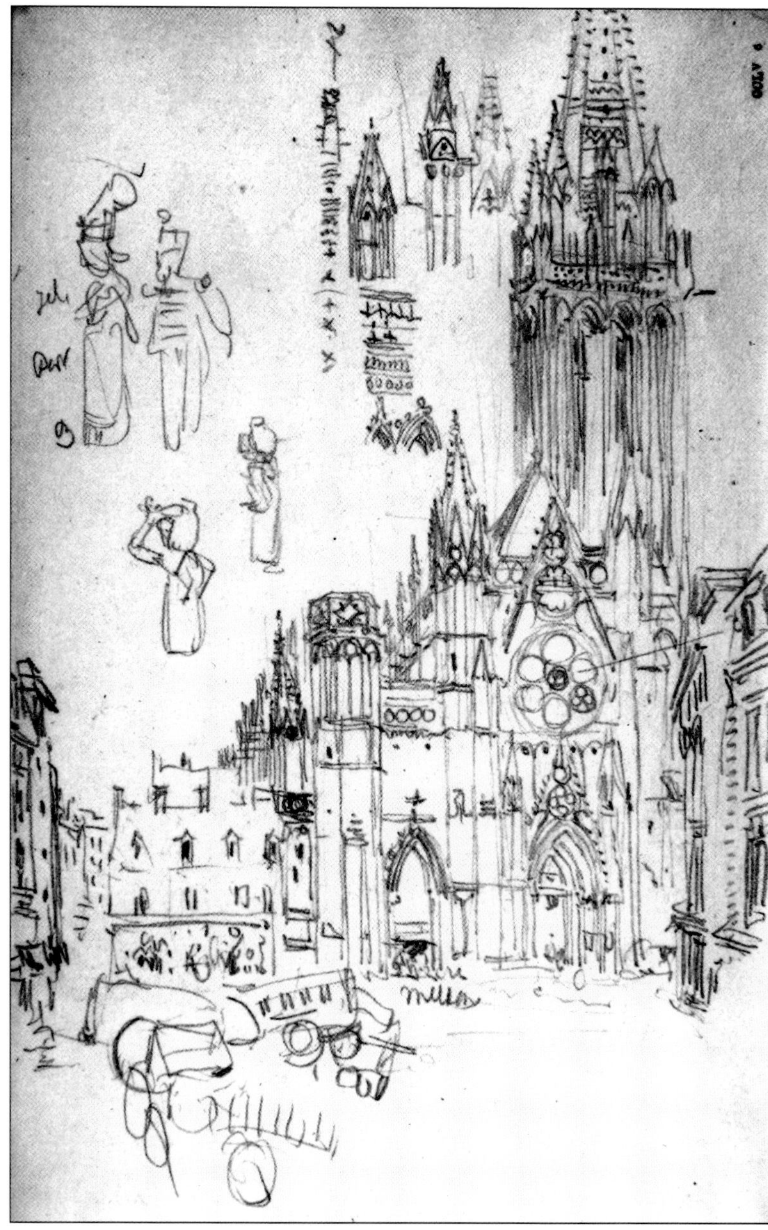

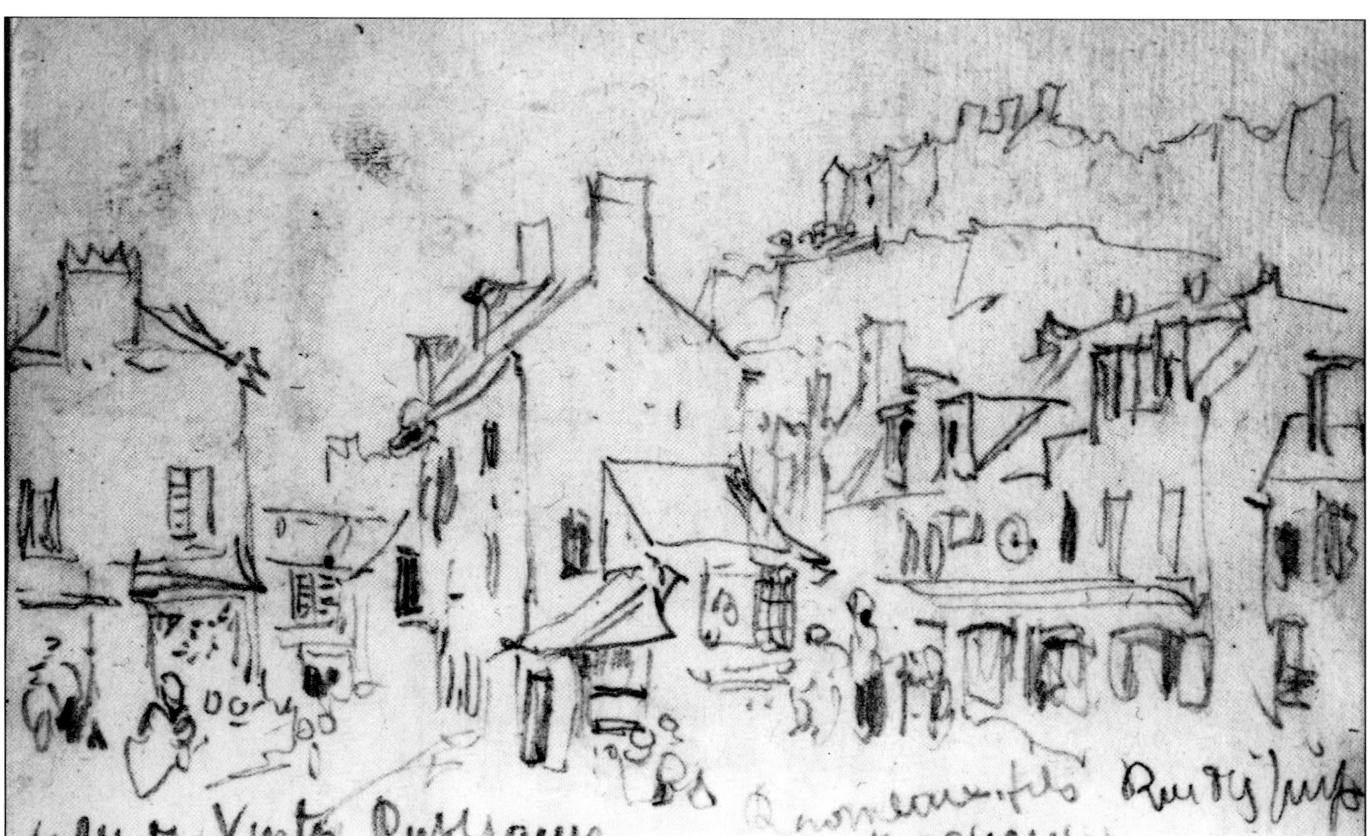
Salle de Ventes Publiques

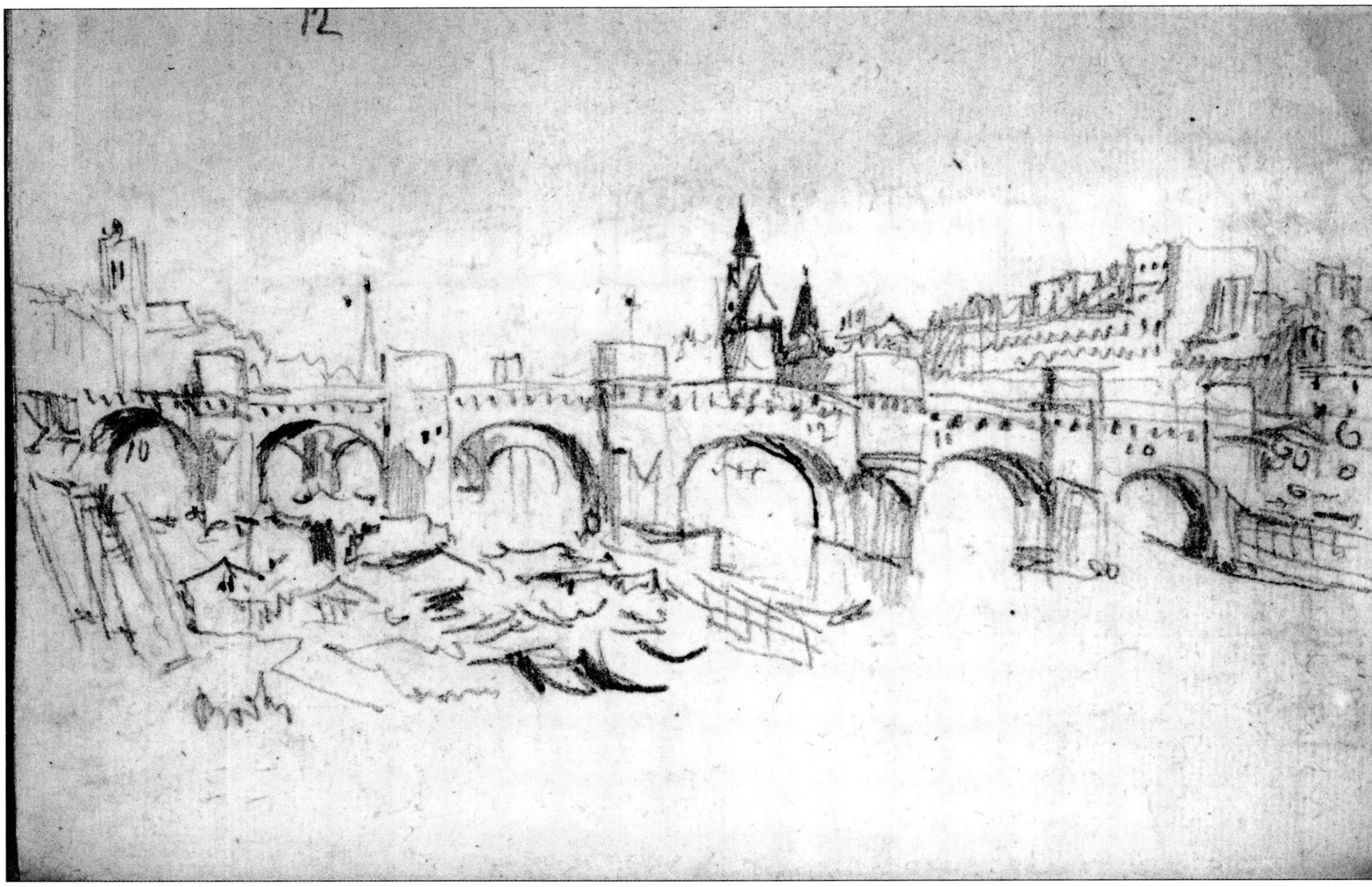

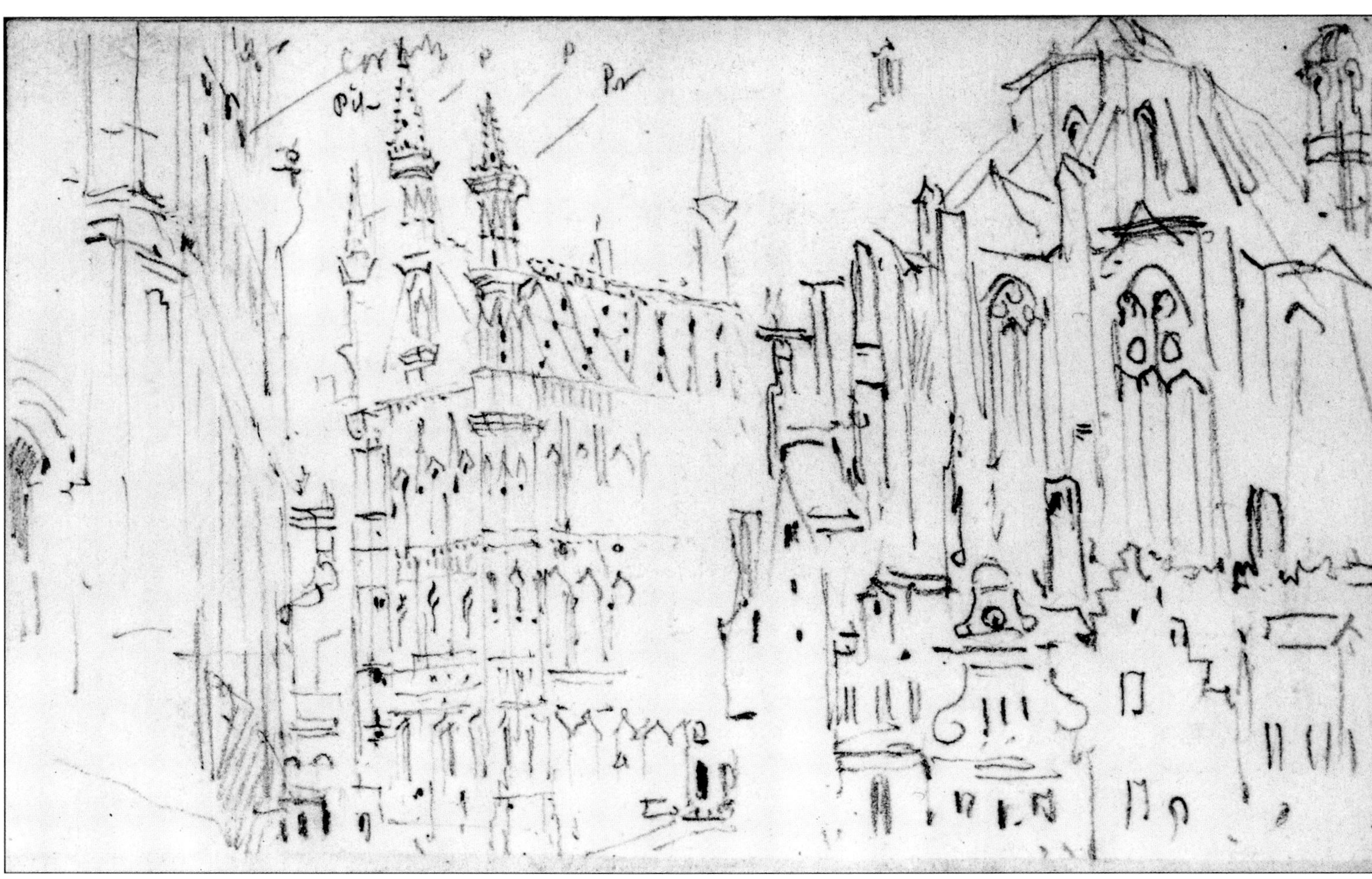

# THE LATE WORK

The Fighting »Temeraire«, tugged to her last berth to be broken up. (detail). 1838
Oil on canvas, 91 x 122 cm
Turner Bequest, National Gallery, London

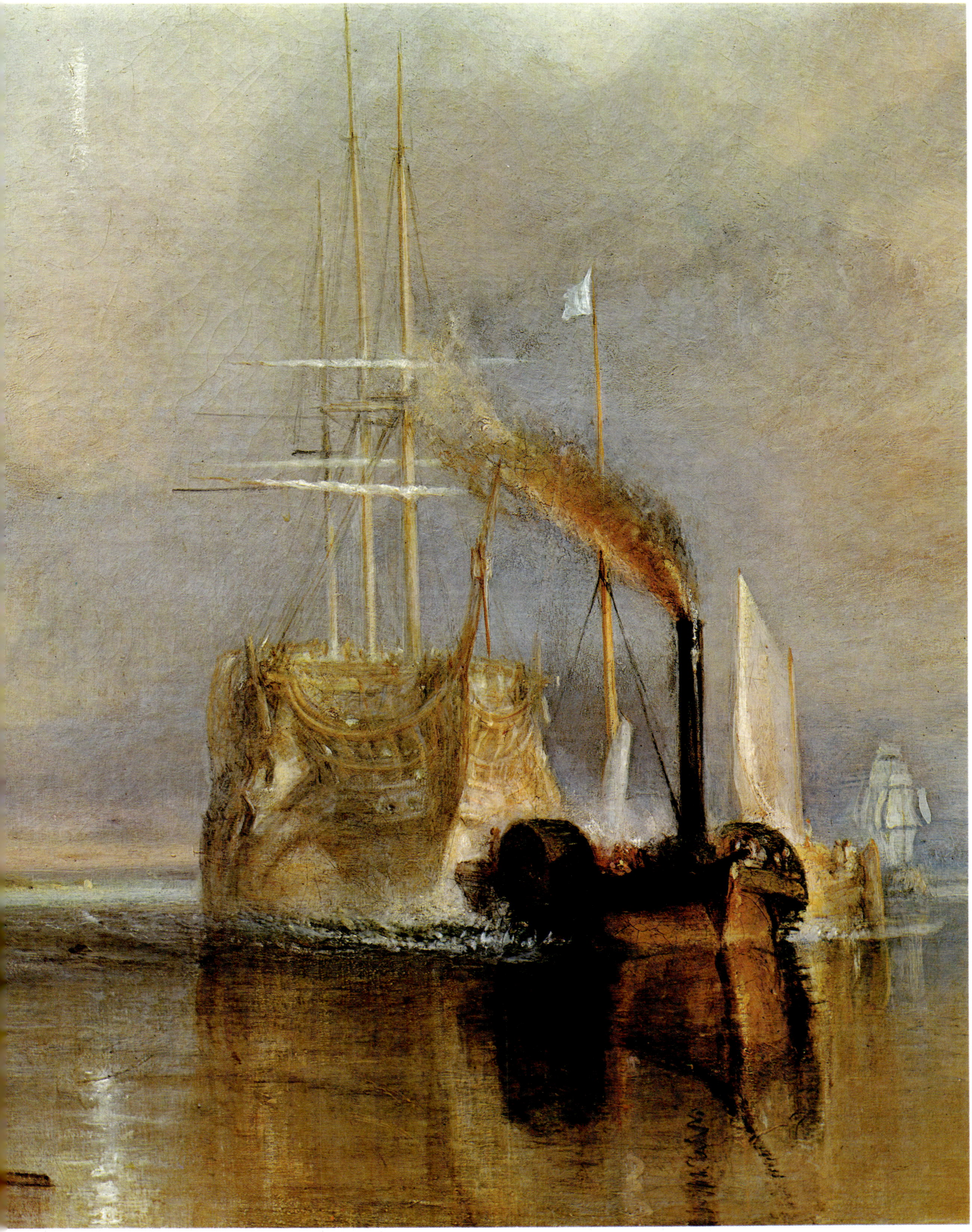

Yacht approaching the coast. Ca. 1835—1840
Oil on canvas, 102 x 142 cm
The Tate Gallery, London

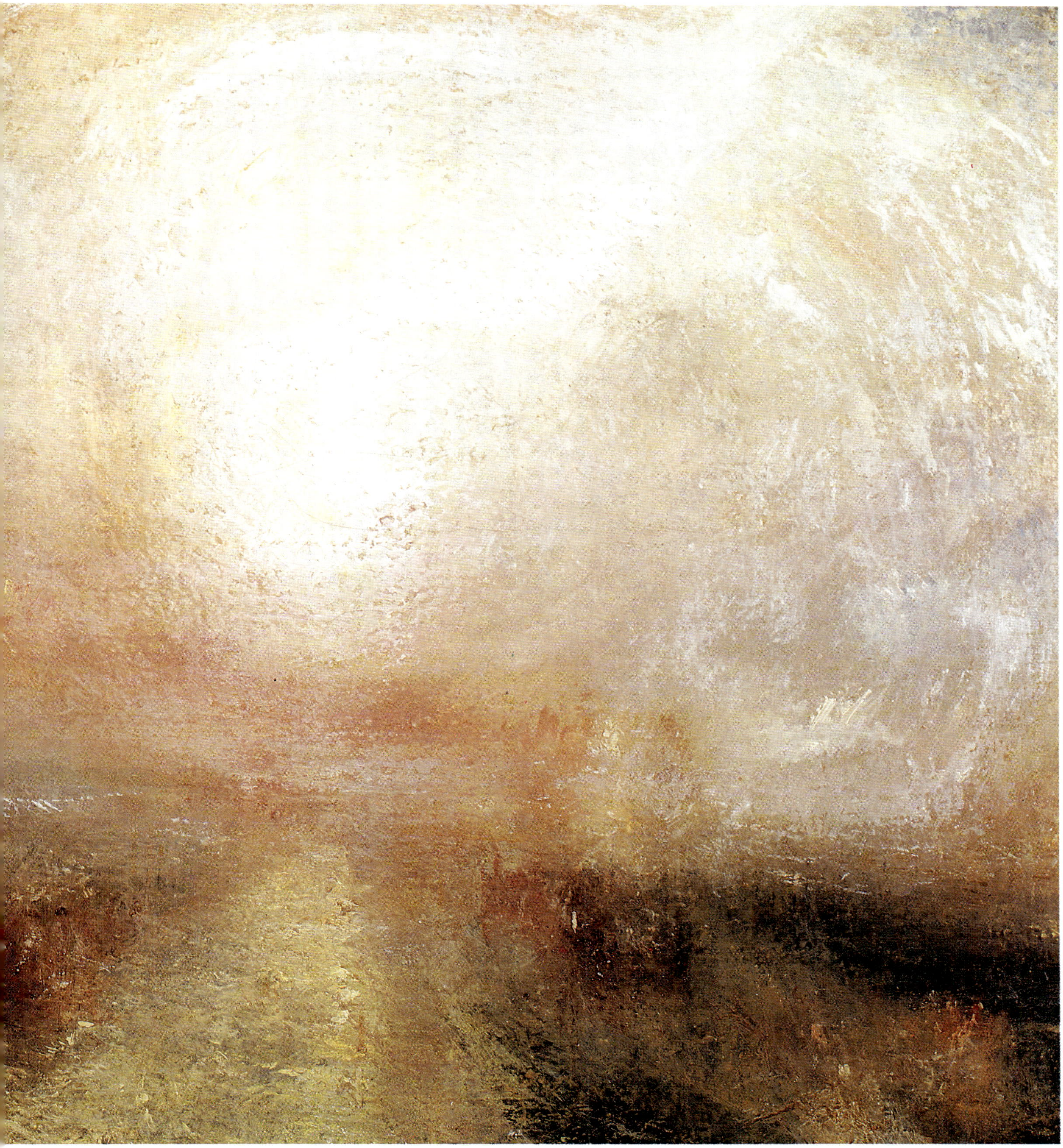

Peace — burial at sea. 1842
Oil on canvas, 87 x 86.5 cm
The Tate Gallery, London

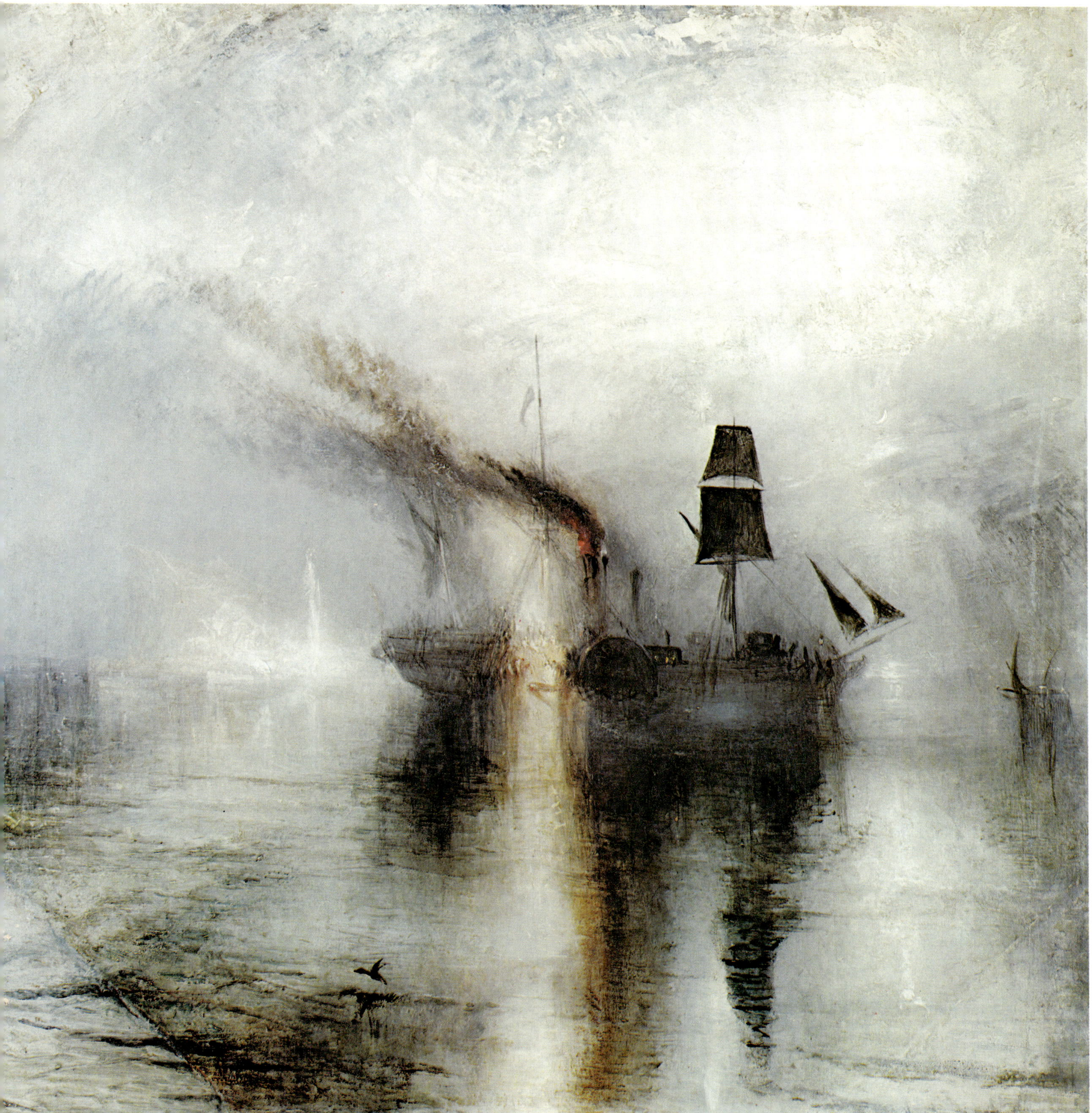

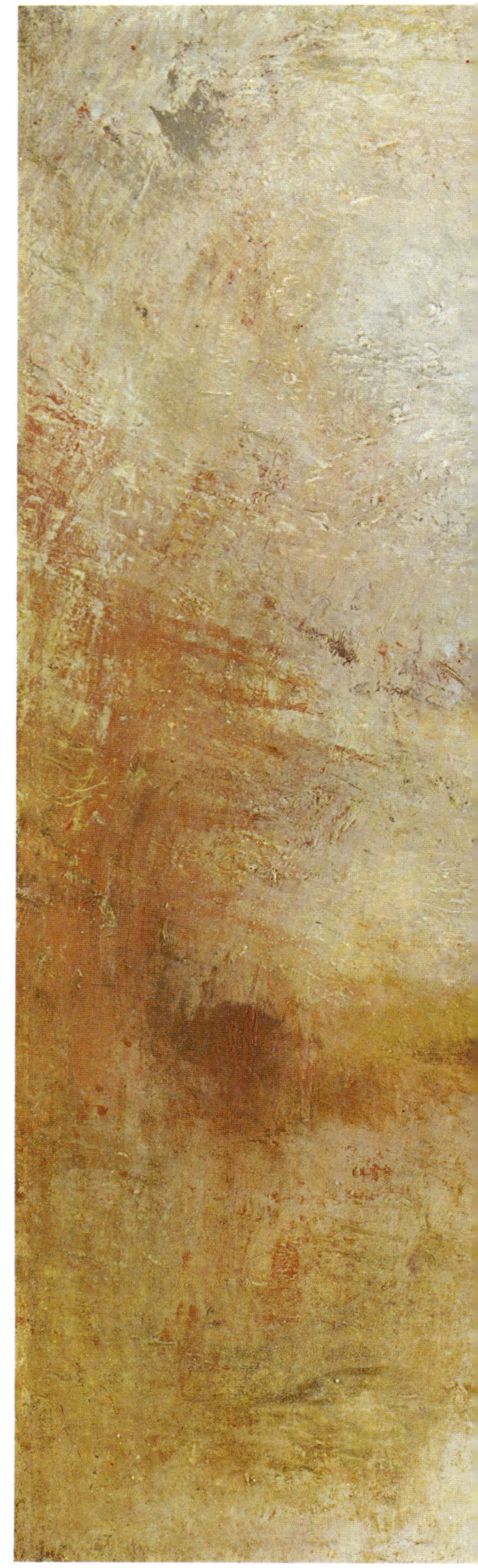

Sun setting over a lake. 1840
Oil on canvas, 91 x 122.5 cm
Turners Bequest, Tate Gallery, London

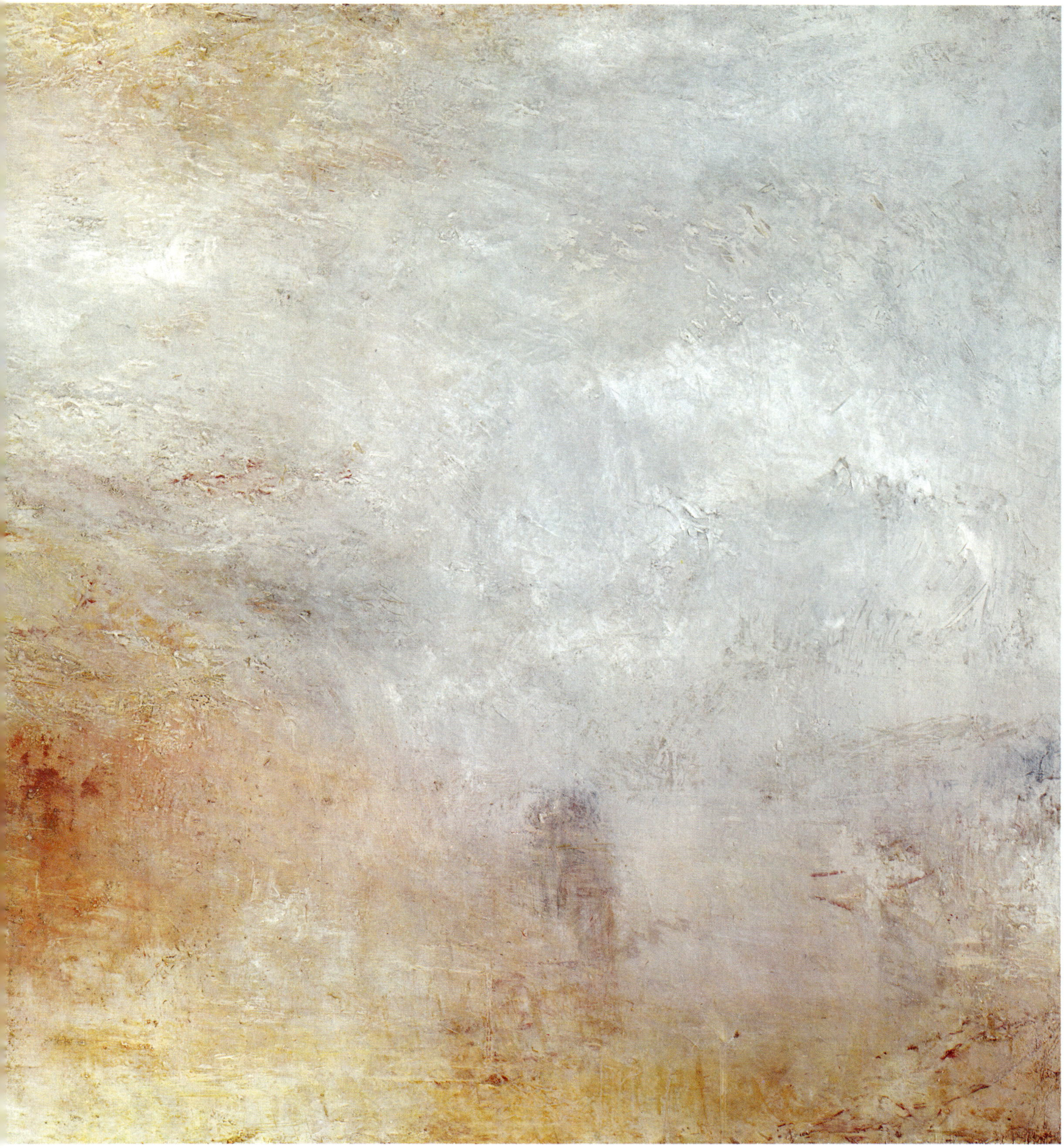

Light and colour (Goethe's Theory)
— the morning after the Deluge —
Moses writing the book of Genesis. 1843
Oil on canvas, 78.5 x 78.5 cm
The Tate Gallery, London

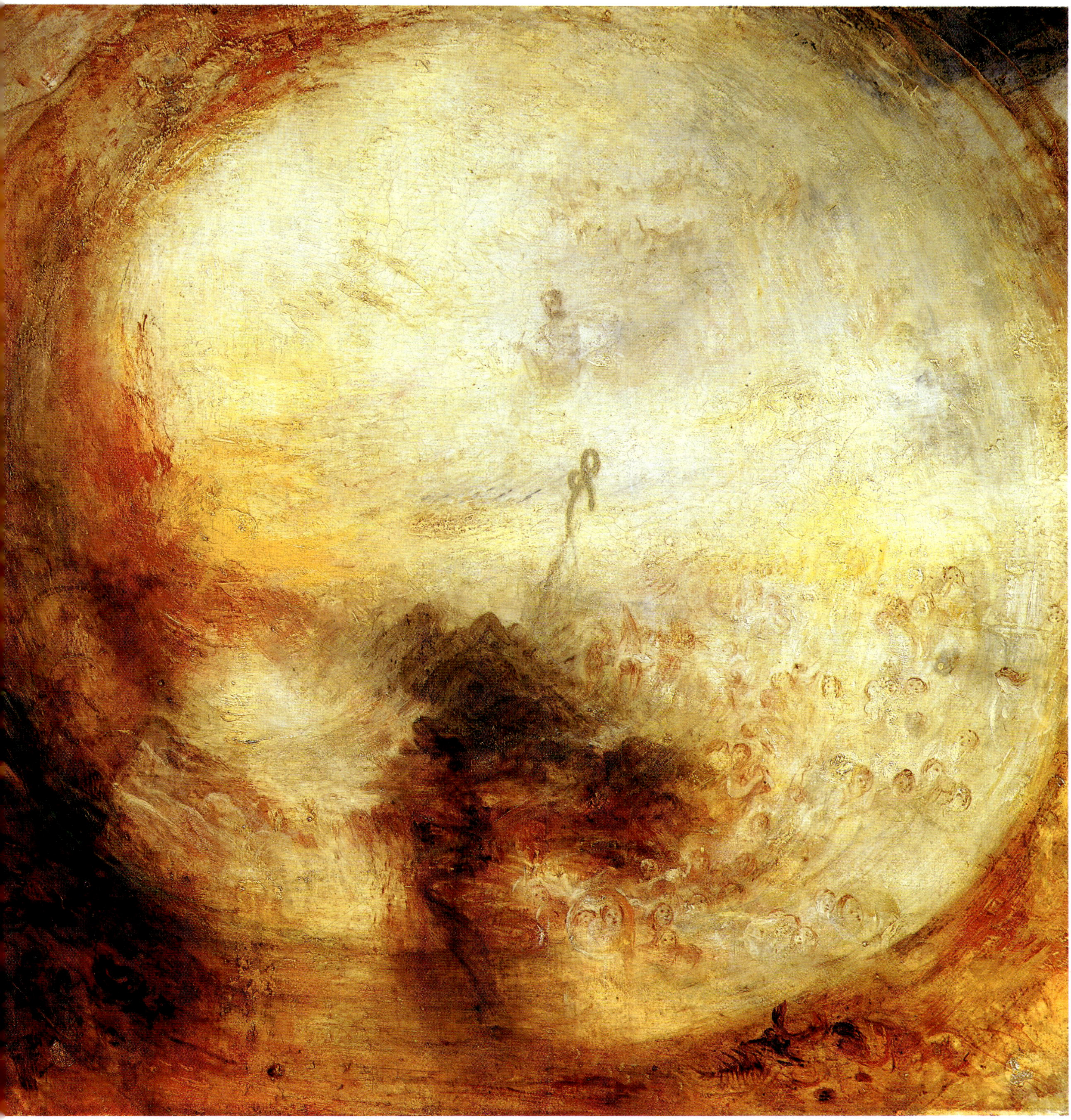

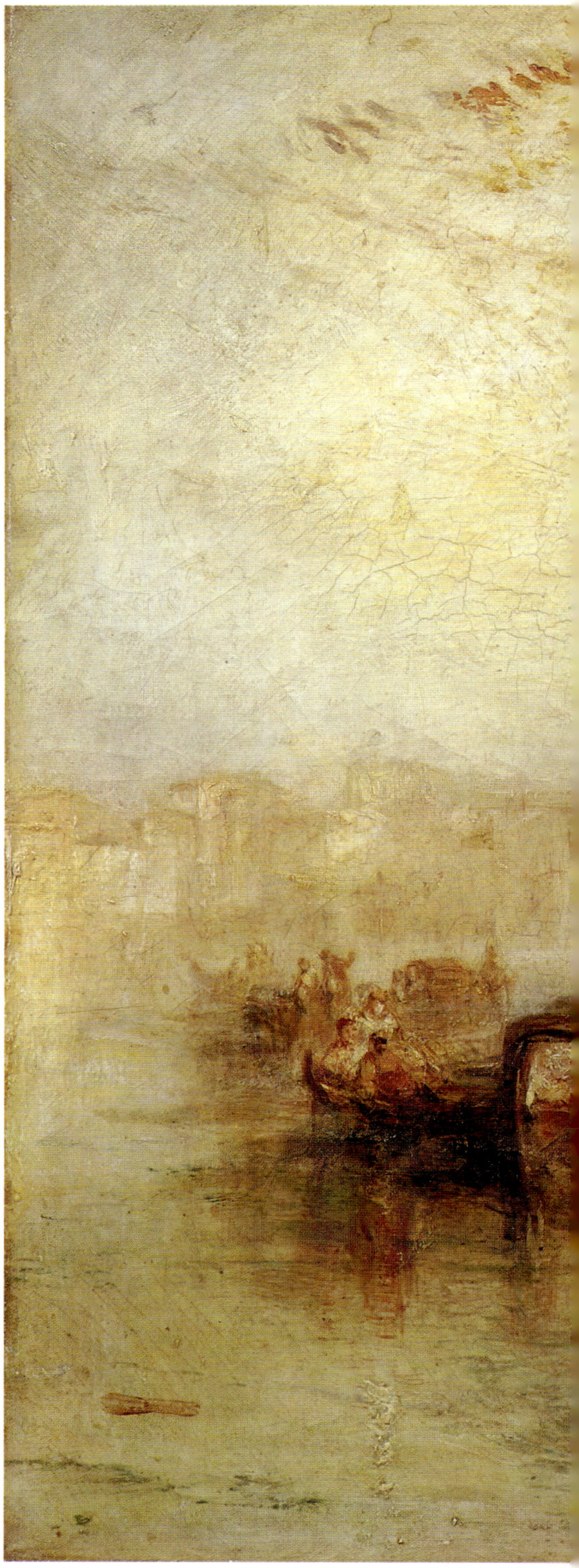

St. Benedetto, looking towards Fusina. 1843
Oil on canvas, 61.5 x 92 cm
The Tate Gallery, London

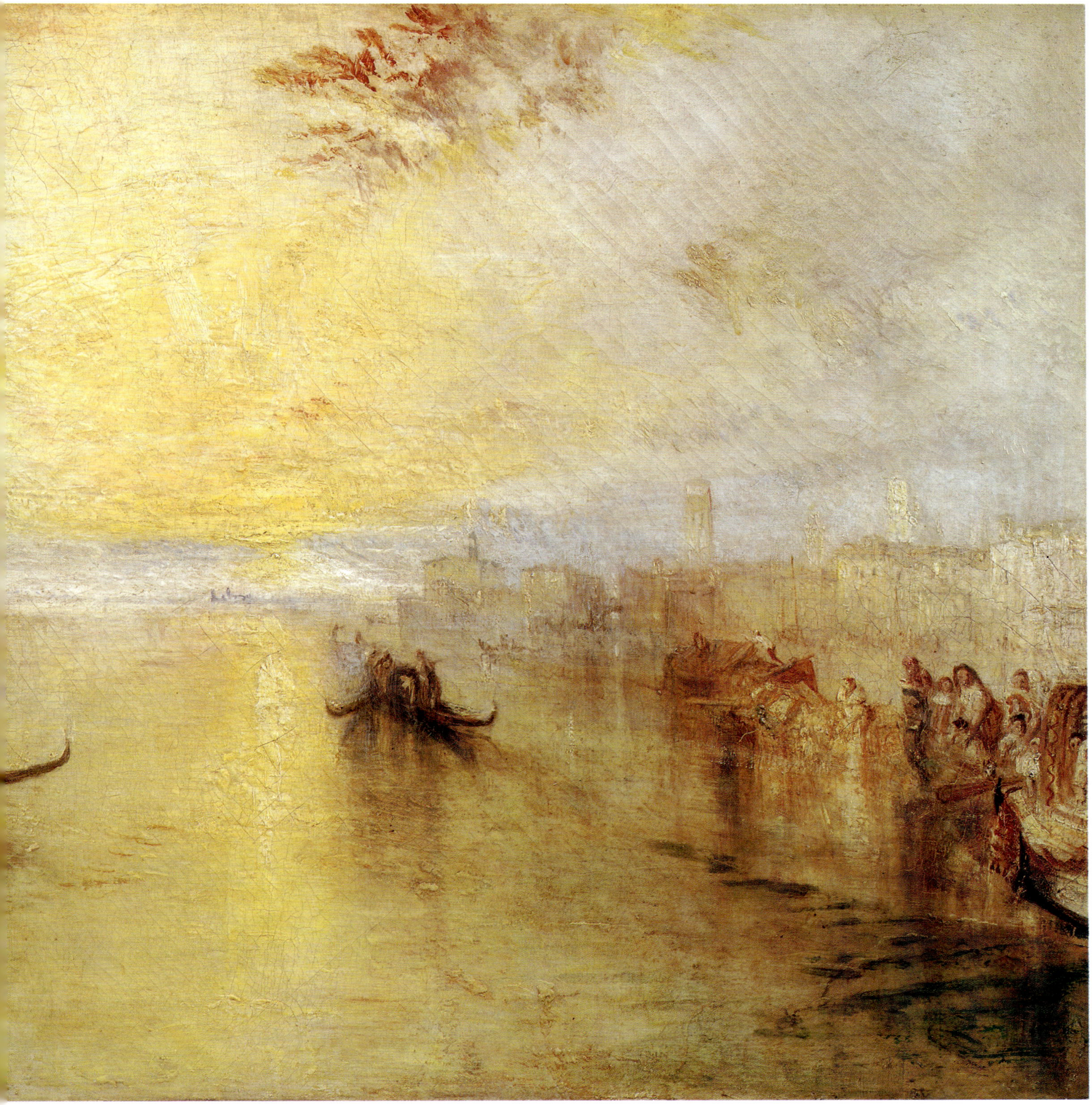

»The Sun of Venice« going to sea, (detail). 1843
Oil on canvas, 61.5 x 92 cm
The Tate Gallery, London

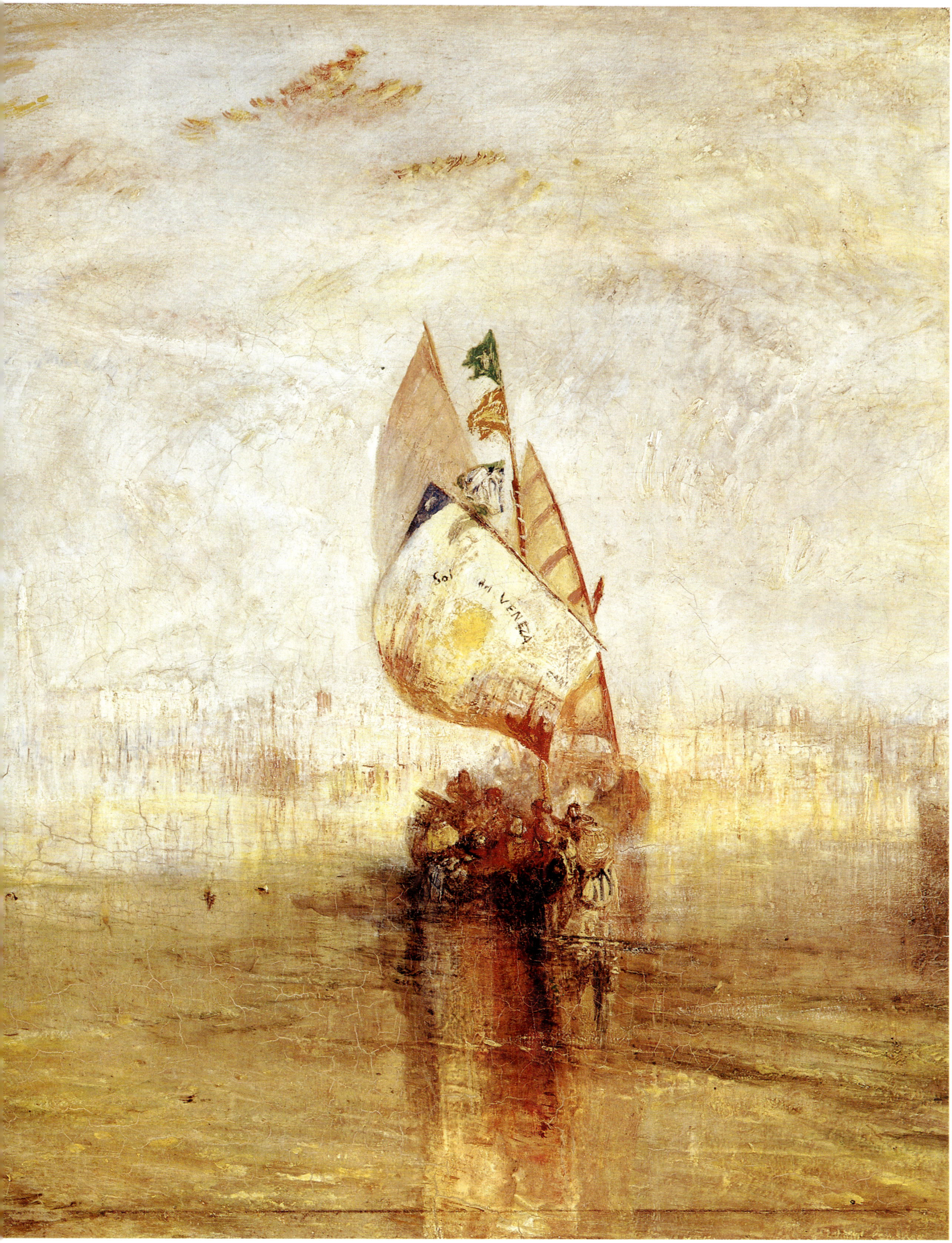

Rain, Steam and Speed —
The Great Western Railway. 1844
Oil on canvas, 91 x 122 cm
Turner Bequest, National Gallery, London

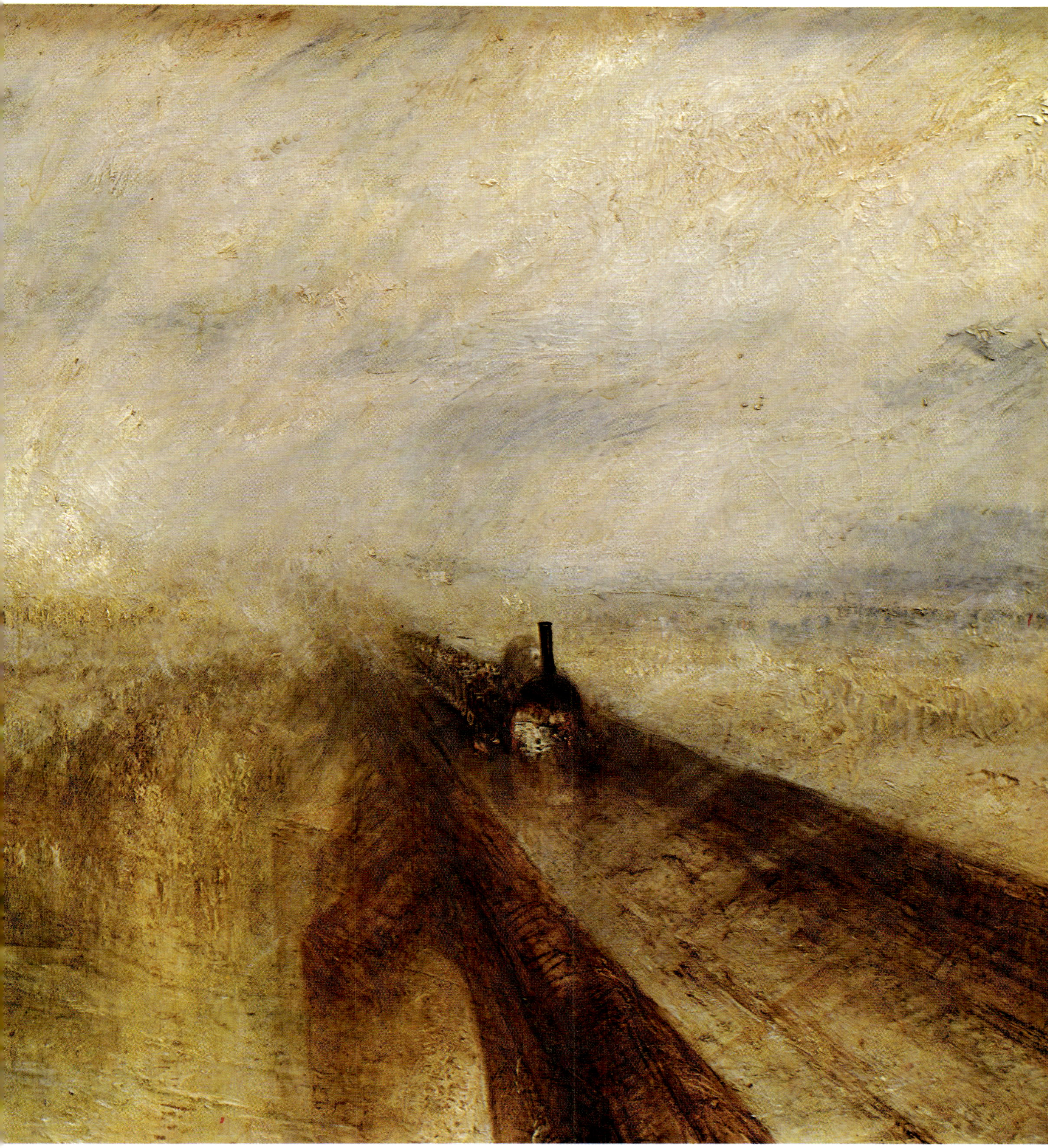

Van Tromp, going about to please his masters, ships at sea, getting a good wetting (detail). 1844
Oil on canvas, 91.4 x 121.9 cm
Royal Holloway College, Englefield Green

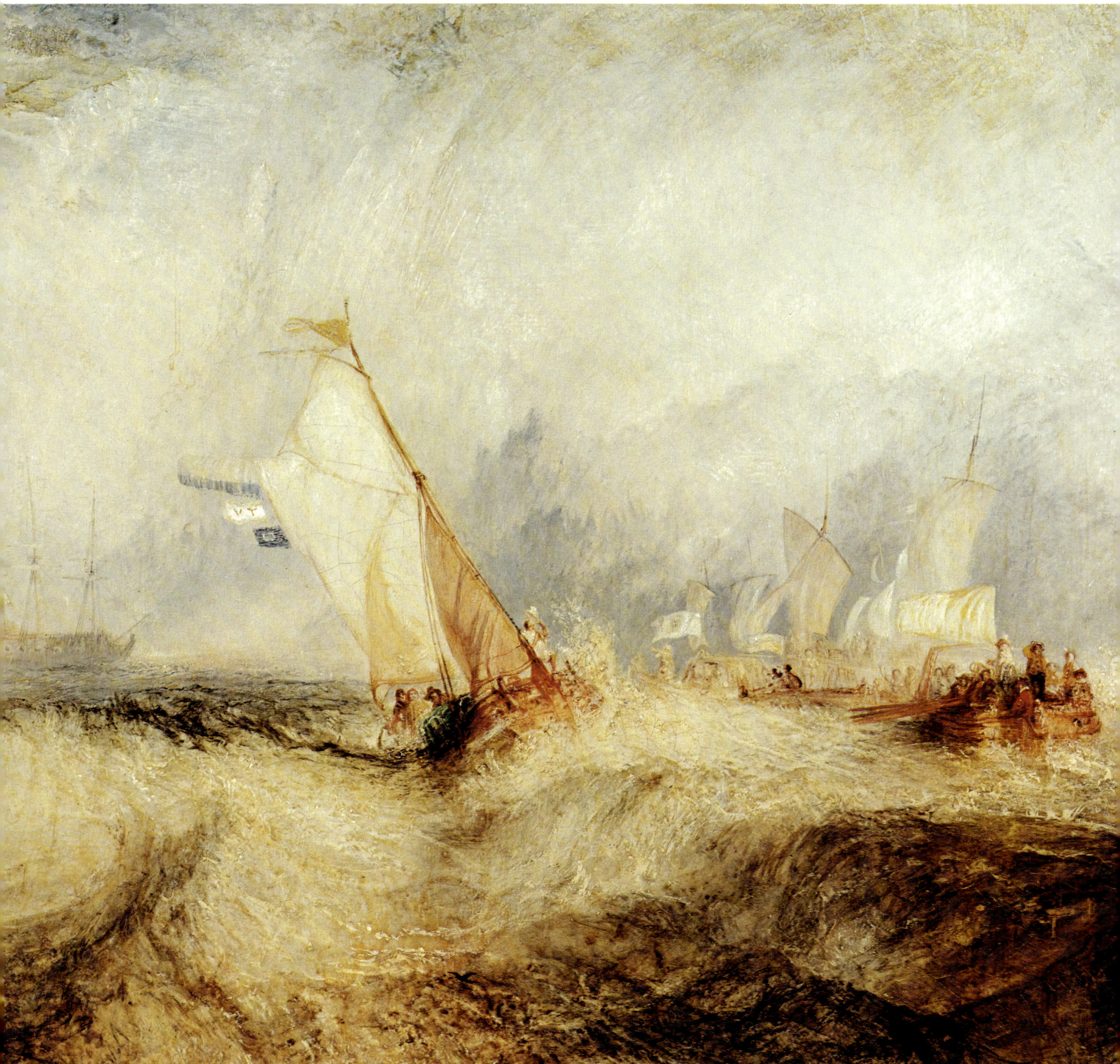

Festive Lagoon scene, Venice? Ca. 1845
Oil on canvas, 91 x 121 cm
Turner Bequest, Tate Gallery, London

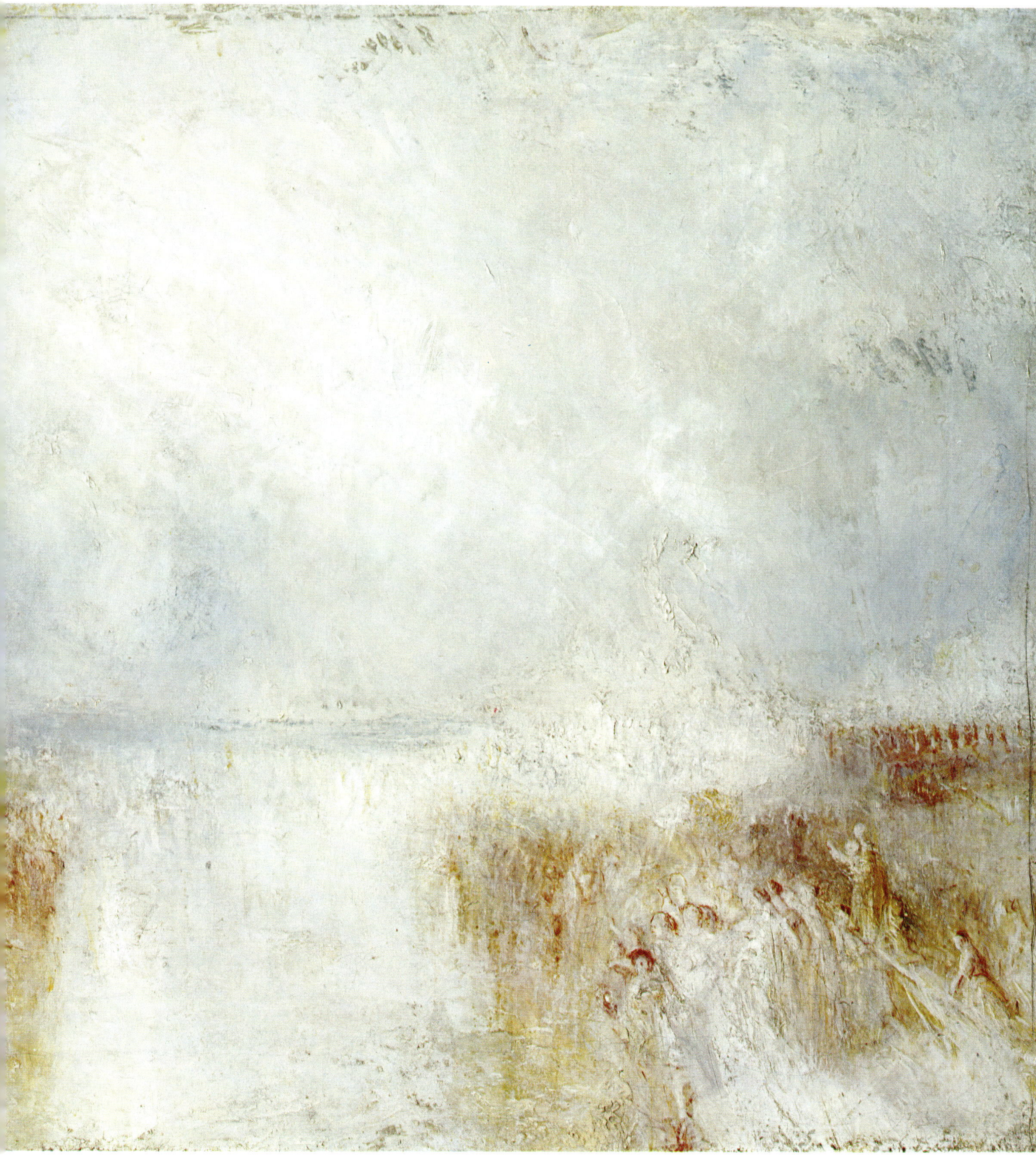

Whalers (detail). 1845
Oil on canvas, 91 x 122 cm
The Tate Gallery, London

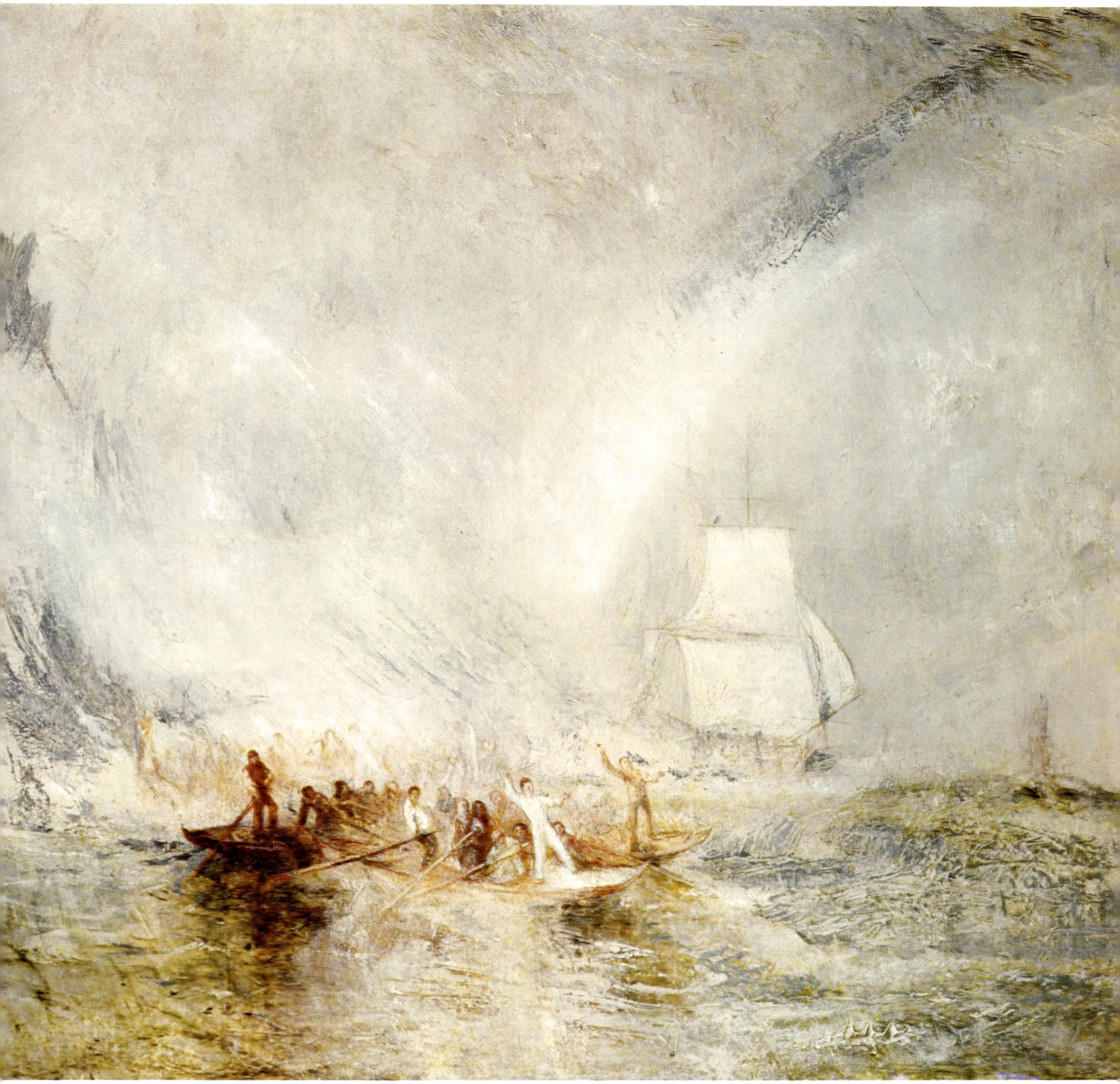

Undine giving the ring to Masaniello,
fisherman of Naples. 1846
Oil on canvas, 79 x 79 cm
The Tate Gallery, London

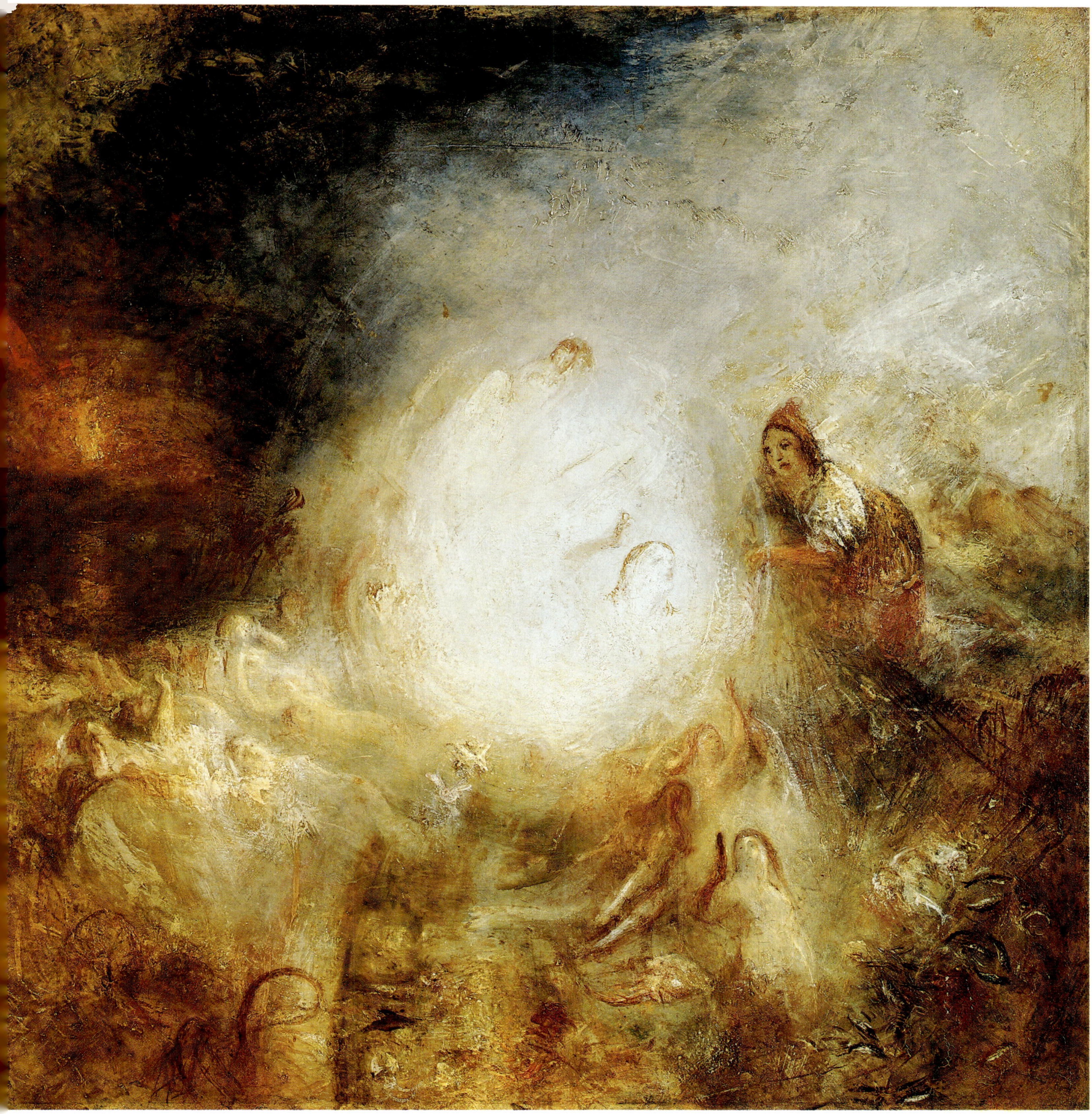

# LIST OF ILLUSTRATIONS

A Memorandum of Coastal Scenery. Ca. 1812 — 79 below
Pen and ink, 12.6 x 20.2 cm
Sketchbook CXXVII, page 33

Aysgarth Force. Ca. 1816 — 80 above
Pencil, 12.8 x 21.2 cm
Sketchbook CXLVII, page 11

Design for a Sea-Piece. Ca. 1816—18 — 80 below
Pencil, 11.1 x 18.5 cm
Sketchbook CLIII, page 89a

River scene, wooden bridge with stone supports, boats and figures (seated in foreground). — 81 above
Possibly Old Chelsea Bridge. Ca. 1827
Pencil, 11 x 18.5 cm
Sketchbook CCXXVII, page 40a

Shipping of the Thames; Two sketches, one with St. Pauls in distance.
Pencil, 11 x 18.5 cm
Sketchbook CCXXVII, page 12a

The High Street Oxford, with Queen's College etc. 1834 — 82 above
Pencil, 23.5 x 14.5 cm
Sketchbook CCLXXXV, page 4

Harbour, Ramsgate. Ca. 1832 — 82 below
Pencil, 8.6 x 20.6 cm
Sketchbook CCLXXIX, page 39

The passage of Mount St. Gothard, taken from the centre of the Teufels Broch Switzerland 1804 (Turners Galerie) — 85
Watercolour, 98.5 x 68.5 cm
Abbot Hall Art Gallery, Kendal, Cumbria

The fall of an Avalanche in the Grisons. 1810 (Turners Gallery) — 87
Oil on canvas, 90 x 120 cm
The Tate Gallery, London

Cologne, the arrival of a packet boat; evening. 1826 — 89
Oil and maybe watercolour on canvas, 168.6 x 224.1 cm
Frick Collection, New York

Normandy Costumes. Ca. 1830 — 104 above
Pencil, 13.3 x 9.1 cm
Sketchbook CCL, page 22

Mont St. Michel. Ca. 1830 — 104 below
Pencil, 11.5 x 18.2 cm
Sketchbook CCLV, page 17

St. Maclou (?), Rouen. Ca. 1830 — 105 above
Pencil, 18.2 x 11.5 cm
Sketchbook CCLV, page 6

Salle de ventes publiques. Rue du Juif. Ca. 1830 — 105 below
Pencil, 9.1 x 13.3 cm
Sketchbook CCL, page 26a

Pont Neuf. Ca. 1830 — 106 above
Pencil, 12.7 x 17.5 cm
Sketchbook CCLVII, page 55a

Hotel de Ville, Louvain also the Gothic Church
of St. Pierre. Ca. 1836 — 106 below
Pencil, 9.4 x 15.4 cm
Sketchbook CCLXXXVII, page 2a

The Righting »Temeraire«, tugged to her last berth — 109
to be broken up. (detail). 1838
Oil on canvas, 91 x 122 cm
Turner Bequest, National Gallery, London.

Yacht approaching the coast. Ca. 1835—1840 — 111
Oil on canvas, 102 x 142 cm
The Tate Gallery, London

Peace — burial at sea. 1842 — 113
Oil on canvas, 87 x 86.5 cm
The Tate Gallery, London

Sun setting over a lake. 1840 — 115
Oil on canvas, 91 x 122.5 cm
The Tate Gallery, London

Light and colour (Goethe's Theory) — the morning — 117
after the Deluge — Moses writing the book of Genesis. 1843
Oil on canvas, 78.5 x 78.5 cm
Turner Bequest, Tate Gallery, London

The publishers wish to thank the respective museums and galleries for allowing the use of photographic material on the following pages:

The Tate Gallery, London: p. 29, 41, 55, 57, 69, 73, 95, 119, 131. In addition, all the photographs for illustration from sketchbooks.
Abbot Hall Art Gallery, Kendal: p. 85
Frick Collection, New York: p. 89
Sheffield City Art Galleries, Sheffield: p. 2
Colorphoto Hans Hinz SWB, CH-Allschwil: p. 53, 63
The Bridgeman Art Library, London: p. 31, 43, 59, 61, 91, 93, 97, 98, 111, 117, 121.
All other reproductions where no source is mentioned are taken from the Berghaus archives.